TIMOTHY GREENFIELD-SANDERS

LOOK

PORTRAITS BACKSTAGE AT OLYMPUS FASHION WEEK

pH powerHouse Books Brooklyn, NY

OLYMPUS

In memory of
JOHN MICHAEL MAHANEY
1949–2006

—TG-S

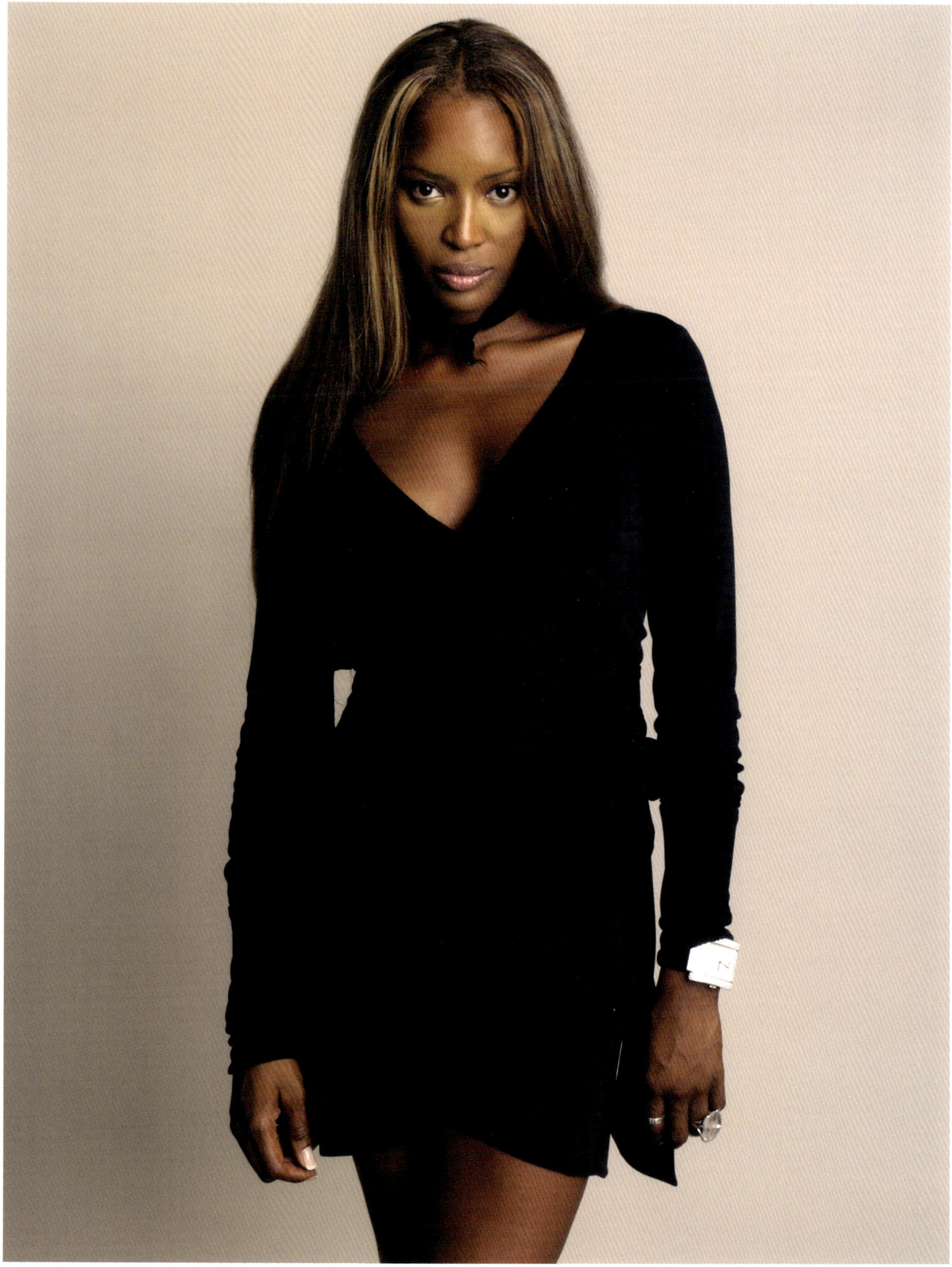

NAOMI CAMPBELL Supermodel

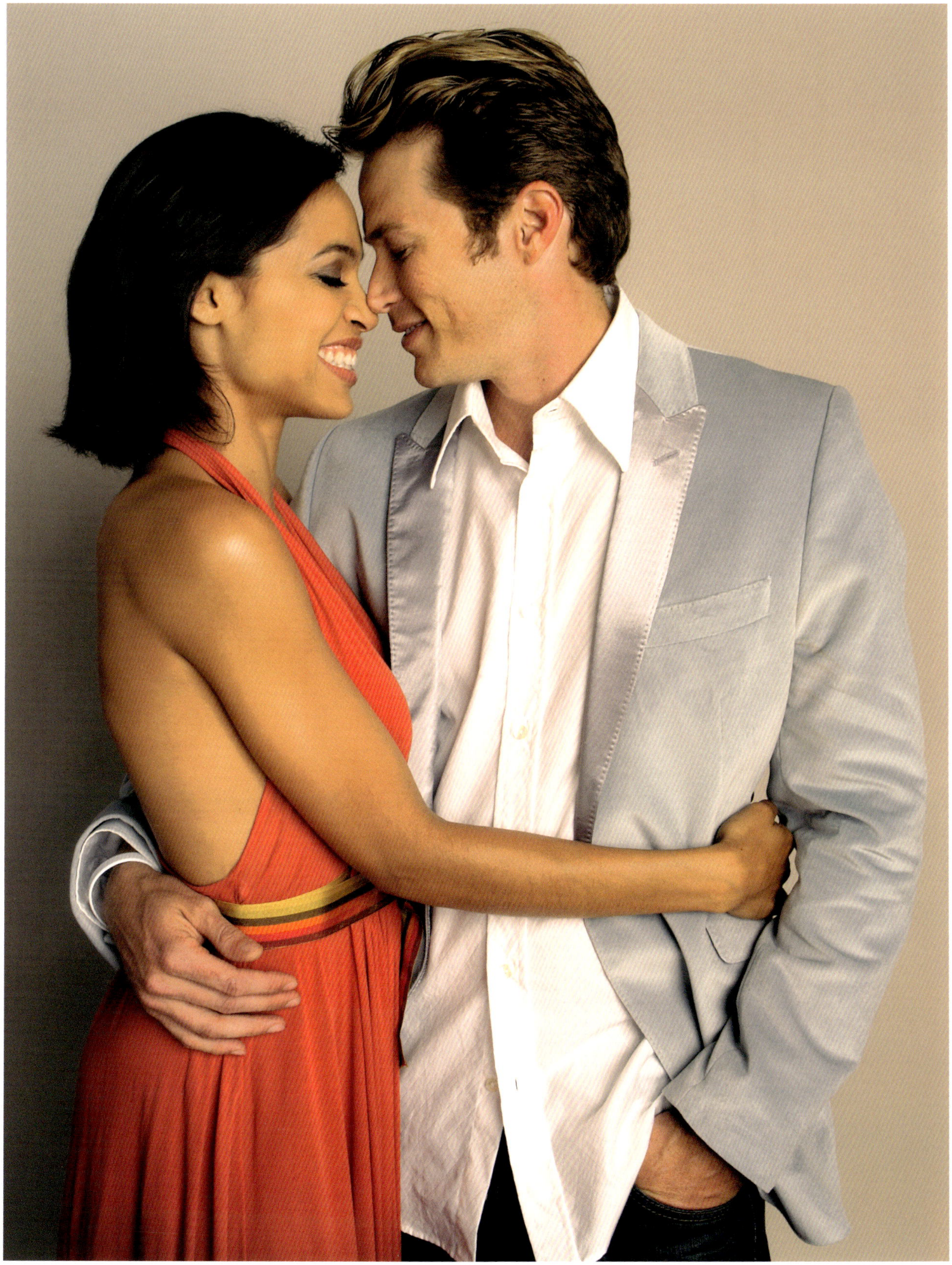

ROSARIO DAWSON & JASON LEWIS Actors

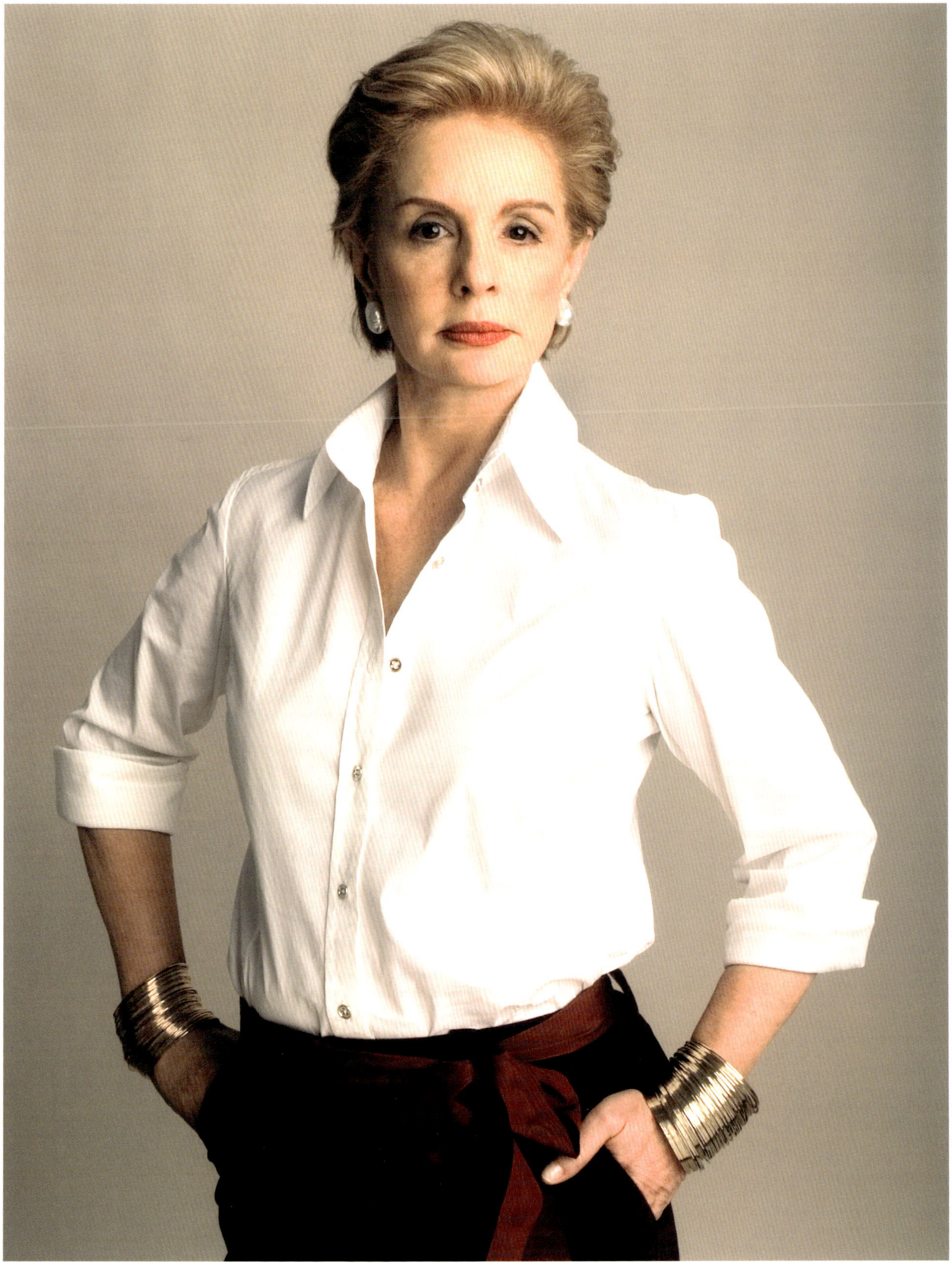

CAROLINA HERRERA Designer

For me, fashion isn't about the clothes. I'm interested in the people who know what goes with what. I admire great style in front of the lens, but I'm personally more comfortable hiding behind the viewfinder in safe and boring basic black. Let's face it: Bill Cunningham wouldn't waste a frame of film on my outfits.

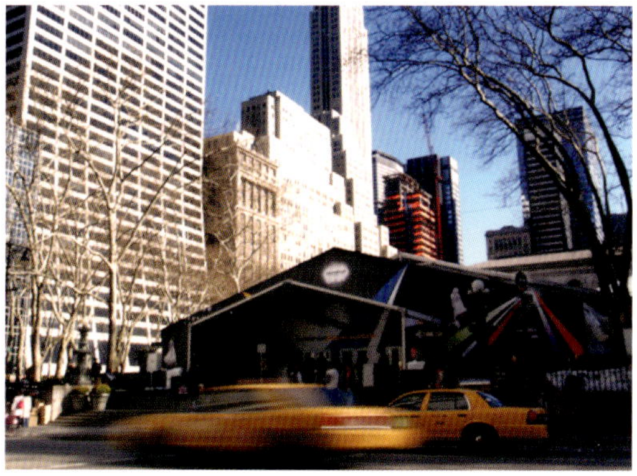

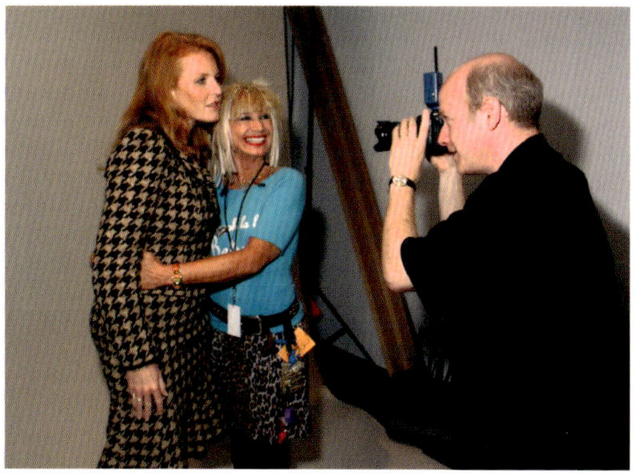

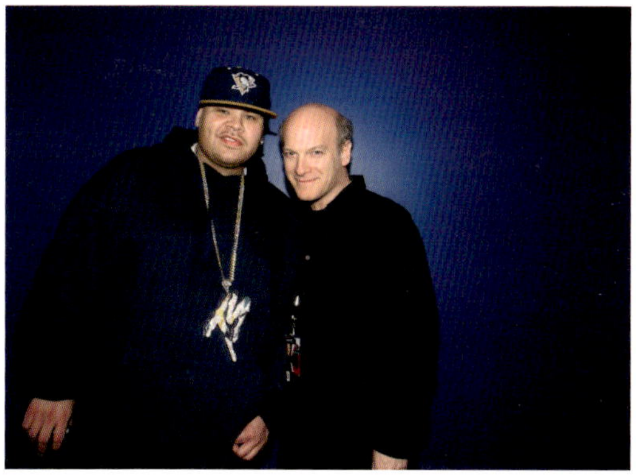

from top: Bryant Park, Feb. 2005; with Sarah Ferguson & Betsey Johnson; with Fat Joe

I'm fascinated by the folks who love and obsess over fashion—they're the intriguing ones for me.

I've always tried to find intensely driven subjects—artists, actors, musicians, politicians, writers...even, lately, porn stars. But in many ways the fashion world, with its frenetic energy, its extravagance, its fanatical devotion, rivals any realm I've ever focused on. The heady, intoxicating mix of creativity and commerce, art and money—that's a roller coaster worth watching.

I was invited into the fashion world in 1986 when Rei Kawakubo of Comme des Garçons asked me to photograph my artist friends wearing her clothes. With an antique 11x14-inch large-format view camera, I shot black-and-white portraits of dozens of art-world talents, including de Kooning, Schnabel, Rauschenberg, and Halley. Barneys soon wanted a "fashion portrait" campaign, and then Grace Mirabella hired me to shoot for her new magazine, *Mirabella*. My images were never really fashion photos—they were portraits of people who happened to be wearing the clothes of the moment. For me, it was about the sitter, not the sartorial.

In 1993 Fern Mallis, who was then executive director of the Council of Fashion Designers of America, commissioned me to photograph portraits for the CFDA's annual awards gala. Fern and I became fast friends, and shortly thereafter we discussed a portrait series that would document the great American fashion designers. Fern is a visionary and a unifier, and she opened doors for me. By now, I've photographed well over 100 of America's most revered designers, including those we're all on a first-name basis with: Calvin, Donna, Oscar, Betsey, Diane...

Not long after we met, Fern organized the first collection of fashion shows held under tents in Manhattan's Bryant Park. Now, in 2006, New York Fashion Week is owned by IMG—the sports and entertainment powerhouse—and has become a twice-a-year spectacle of fashion and celebrity watched from around the world.

In 2004 Fern introduced me to Olympus, the camera brand that had just signed on as title sponsor of the tents at Bryant Park. The company recognized the influence fashion and design have over the country (and the world), and they invited me to document the many boldface names that drive what was rechristened

Olympus Fashion Week. They armed me with Olympus E-Series digital cameras, built a backstage photography studio especially for me, and provided unprecedented access to designers, models, pop-culture icons (from rap stars to Oscar winners), and industry leaders.

I was more than a little hesitant at first to be shooting digital, since I was known for my love of film and large-format photography, but over the past two years I've been impressed with the results. Instant feed-back and instant gratification are what digital photography is all about.

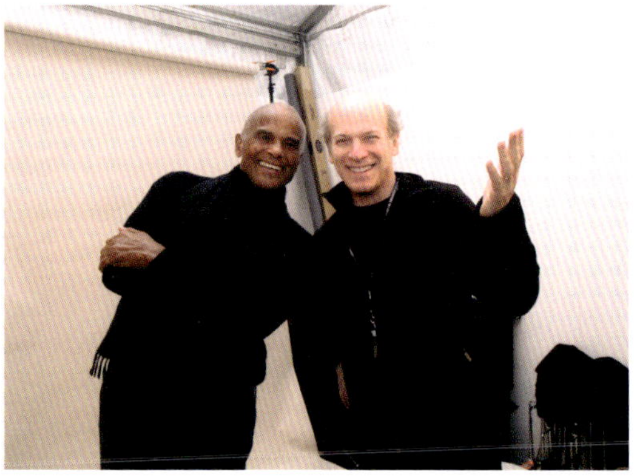

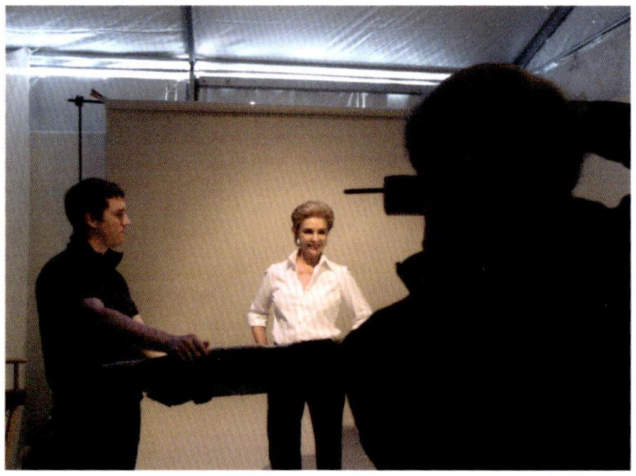

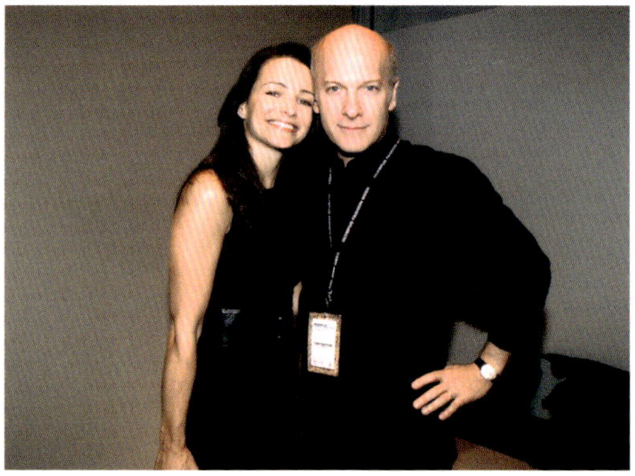

from top: with Harry Belafonte; with Carolina Herrera; with Kristin Davis

Fashion Week has changed tremendously since the days when I first attended the occasional show. The dynamic is global and nonstop, with traditional print-media coverage now being supplemented by satellite uplinks, an ever-swelling pack of paparazzi, obsessive blog coverage, live Webcasts, podcasts, and more. Everybody's watching not only to get the early word on tomorrow's fashions today, but also to gawk at the disparate group of A-listers from every walk of life who attend.

I remember Mary J. Blige and tennis greats James Blake and Venus and Serena Williams patiently lining up to get their portraits taken while I photographed Brandy. One season the Secret Service commandeered my studio for First Lady Laura Bush when she attended the Heart Truth's Red Dress fashion show (I was allowed to stay in my own studio despite the swarming Men in Black). We provided refuge for Beyoncé and her mom, who ducked in to escape the crush of (other) cameras. And Duchess Sarah Ferguson felt so at home she kicked off her shoes and sipped cocktails with a mash of male models in my perfectly lit Olympus studio.

The fashion world I have come to know is a complex mix of fun, big business, big egos, and a strong passion for social causes. There are a hell of a lot of talented people under the tents, and I've had a great time meeting and photographing them. Truth be told, it's been fabulous—including a visit from the rapper Fabolous, who was quite fabulous.

The portraits in *Look* are a testament to the power of Olympus Fashion Week. It is an event like no other, an event that brings together the power brokers and the wannabes, the driven and the dreamers, the freakish and the fashionable.

To each of the designers, celebrities, editors, models, and other notables who kindly sat for me, thank you for your time, humor, and cooperation. I hope you enjoy your portrait as much I enjoyed photographing you. You look amazing.

I'll see you again at the tents, camera in hand...

TIMOTHY GREENFIELD-SANDERS

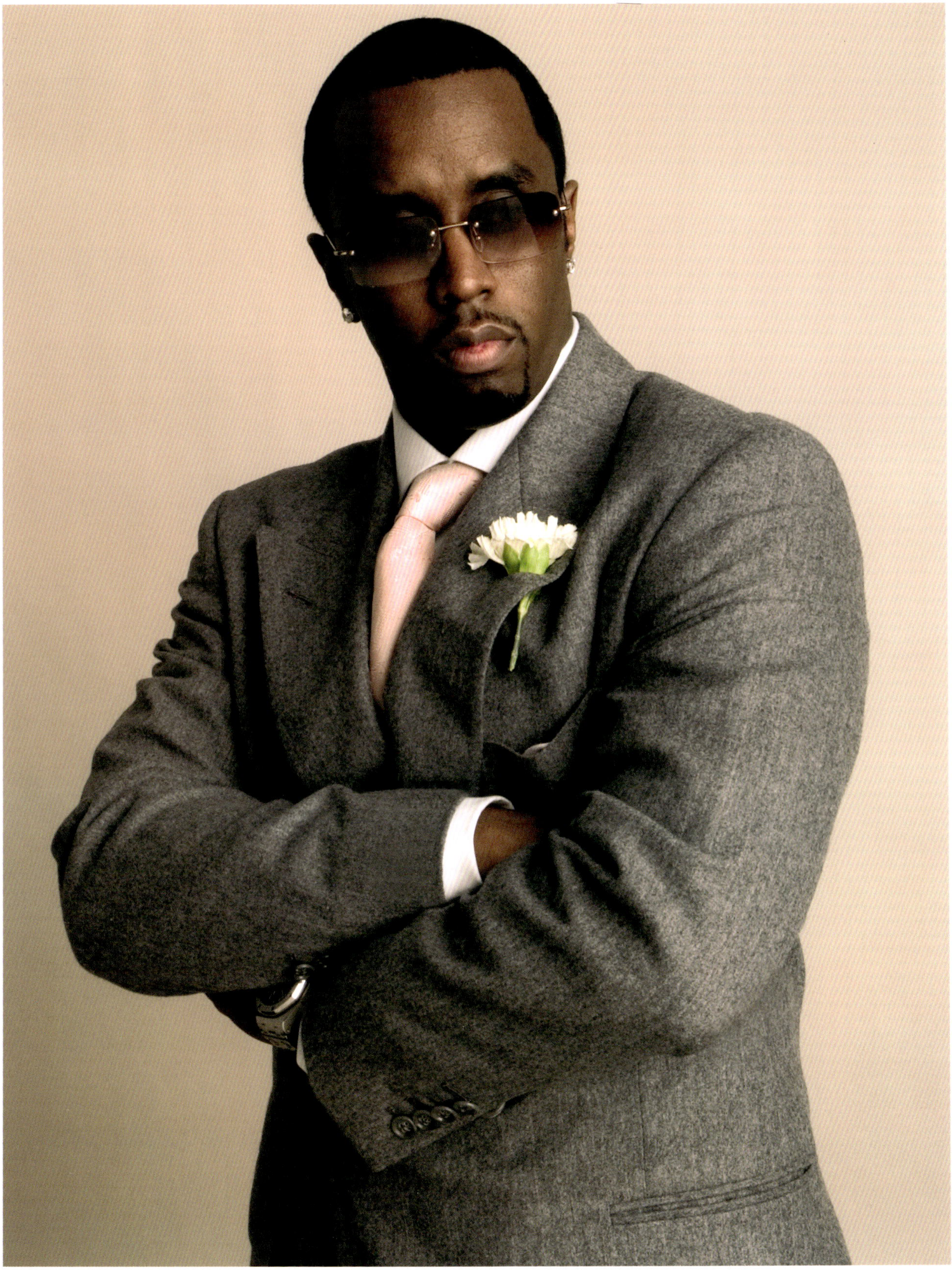

SEAN COMBS Mega-Mogul

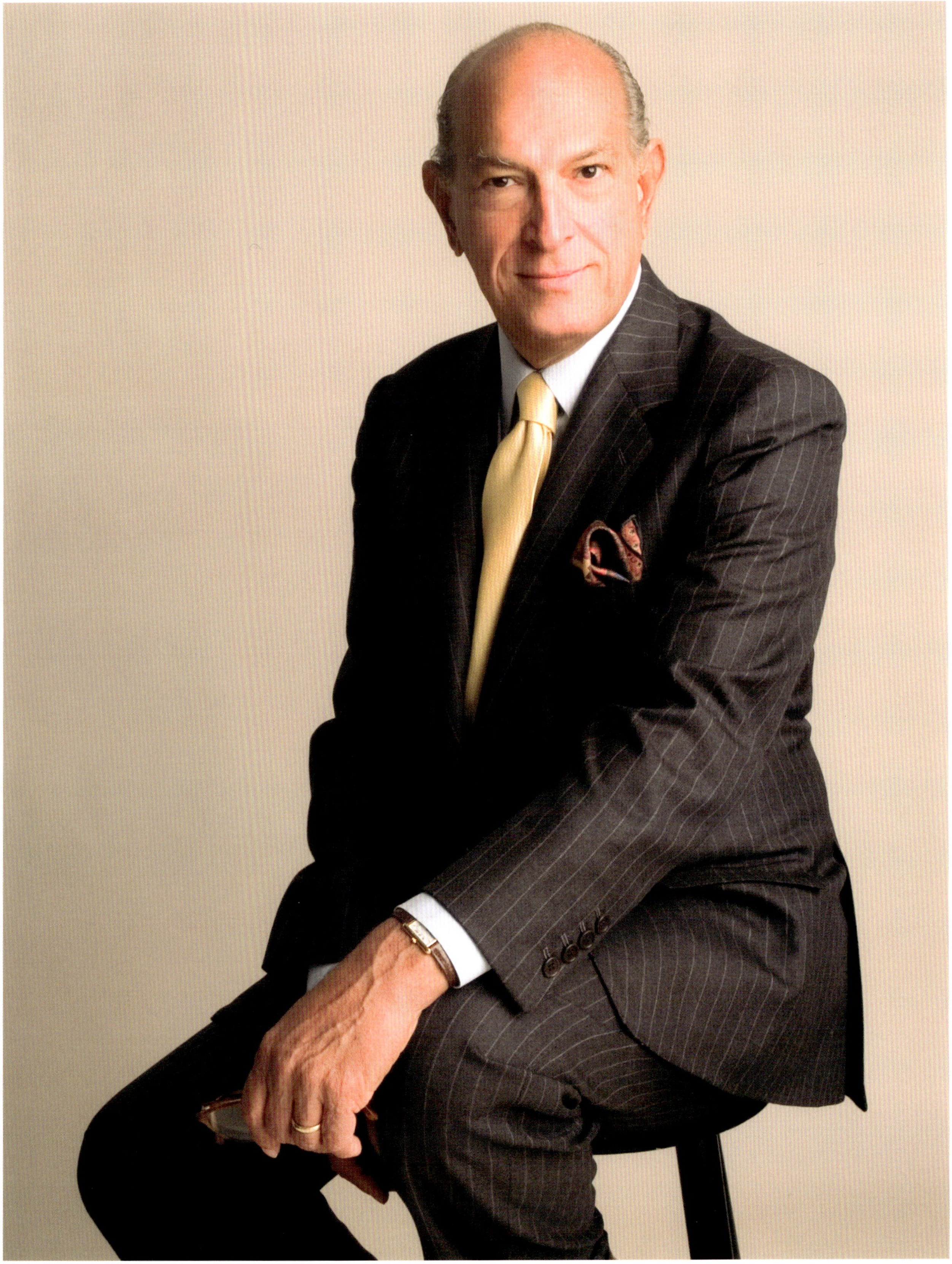

OSCAR DE LA RENTA Designer

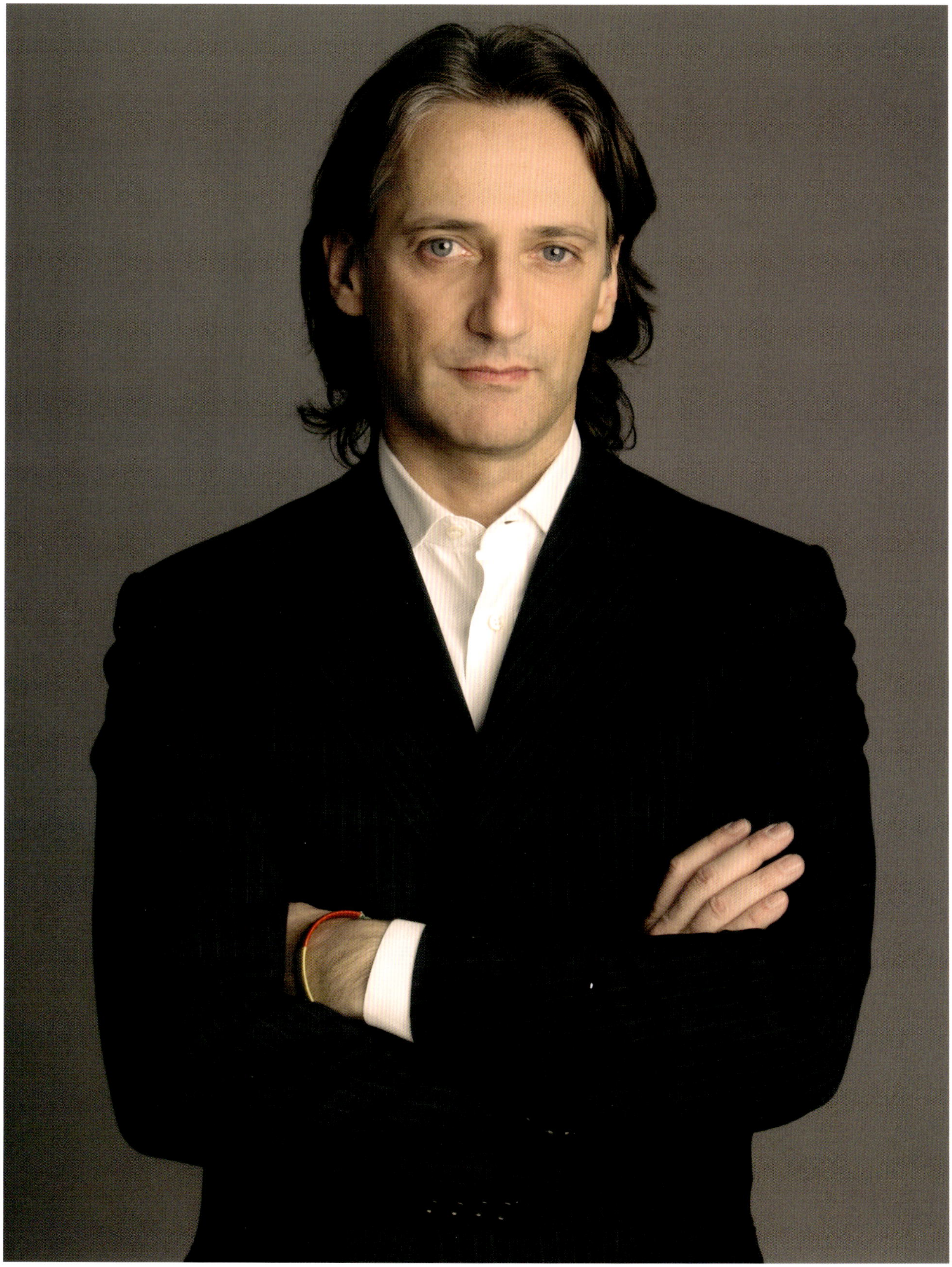

LUCA ORLANDI Designer, Luca Luca

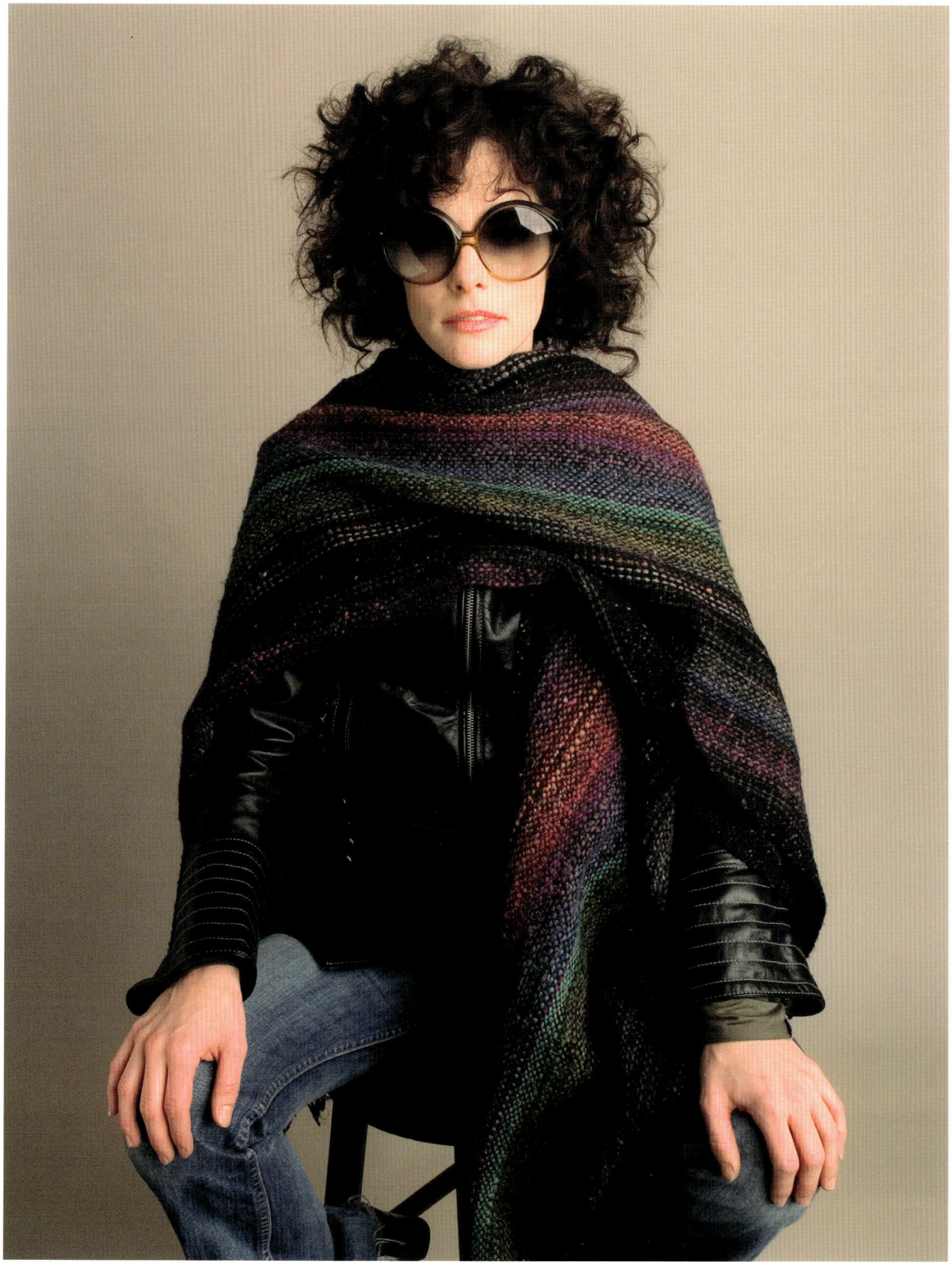

PARKER POSEY Actor

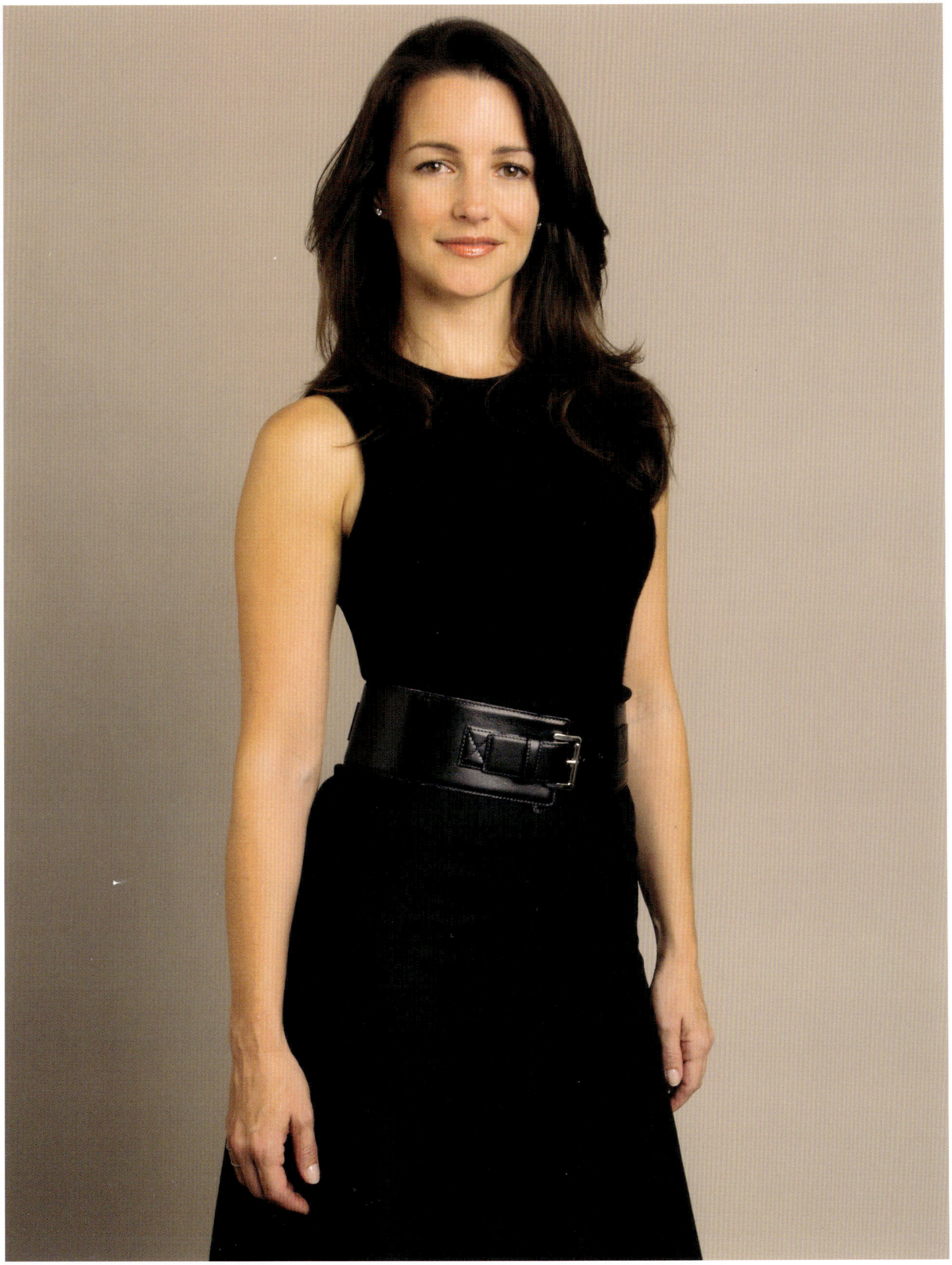

KRISTIN DAVIS Actor

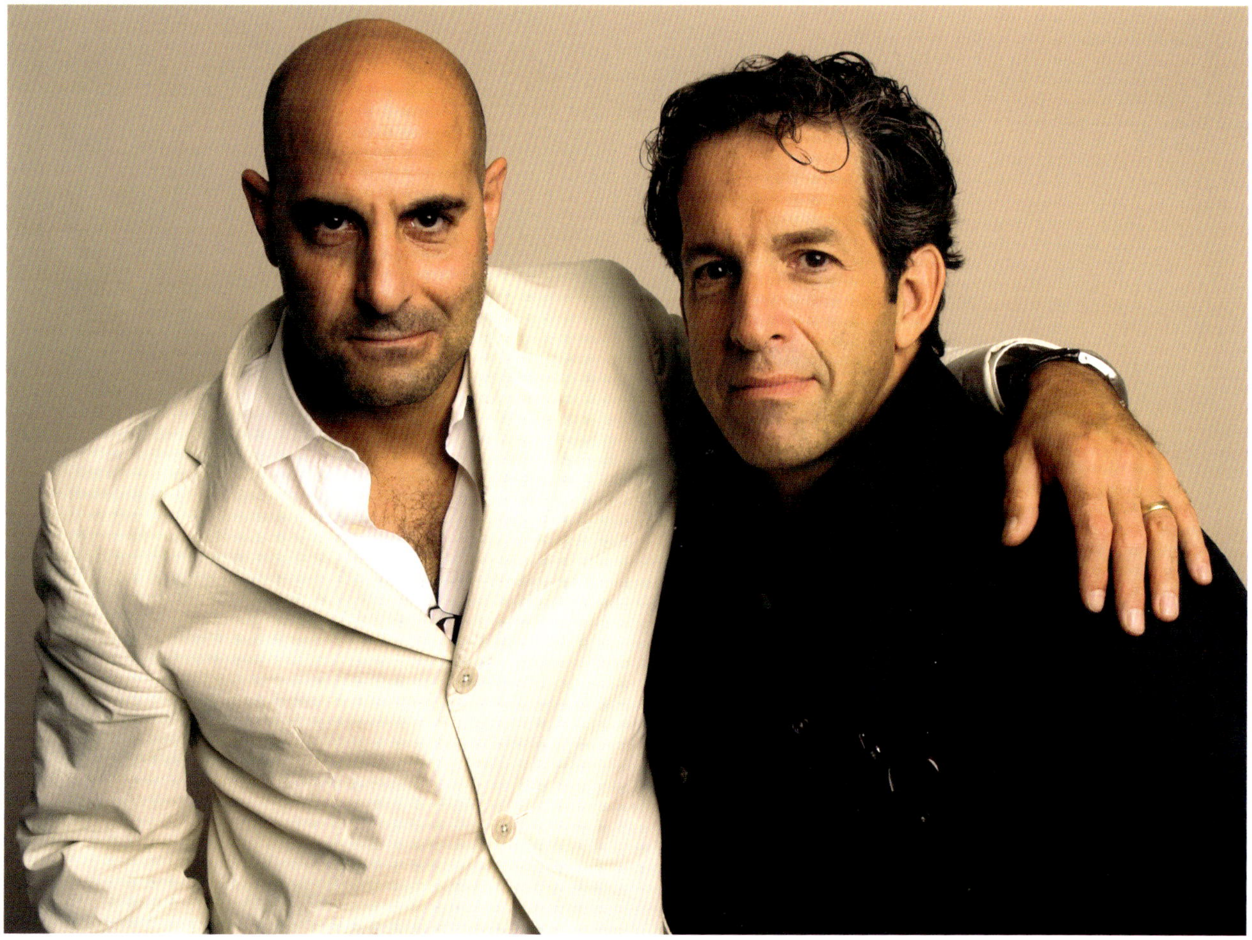

STANLEY TUCCI Actor
KENNETH COLE Designer

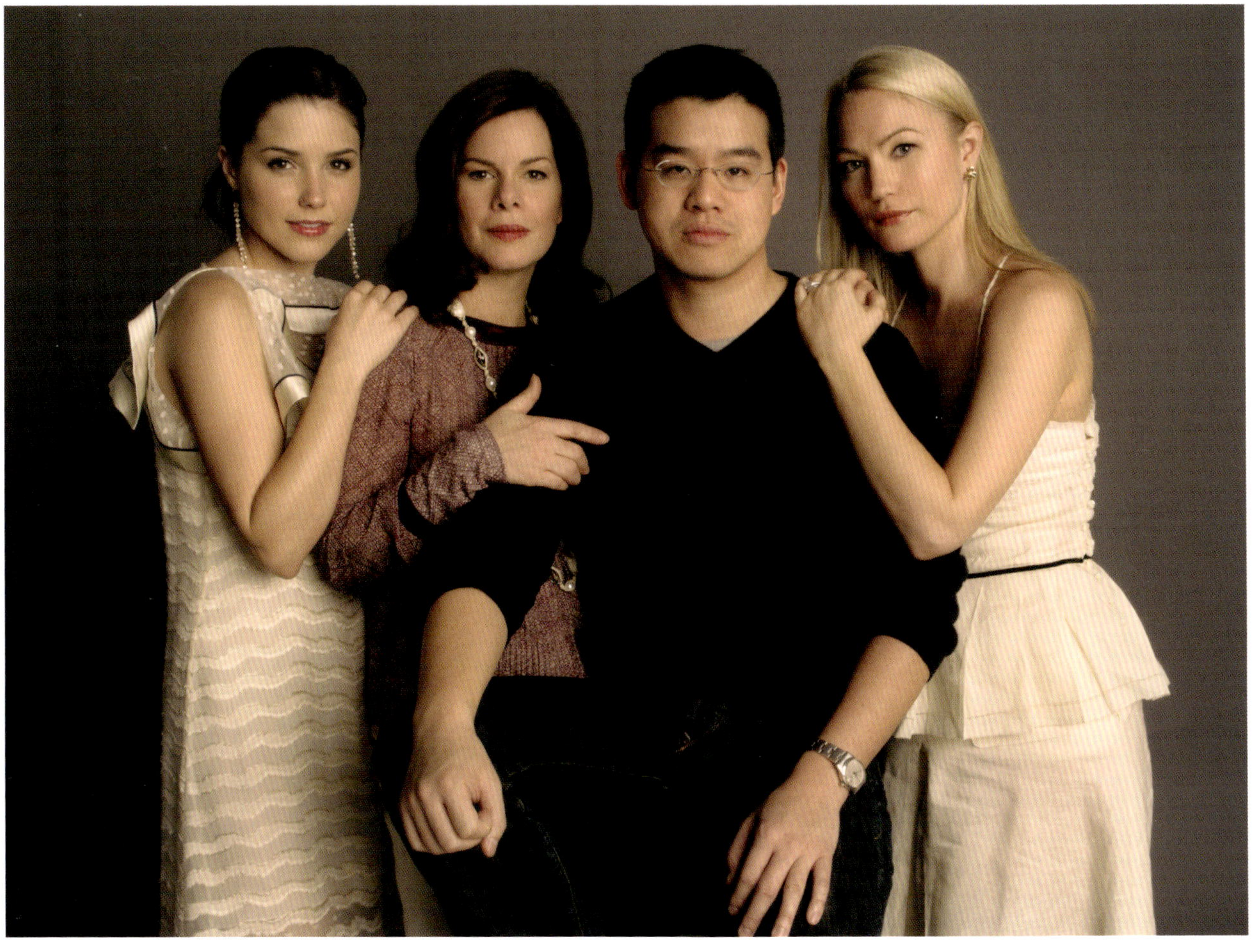

PETER SOM Designer
SOPHIA BUSH, MARCIA GAY HARDEN & SARAH WYNTER Actors

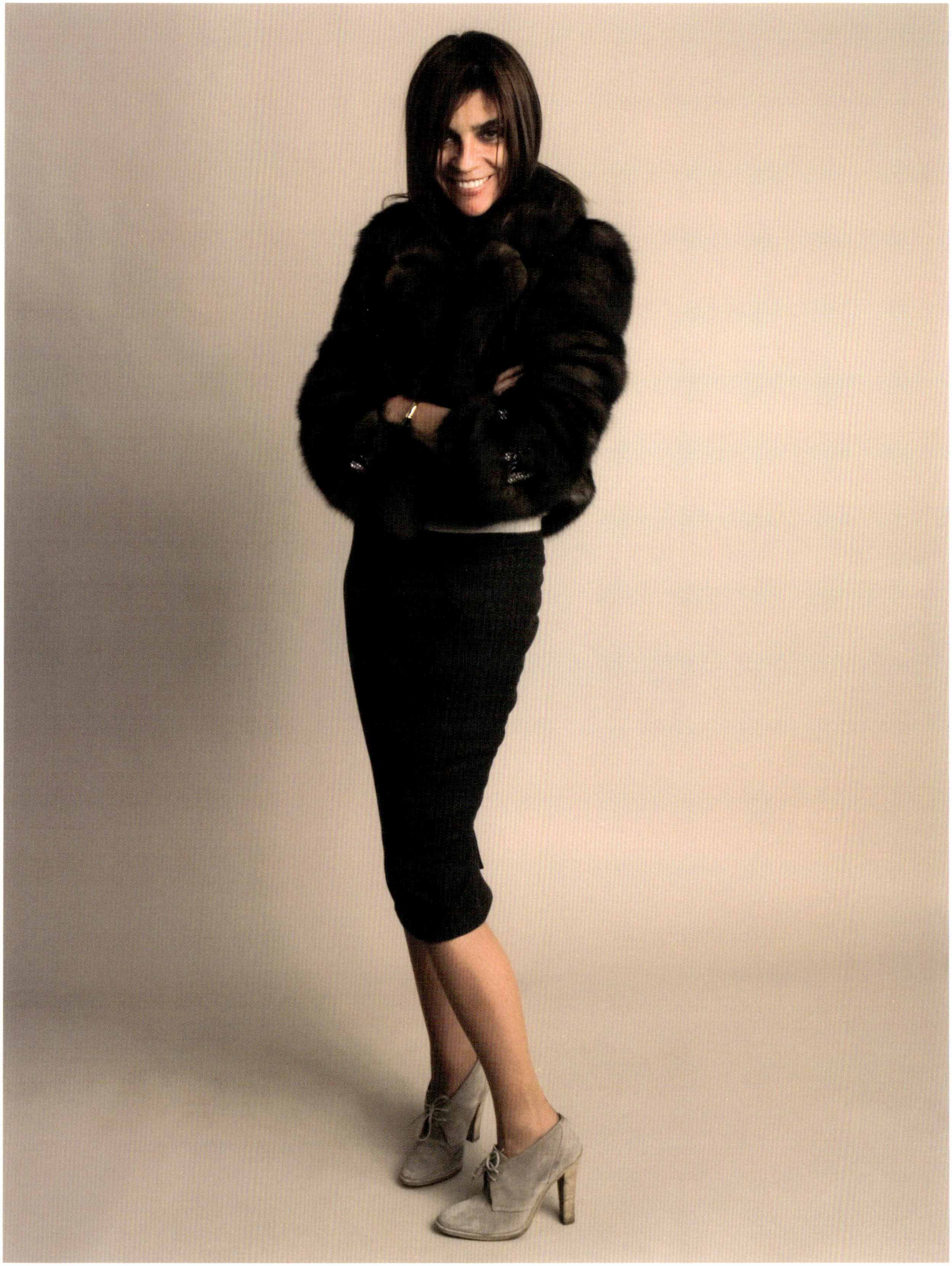

CARINE ROITFELD Editor in Chief, French *Vogue*

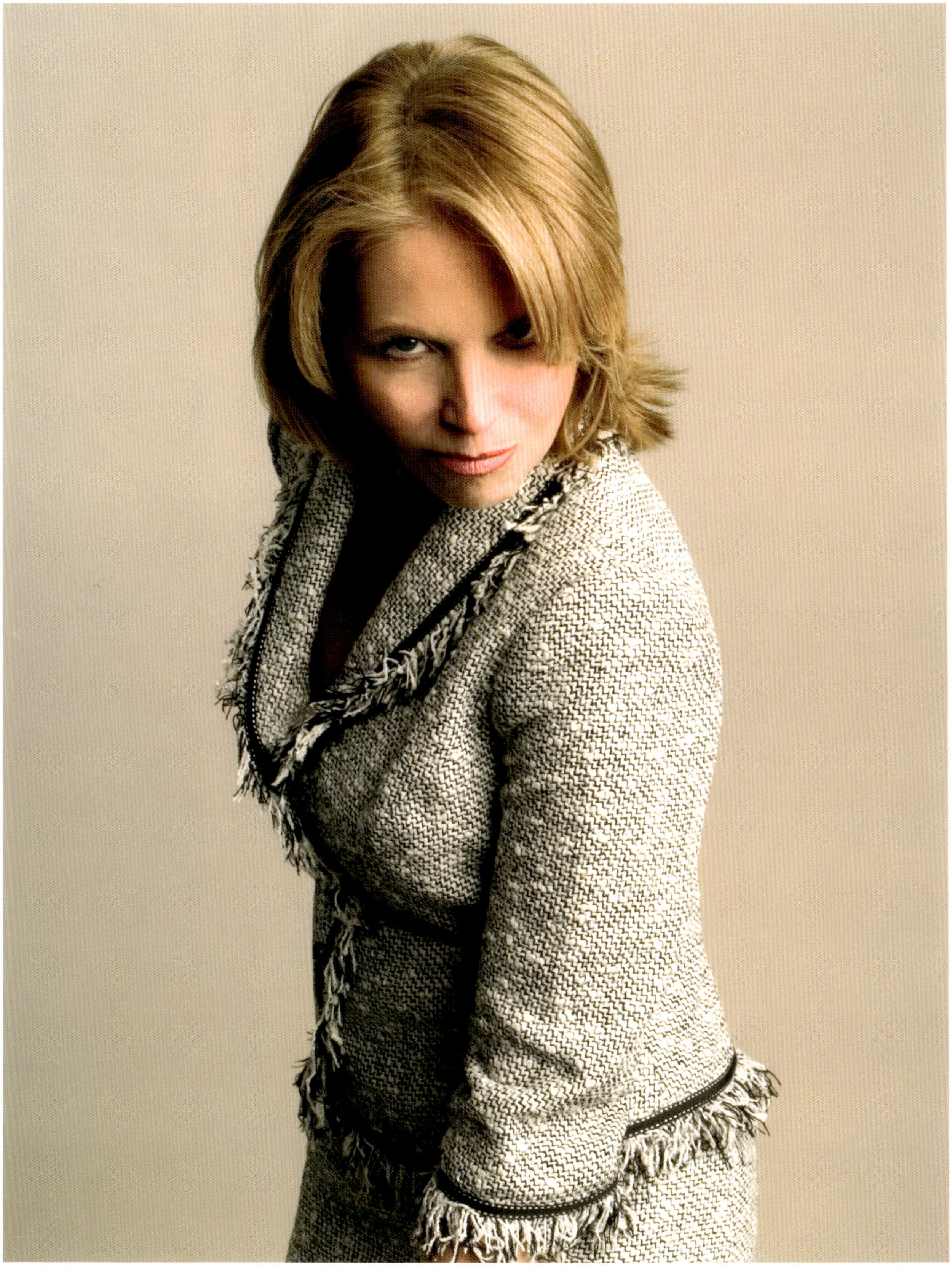

KATIE COURIC Co-founder, National Colorectal Cancer Research Alliance

Since I have a highly visible job in television, my style selections are out there for everyone to see. And given that I get lots of feedback on them, I can personally attest to America's interest in fashion!

The world is a much more fashion-forward place than when I began my career; the fashion industry has moved from niche and exclusive to mainstream and accessible. Fashion is a significant cultural force, and its key players—the designers who create and the models who bring us their work—command attention much like A-list actors and rock stars. Fashion's big names are powerful, and when their influence is channeled in support of a cause, the impact is enormous.

After losing my husband Jay to colon cancer, I joined forces with the Entertainment Industry Foundation and established the National Colorectal Cancer Research Alliance (EIF's NCCRA) in an effort to put my own influence—and that of others in the entertainment industry—to good use. We use the power of celebrity and "buzz" about popular culture to generate awareness of this highly preventable disease.

Colon cancer is the second-leading cause of cancer deaths in America, yet it's curable 90 percent of the time when detected early. SCREENING IS KEY. Men and women are diagnosed in virtually equal numbers, but many women still think of it as a man's disease and underestimate their risk. More than 140,000 people in this country will be diagnosed with colon cancer this year, and 56,000 Americans will lose their lives because of this disease.

I was so moved by the fashion industry's compassion and concern about health crises including AIDS, breast cancer, and heart disease that I enlisted its help, through a partnership with Olympus under the tents at Fashion Week, to focus attention on colon cancer. Fashion Week has provided a wonderful platform for us to spread the word about the importance of screening in combating colon cancer. Our effort, called "BE SEEN, BE SCREENED," is aimed at making it fashionable to talk about colon cancer, and at making sure this is one trend that won't change next season.

Timothy Greenfield-Sanders, who took the portraits you see on these pages, has become an invaluable ally in the fight against colon cancer. In September 2005, Timothy generously donated several of his original photographs—each signed personally by its celebrity subject—to an eBay auction that raised funds to support the NCCRA's work. These portraits, and the others in this book, give you a glimpse backstage at New York Fashion Week, where celebrities let their hair down and models and designers get ready to look cool and unflappable when the music starts and they hit the runway.

With your purchase of *Look*, you'll join our ever-growing family of NCCRA supporters. Timothy and his publisher, powerHouse Books, have agreed to donate a portion of proceeds from sales of *Look* to the NCCRA. And we plan to put the donation to good use: funding the research and the outreach necessary to continue raising awareness of this cancer threat and, ultimately, to save lives.

I am grateful to Timothy for his generosity, and to everyone in the fashion community who has helped with my colon cancer work: Heidi Klum, Iman, Kenneth Cole, Heatherette, Vera Wang, Anna Wintour, and many, many others. Colon cancer survivor and designer extraordinaire Carmen Marc Valvo has a special place in my heart for speaking out about screening's life-saving role in his own life and the importance of knowing your family's medical history.

Thanks to all for so readily embracing this cause, for your generosity, and for your passion to make a difference—all things that will never go out of style.

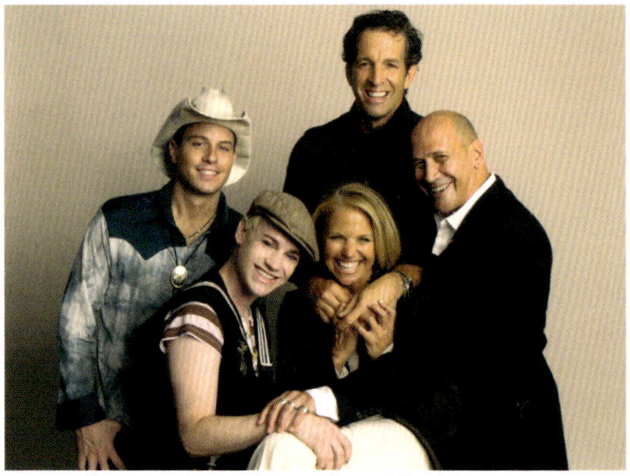

Katie with Heatherette, Kenneth Cole, and Carmen Marc Valvo

KATIE COURIC

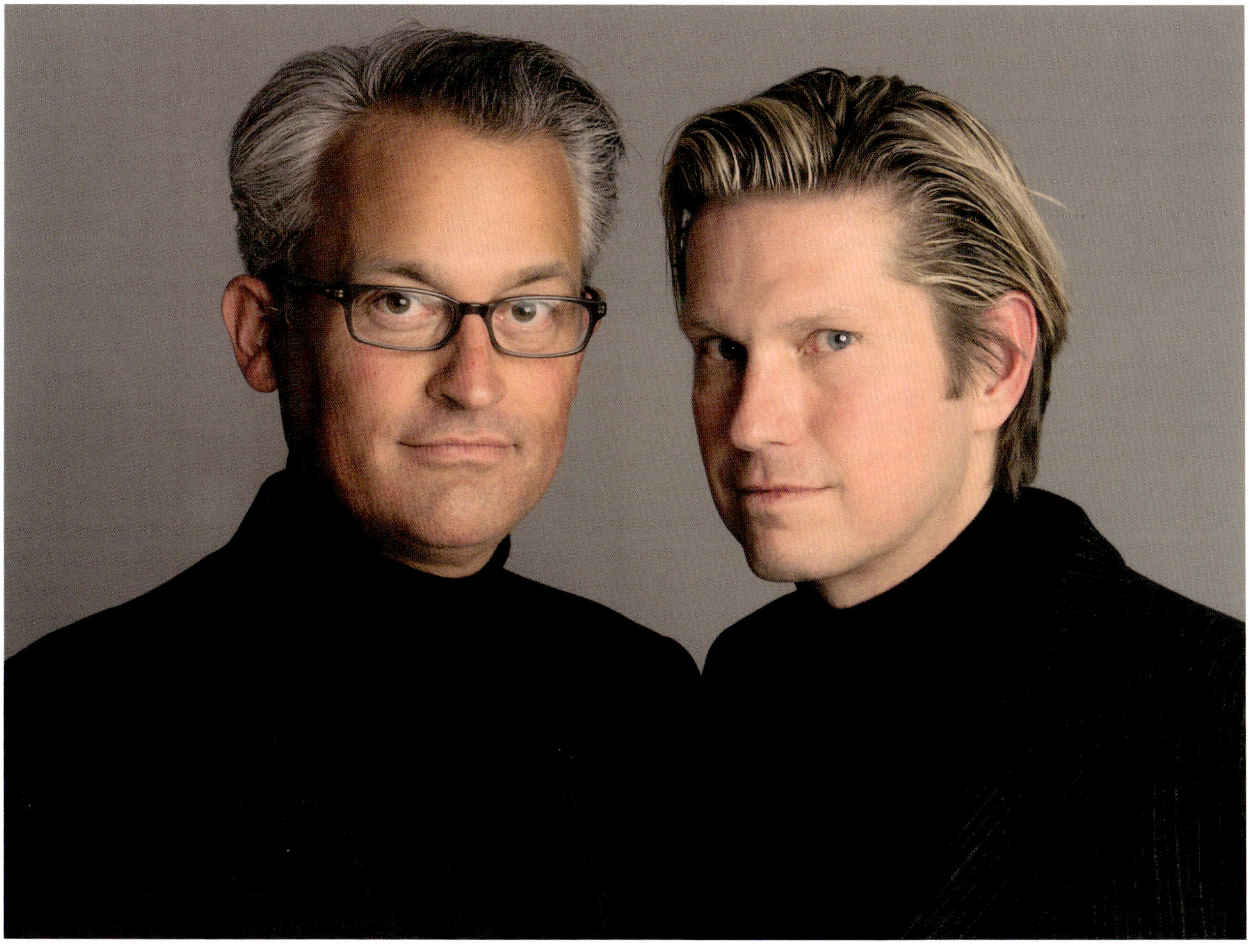

MARK BADGLEY & JAMES MISCHKA Designers, Badgley Mischka

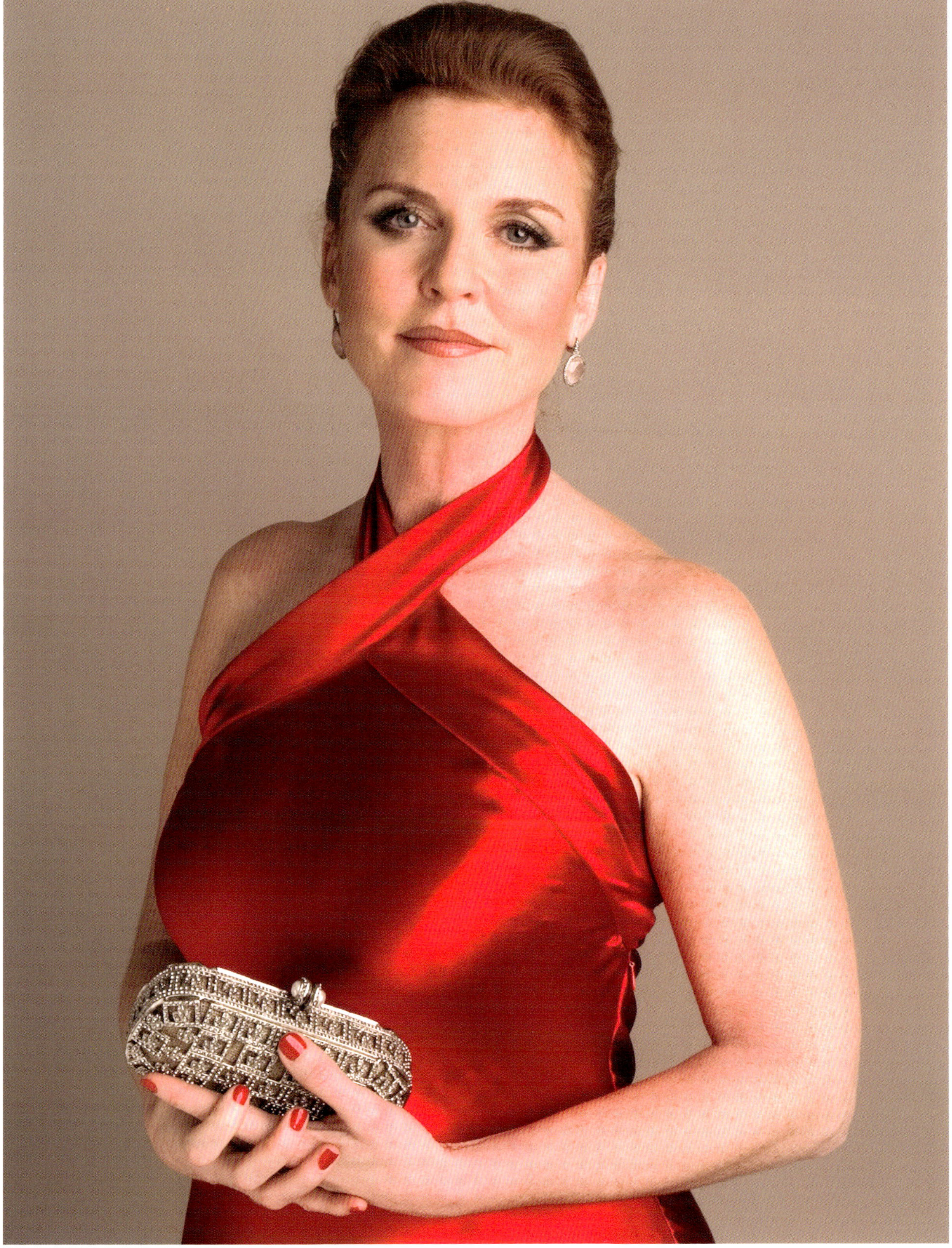

SARAH FERGUSON Duchess of York

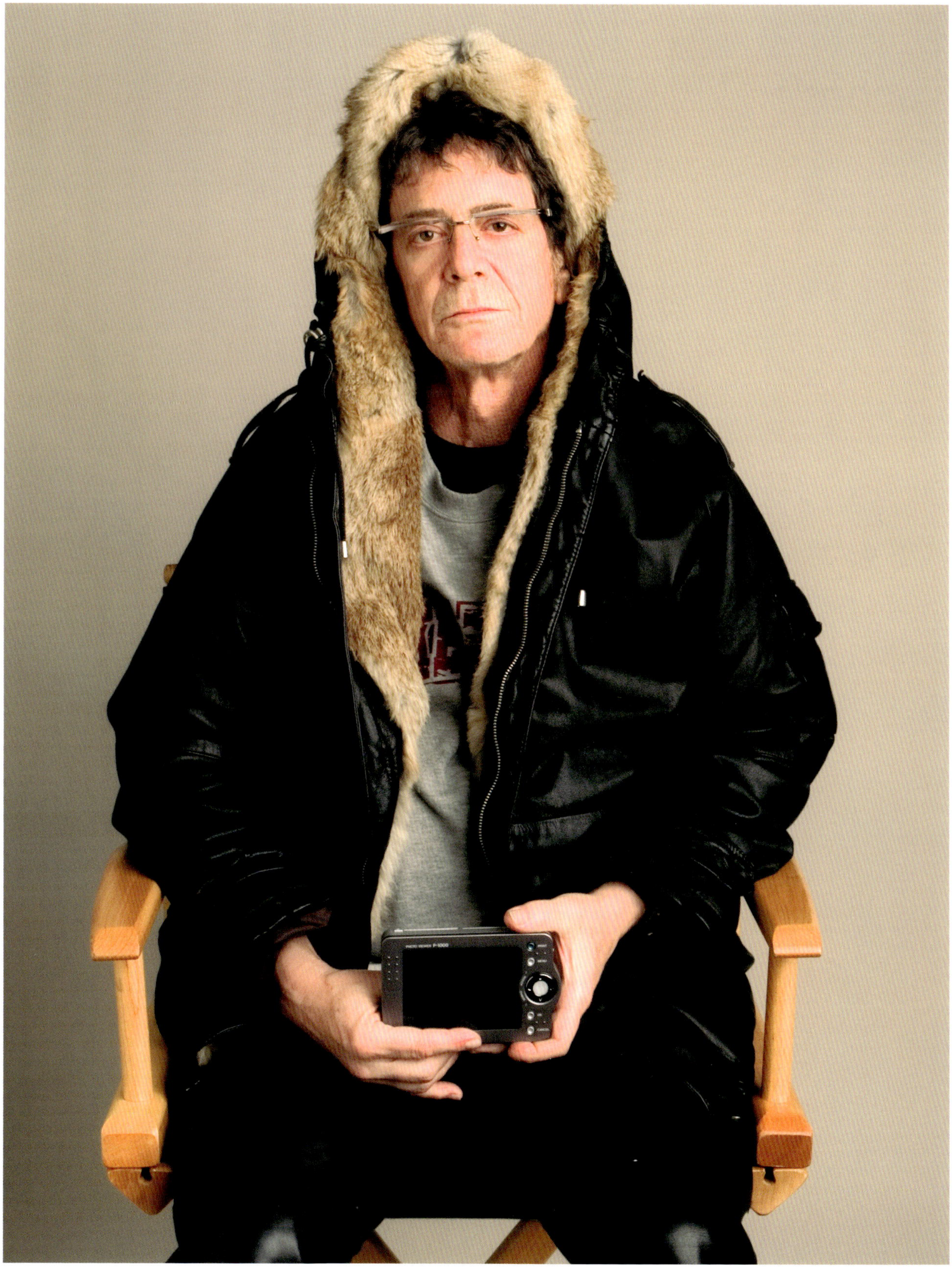

LOU REED

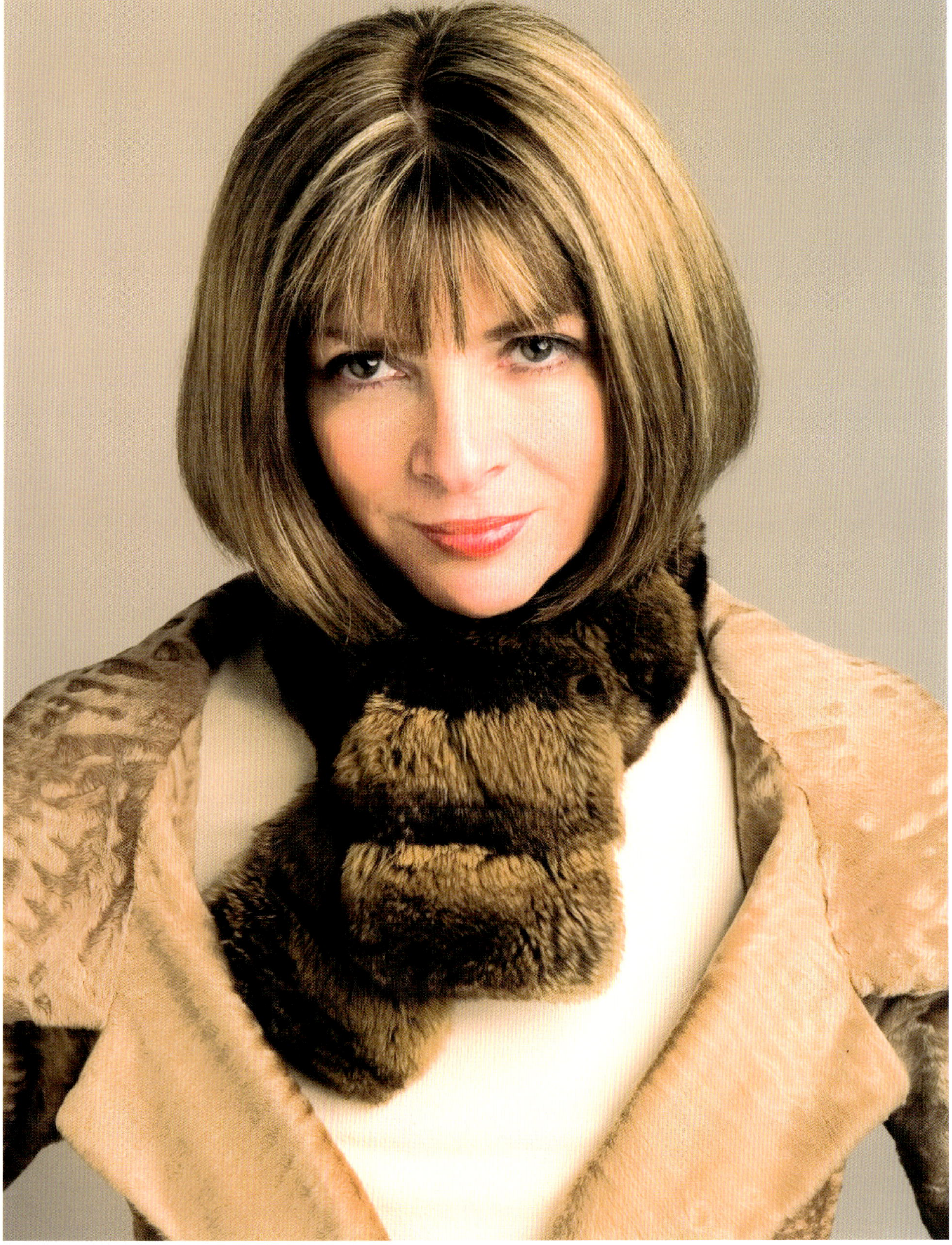

ANNA WINTOUR Editor in Chief, *Vogue*

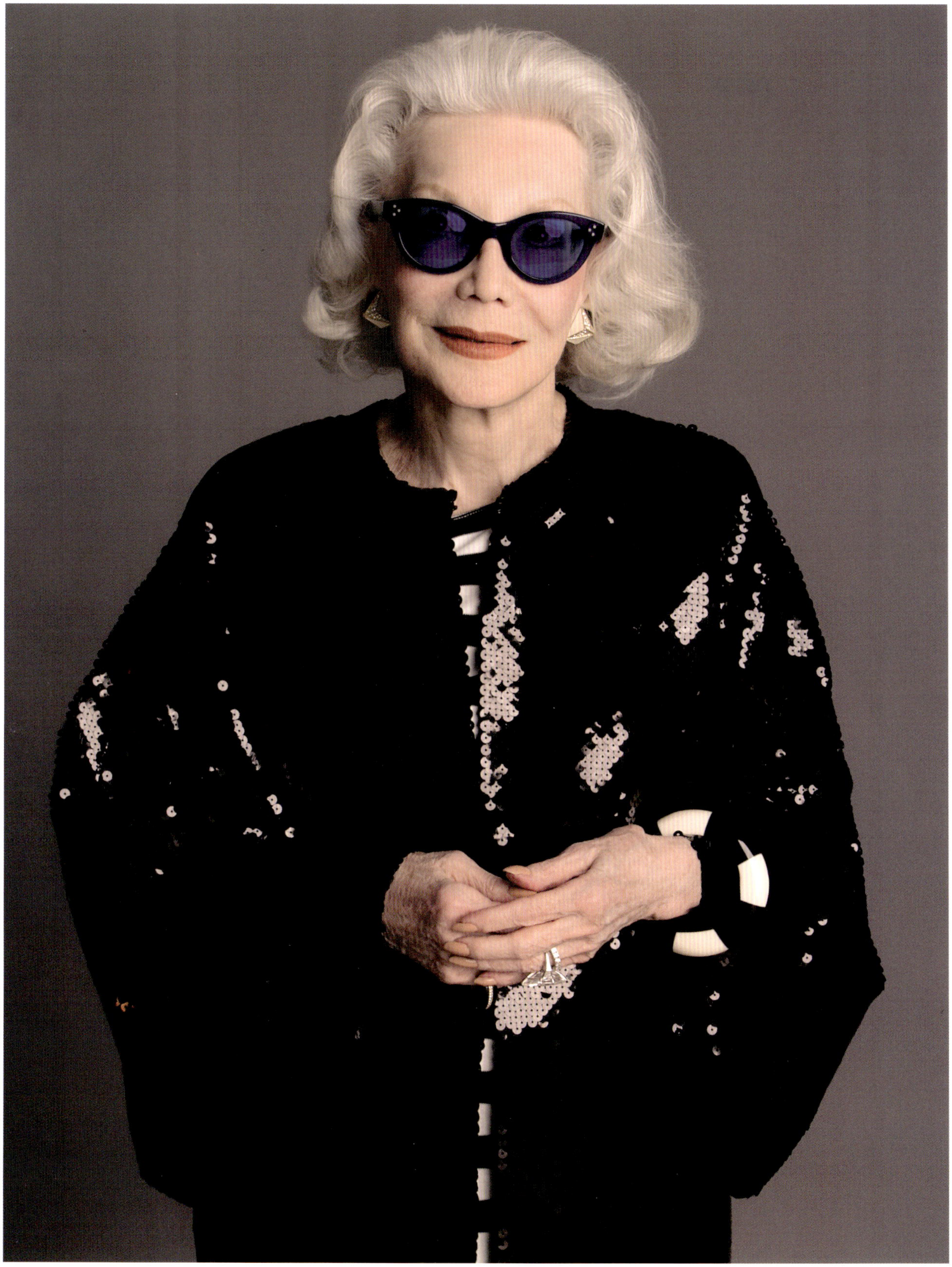

ANNE SLATER Grande Dame

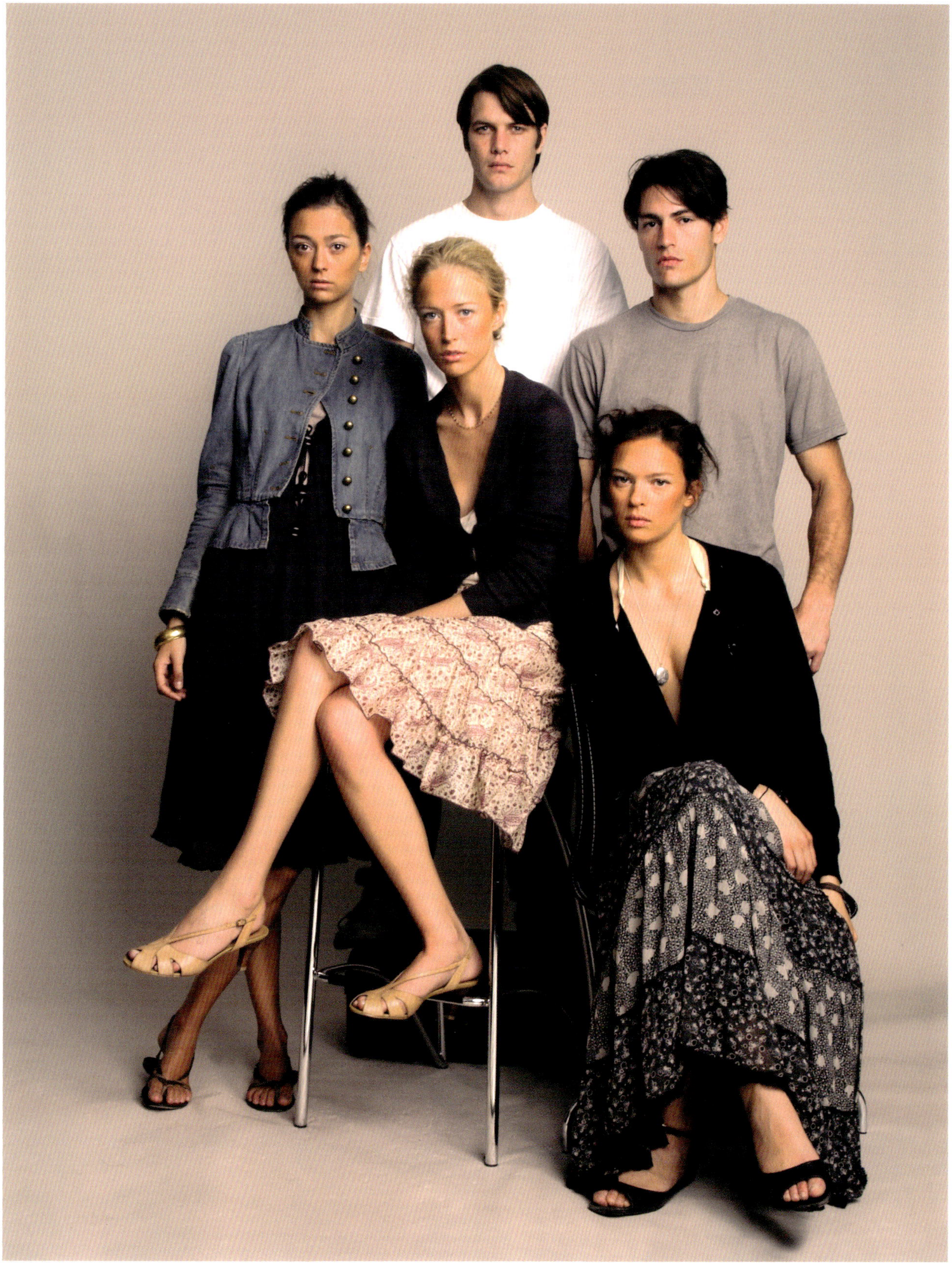

HEATH TOWNSEND & TYSON BALLOU
MORGANE DUBLED, RAQUEL ZIMMERMANN & ELISE CROMBEZ Models

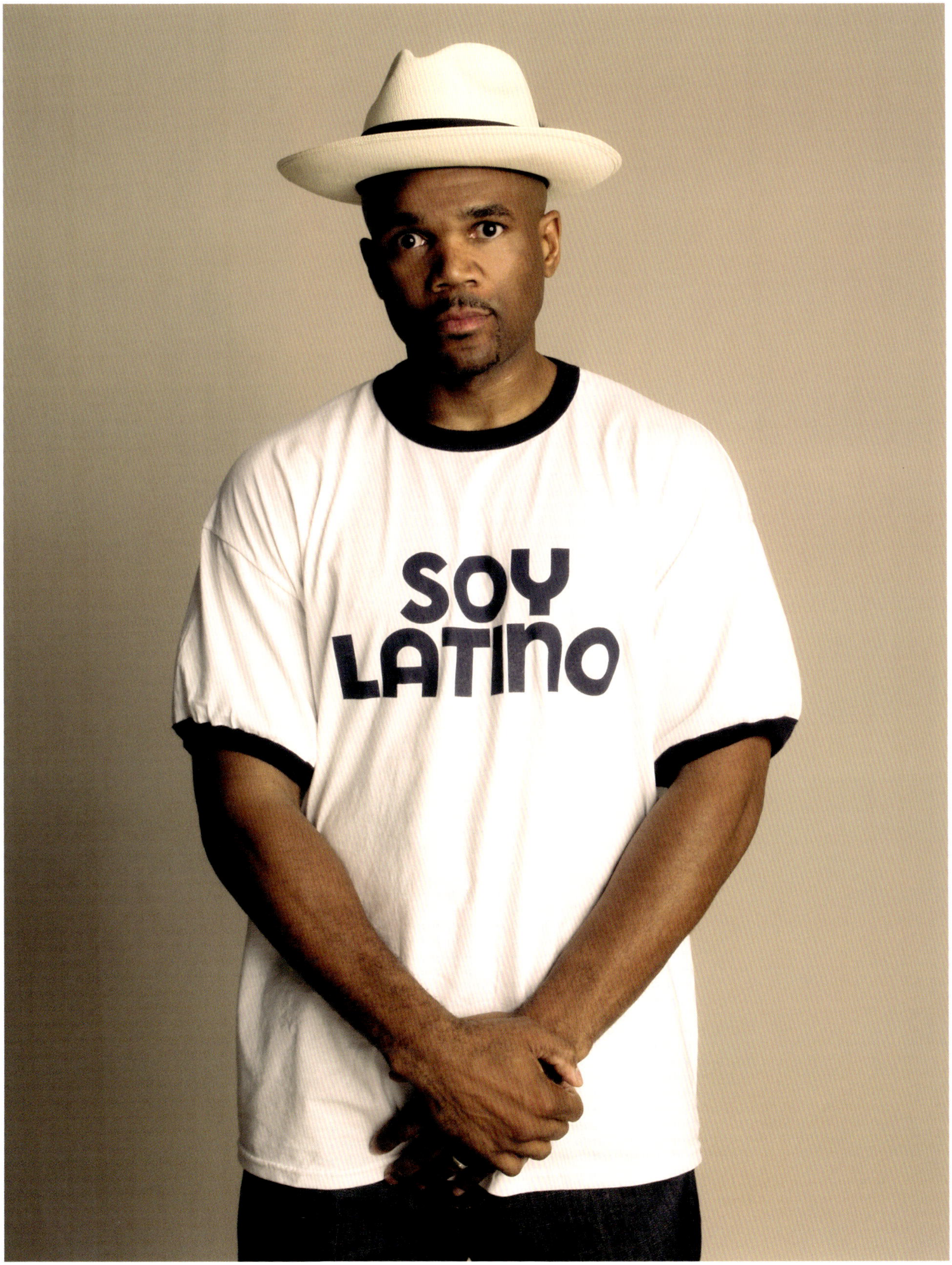

DARRYL MCDANIELS Rap Icon, Run DMC

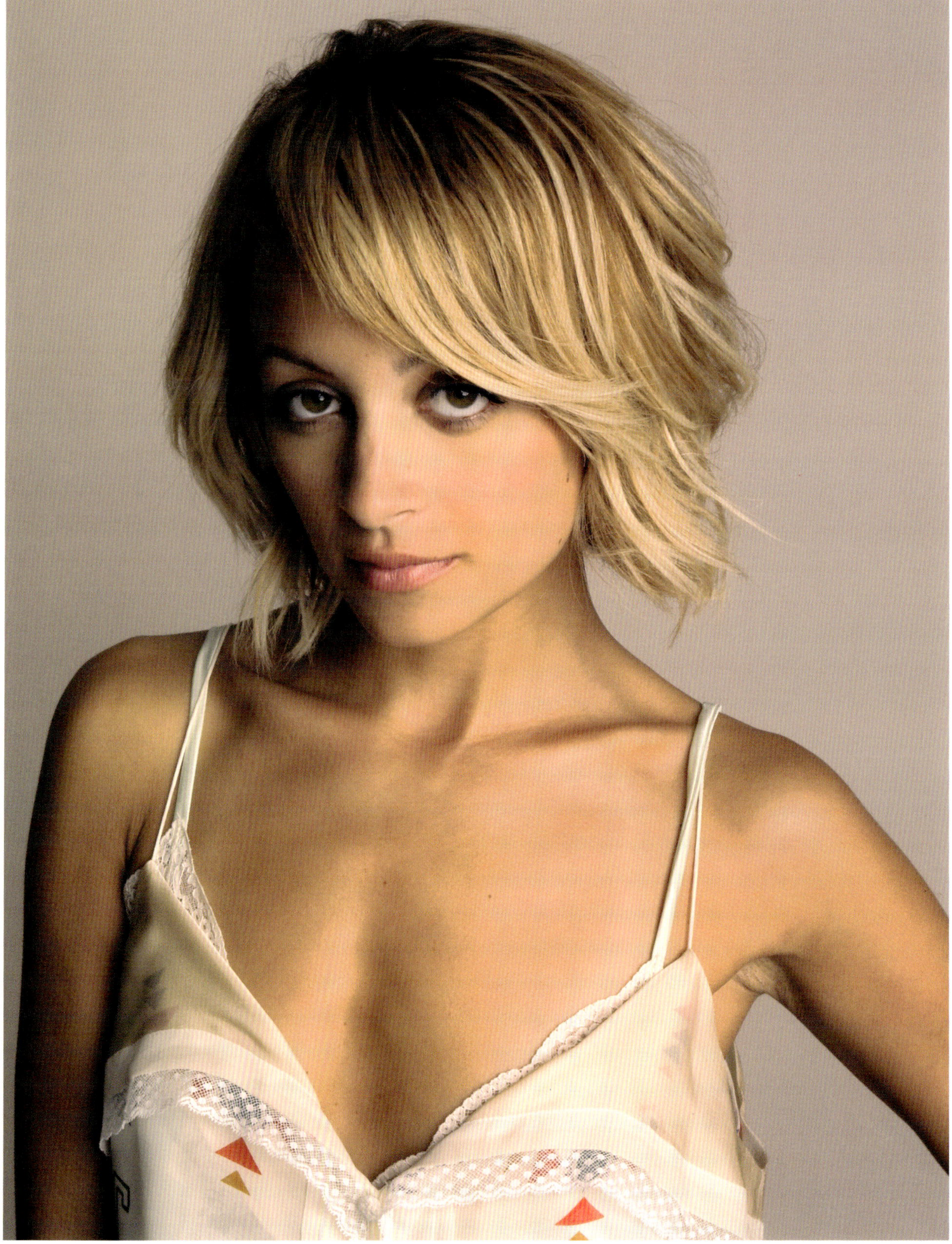

NICOLE RICHIE Starlet

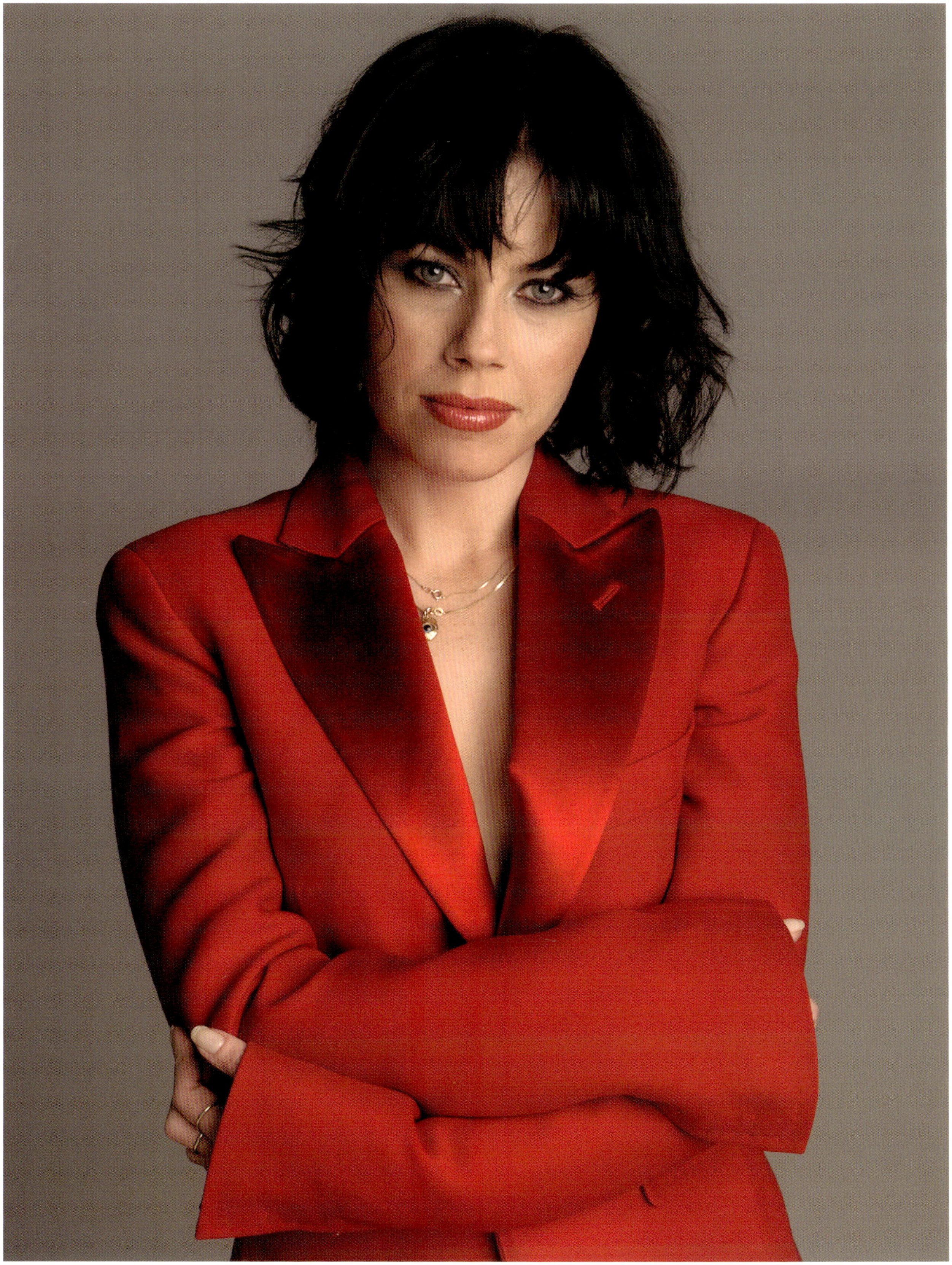

FAIRUZA BALK Actor

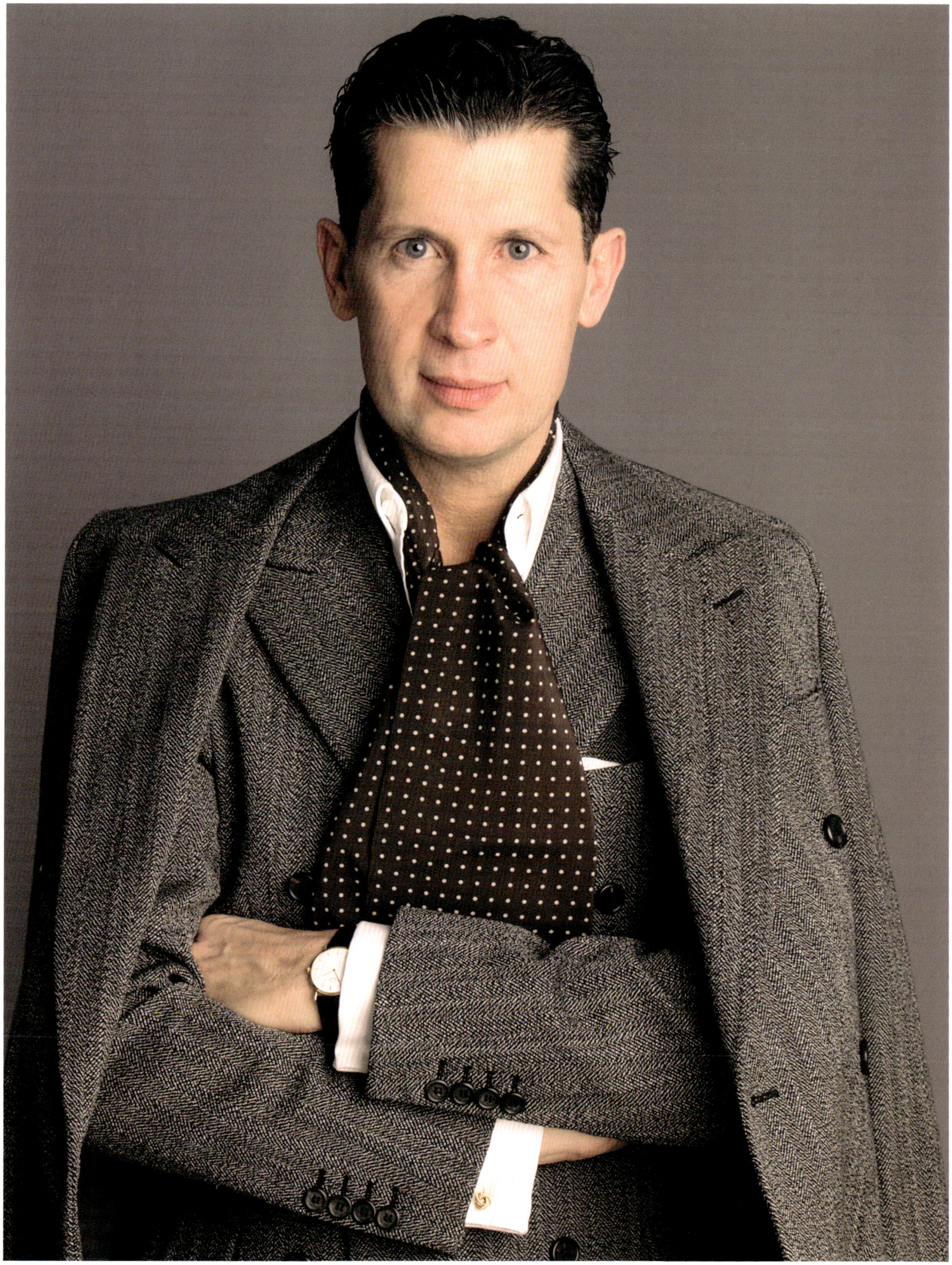

STEFANO TONCHI Editor, *T: The New York Times Style Magazine*

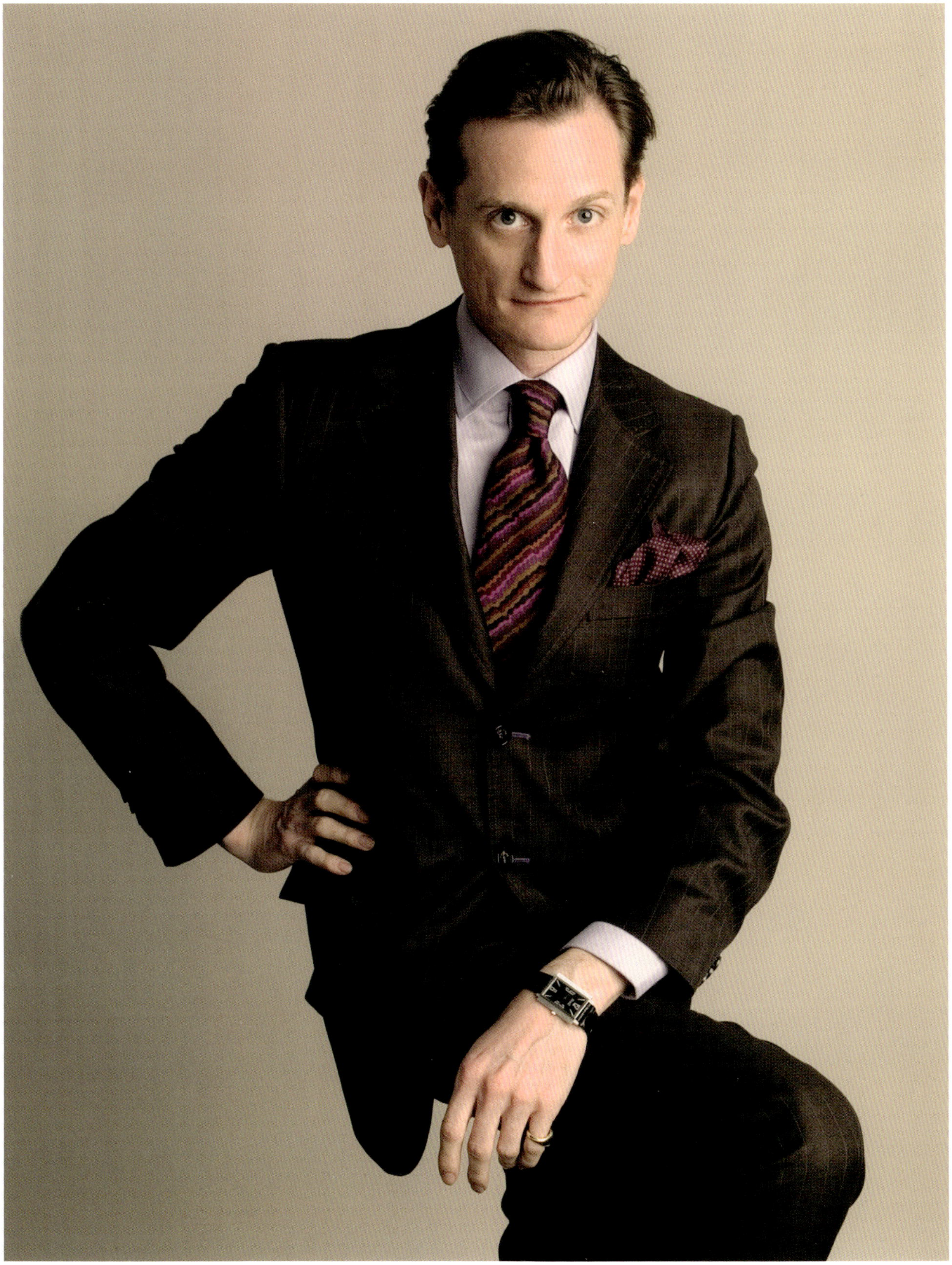

HAMISH BOWLES European Editor at Large, *Vogue*

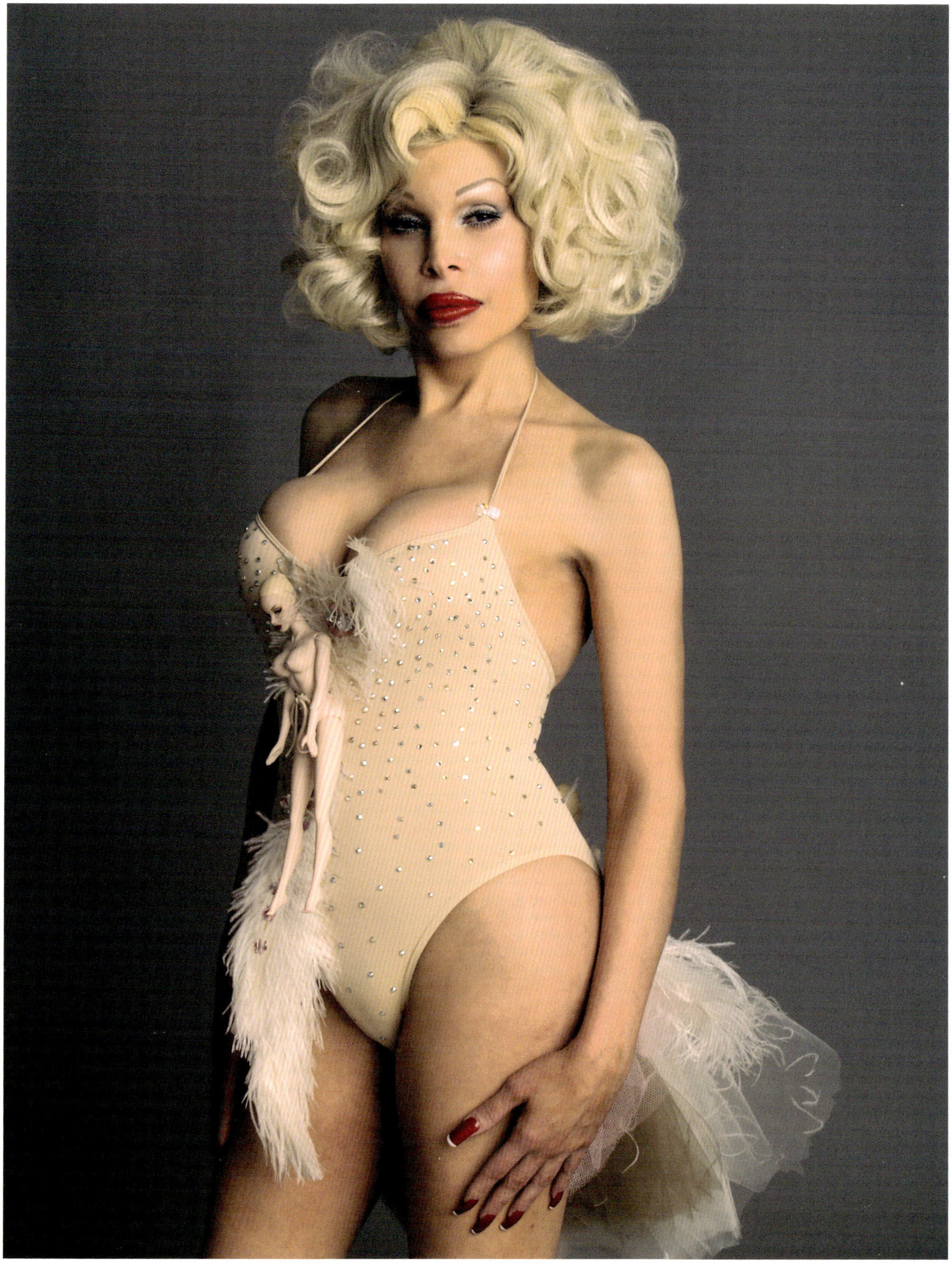

AMANDA LEPORE Muse

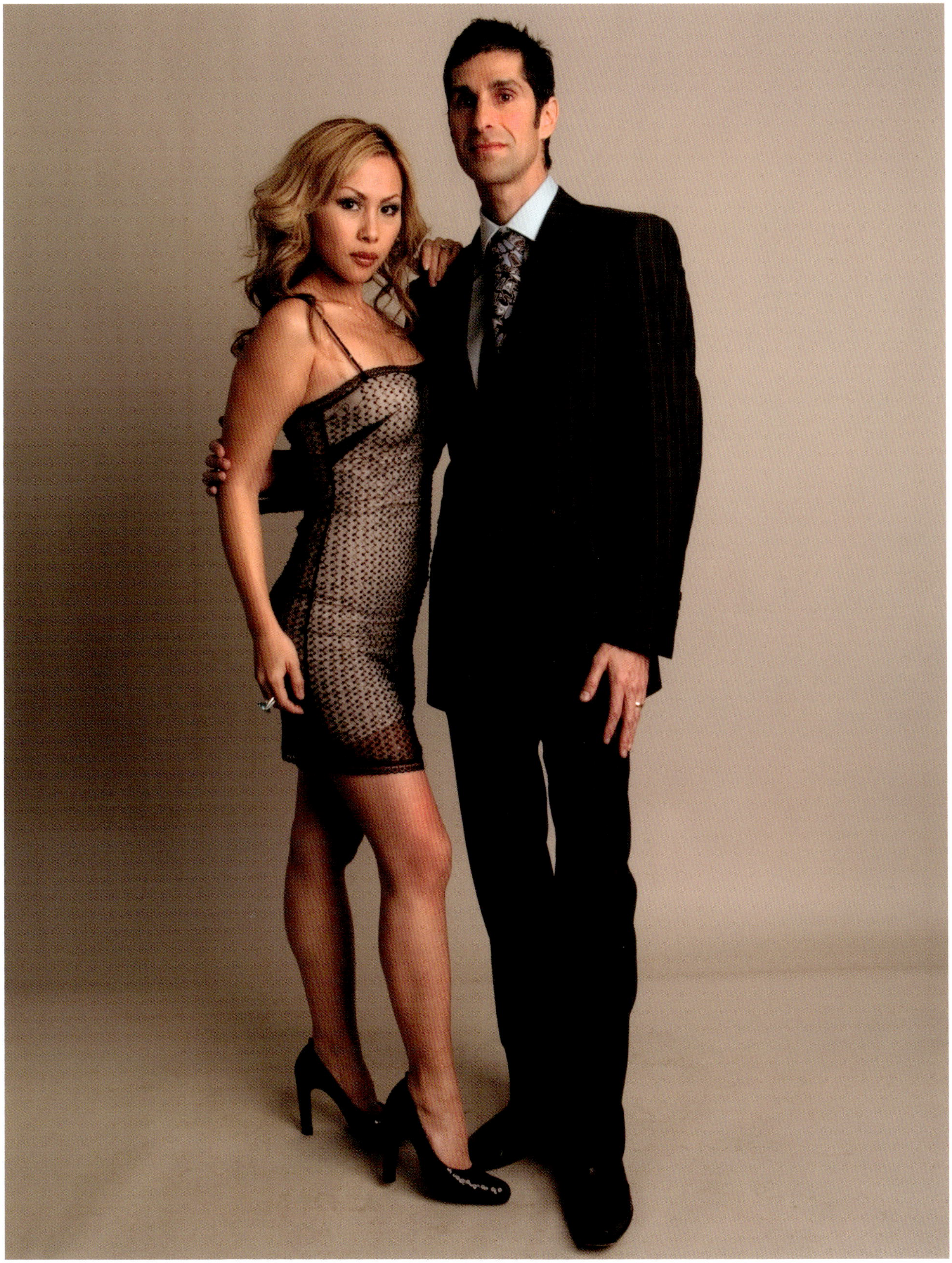

ETTY & PERRY FARRELL Alternative Music Legend with Mrs. F

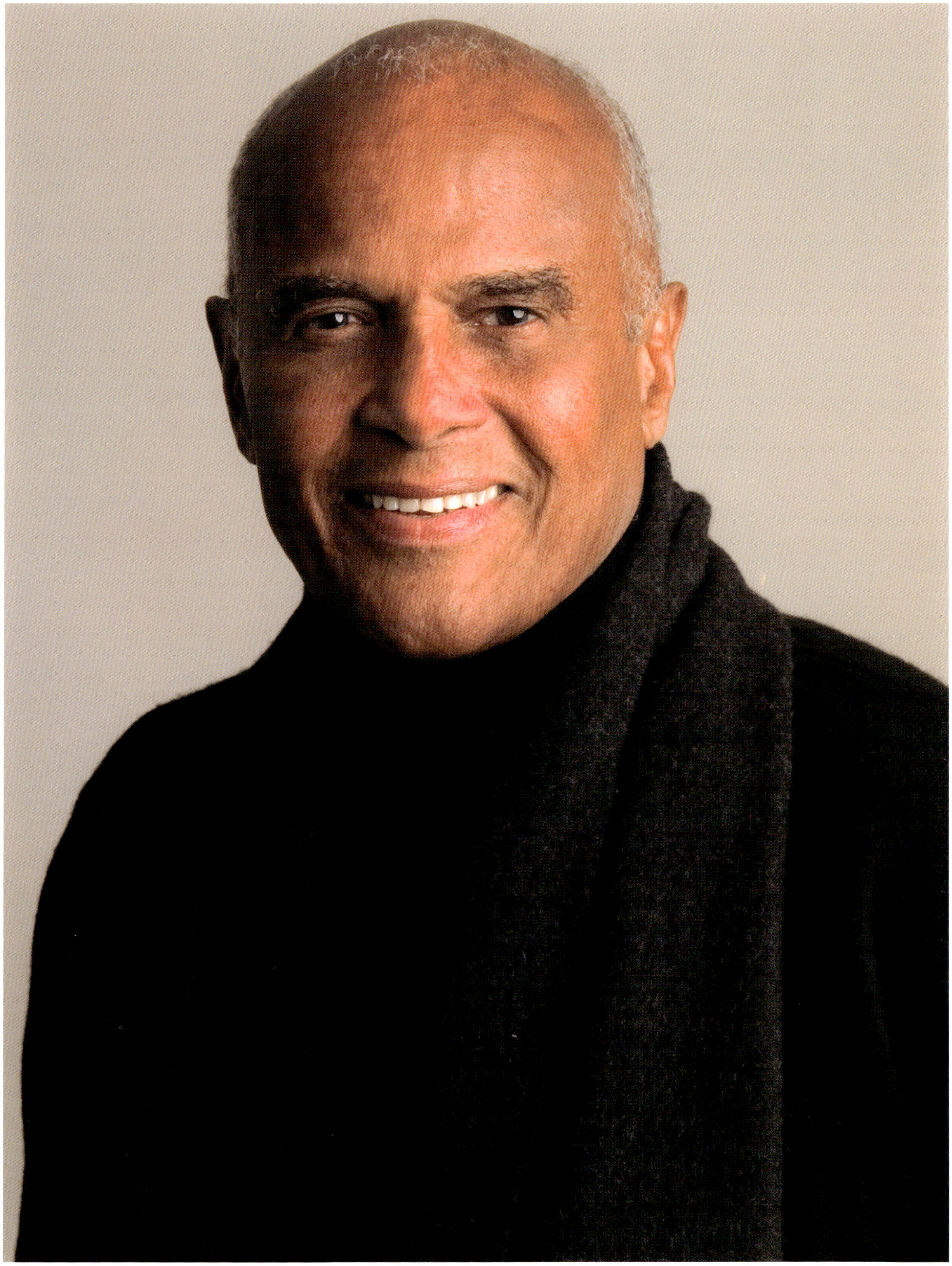

HARRY BELAFONTE Entertainer/Activist

About a year ago I picked up a much-publicized novel by a well-known New York writer, and was delighted to find that the entire first chapter was about how New Year's is not really December 31/January 1. Instead, the New Year starts in September when the iconic white tents go up in Bryant Park and Fashion Week begins. The book followed the comings and goings of a fictional fashion designer, her friends, and other characters in her circle, while chronicling the tremendous amount of work needed to get ready for Fashion Week in New York. While it may have been fiction, for the past 14 years it's been very real for me and all of my IMG Fashion team that works year-round to put on the shows.

Creating what is now known as Olympus Fashion Week in New York still gives me goose bumps: when the first sound check happens and the music booms louder than anything…and when the lighting trusses are raised and the tent-front graphics go up.

When we began, the mission was to organize, centralize, and modernize the runway shows for American designers, but just like New York itself, our tents have grown to include designers from all over the world, reflecting the multiculturalism and excitement of the city and the globalization of fashion. For foreign designers, the tents are "the Ellis Island of Fashion" and the gateway to doing business in America.

While we started out as an industry-only event, over the years Olympus Fashion Week has evolved to become the city's biggest media event. Journalists and retailers from around the globe come to review ten shows a day, eight days straight, from morning until night, with barely a break for lunch or dinner. And today, in addition to the working fashion industry, Fashion Week also attracts captains of business and trade, world leaders, the biggest celebrities, fashionistas, and gatecrashers—all vying to get inside with the fashion people.

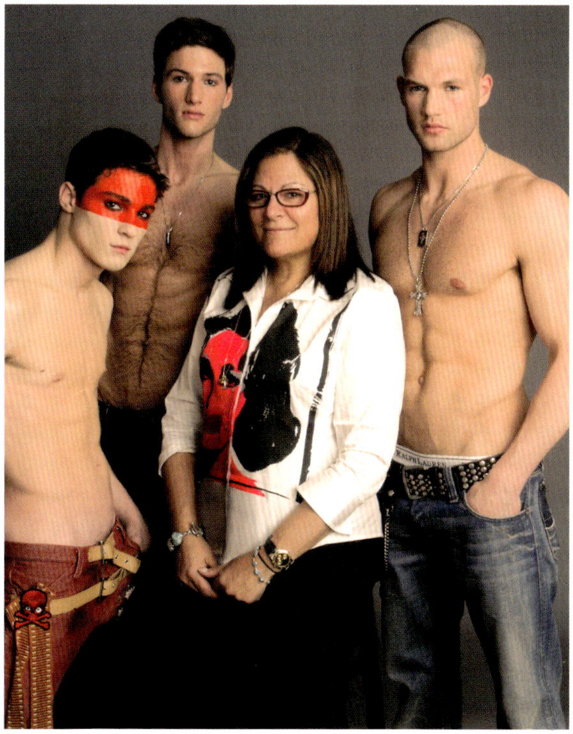

Fern with models Ryan Schira, Chad Dunn, and Lucas Kerr

Everyone is also secretly just *dying* to get their picture taken.

Fashion, and Olympus Fashion Week, is ultimately all about the pictures. Over the last three seasons, one of the hottest spots at the tents has been in the Olympus photo studio with my good friend Timothy Greenfield-Sanders. Backstage in this exclusive space, Timothy has documented the world's elite who've come to the shows. His subjects say it all—and are proof that fashion is at the center of all that is happening.

Fashion is fleeting, it changes constantly, and the tents—well, it's like Brigadoon: there, and then gone. But Timothy's portraits remain, and for that I am eternally grateful.

FERN MALLIS

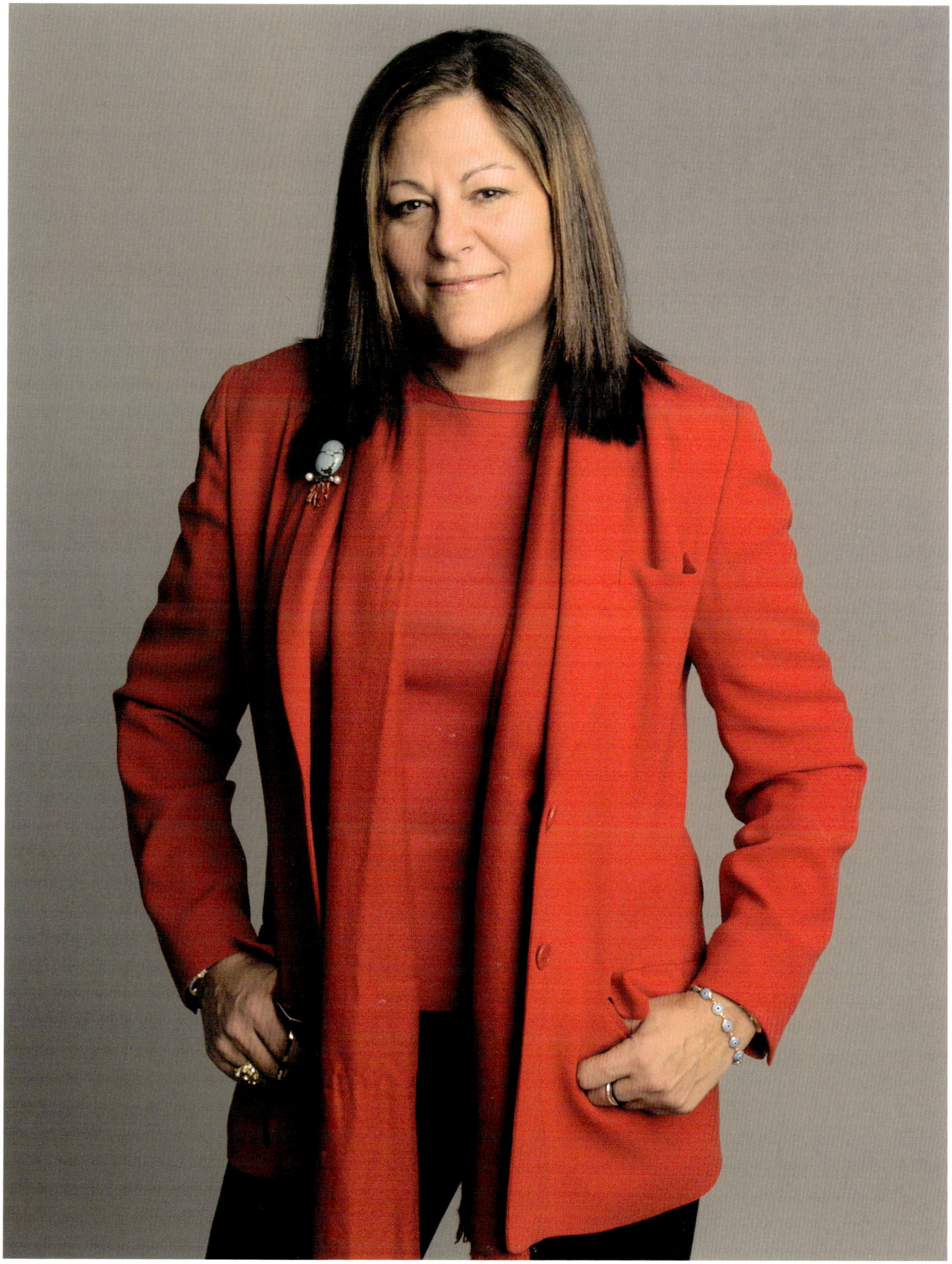

FERN MALLIS Vice President, IMG Fashion

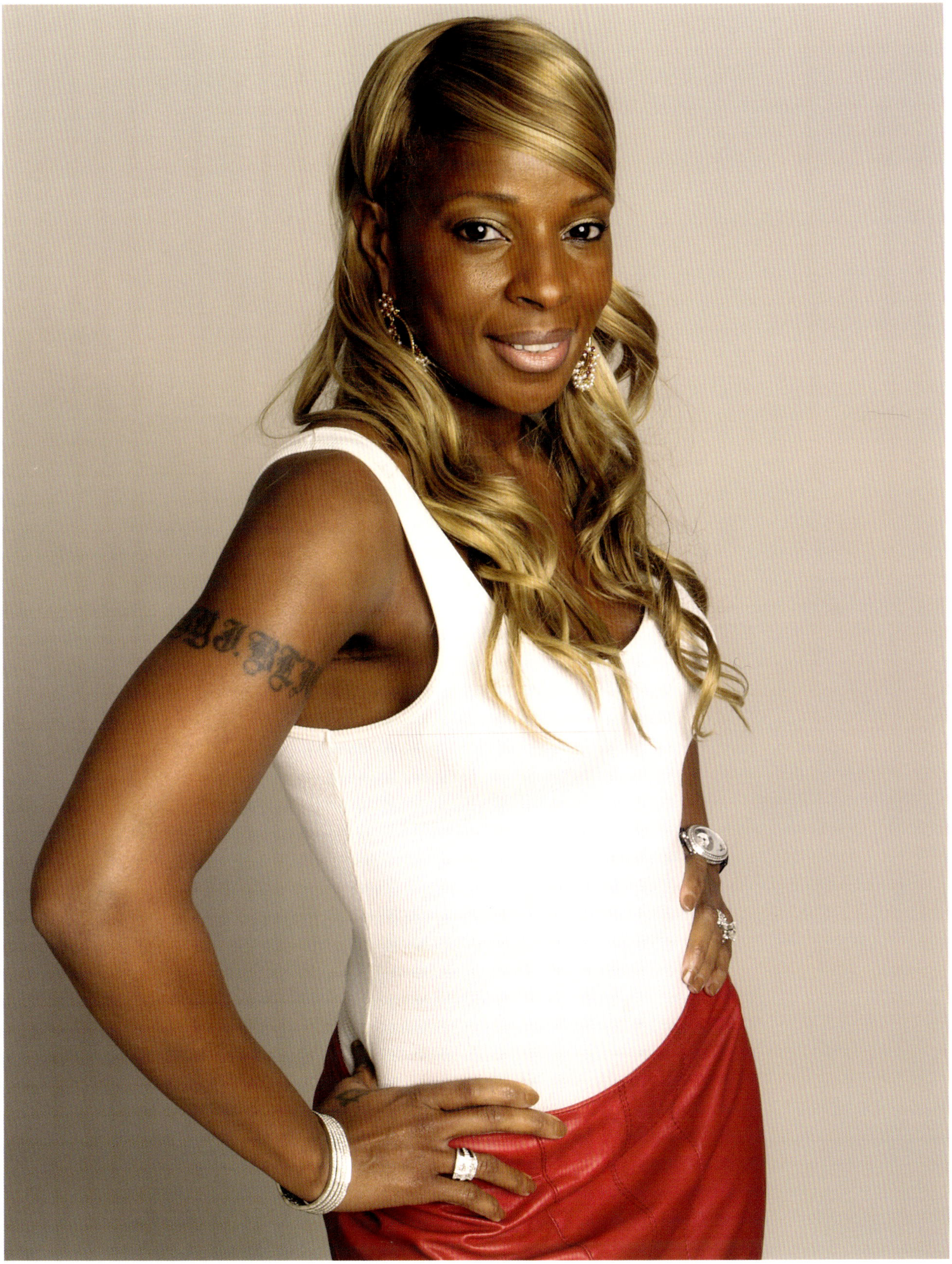

MARY J. BLIGE Queen of Hip Hop Soul

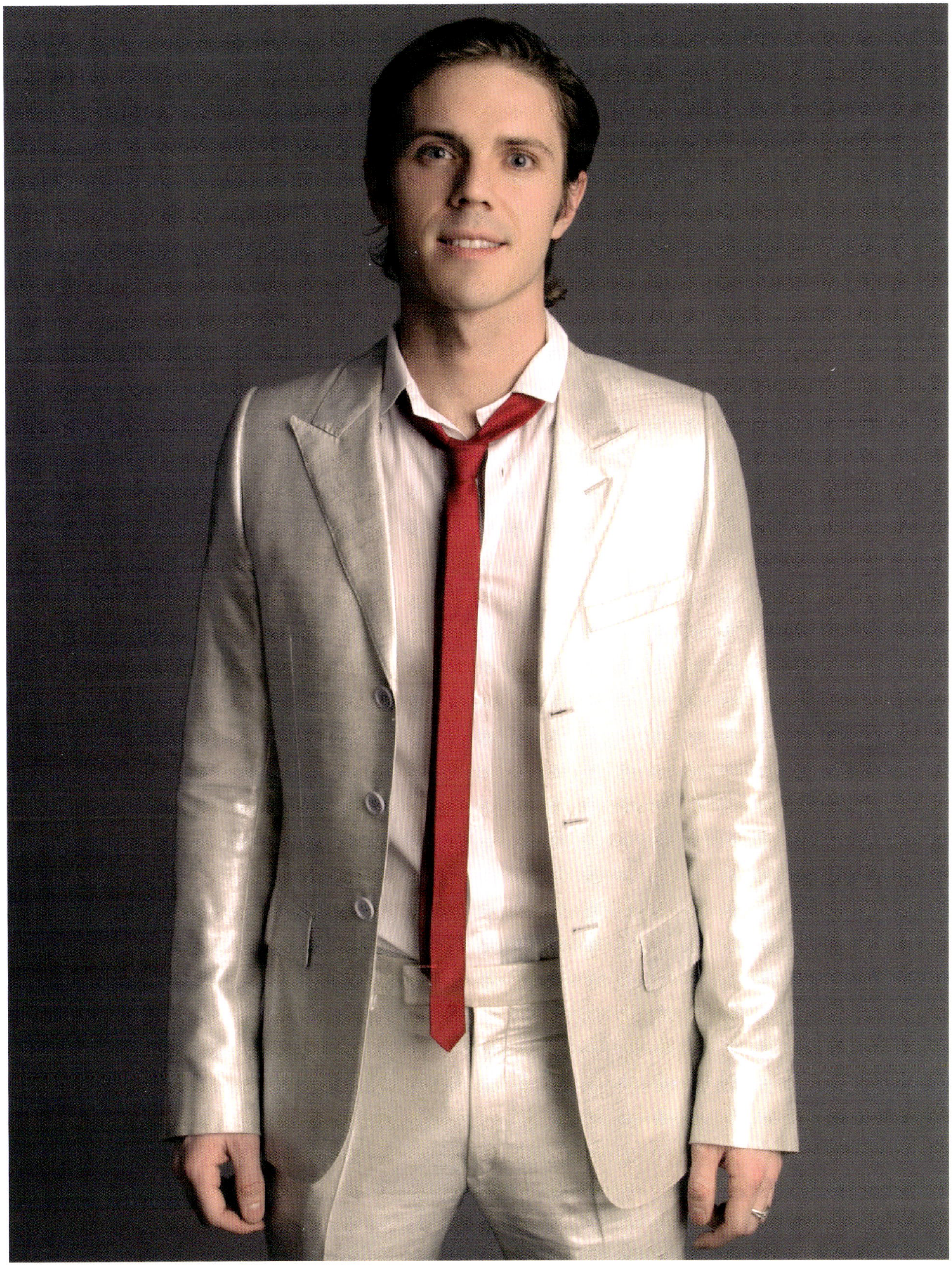

JAKE SHEARS Frontman, Scissor Sisters

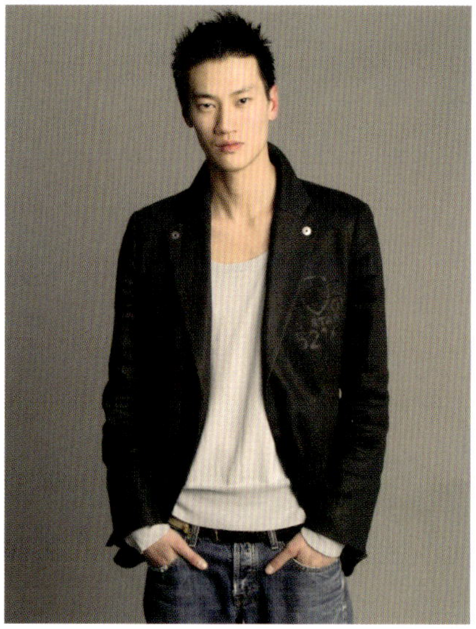

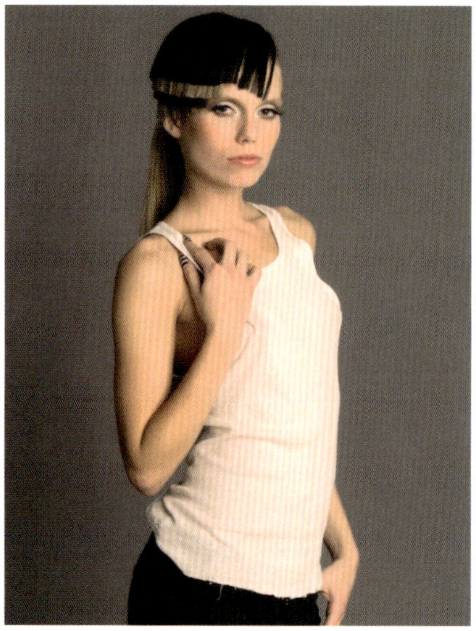

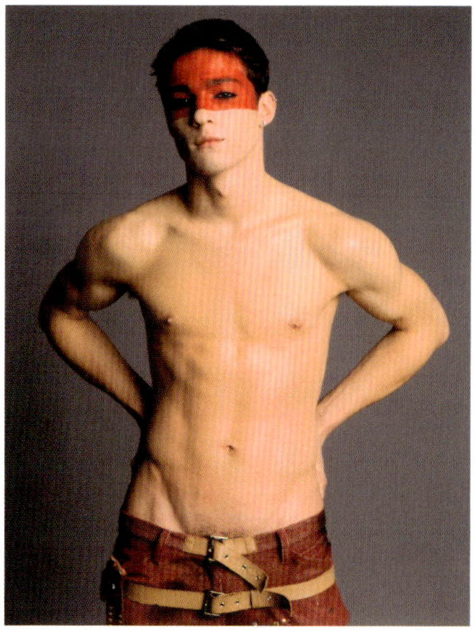

PHILIP HUANG
THEODORA RICHARDS
RYAN SCHIRA

LIYA KEBEDE
BRAD KROENIG
ANDREW COOPER

MICHAEL BRAGER
MICHELLE BUSWELL & TIIU KUIK
FREJA BEHA ERICHSEN

HILARY RHODA
DIANA DONDOE
FABIAN ELSNER Models

(top to bottom, left to right columns)

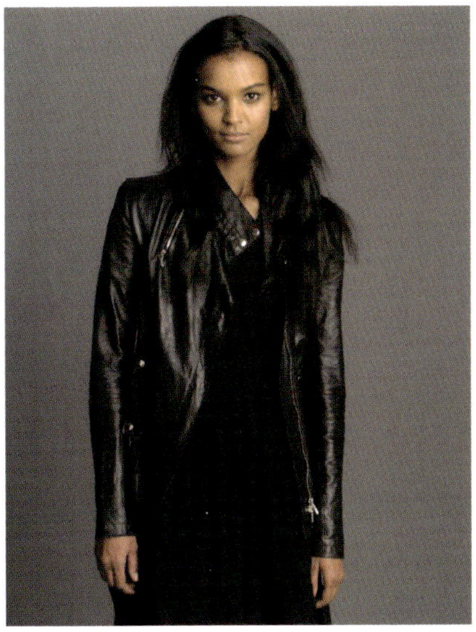
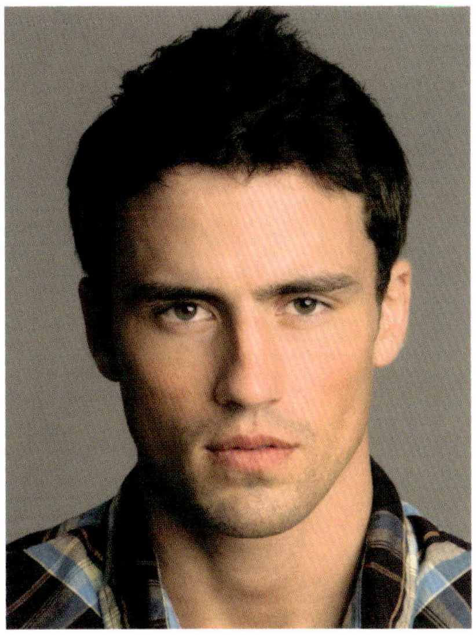
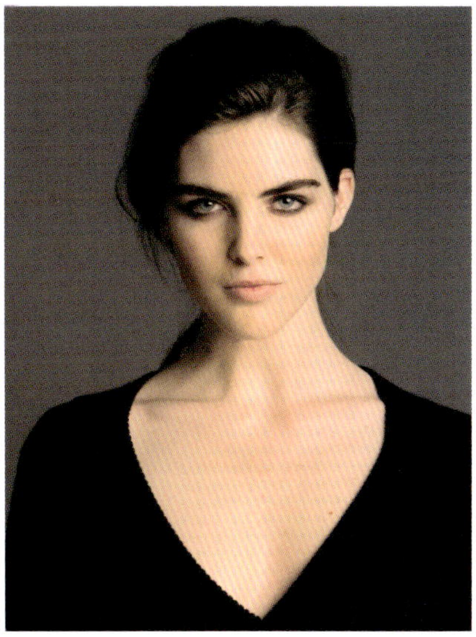
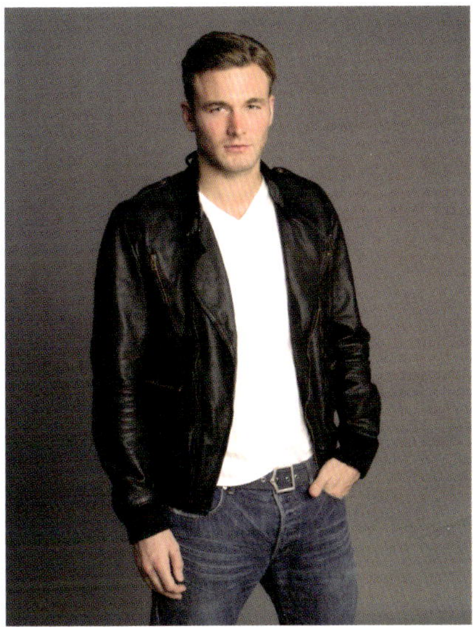
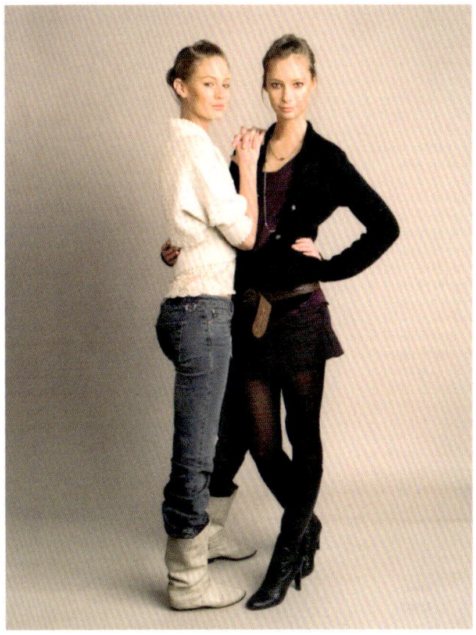
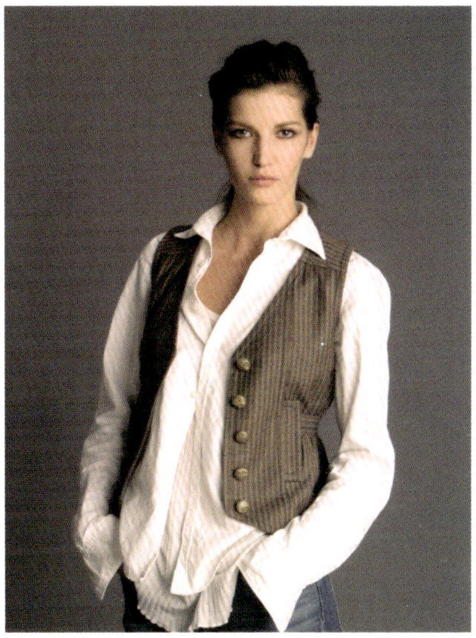
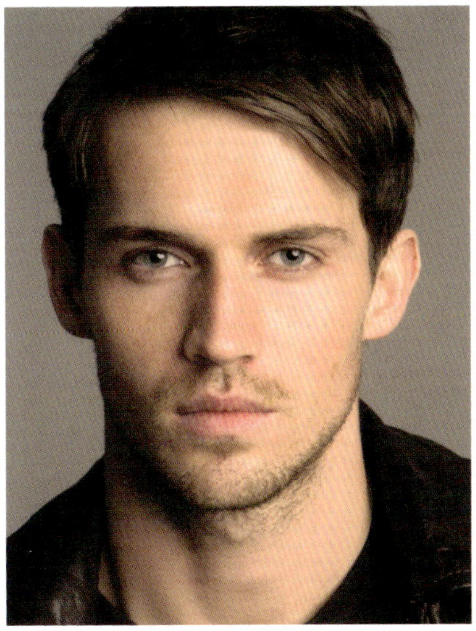
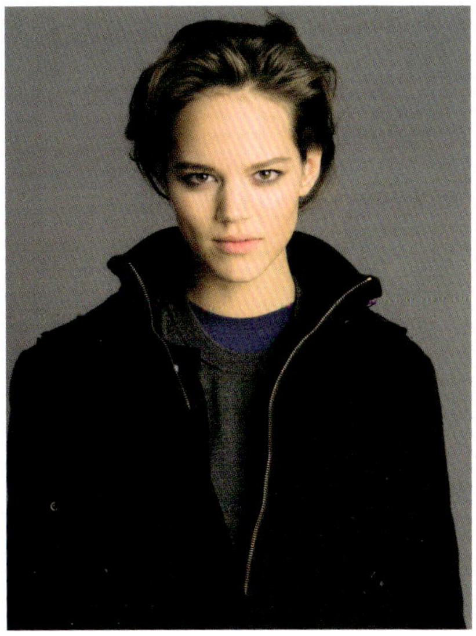
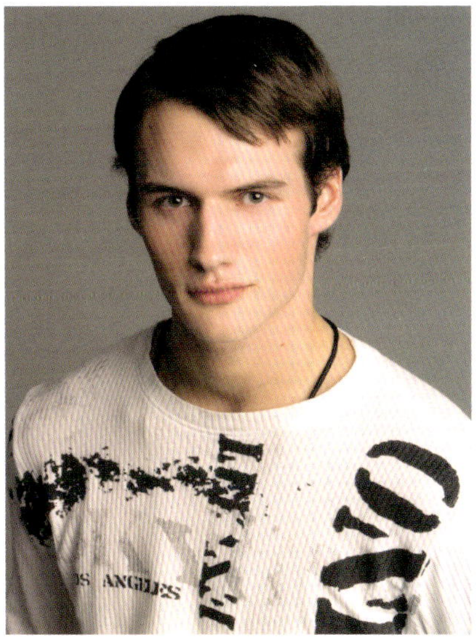

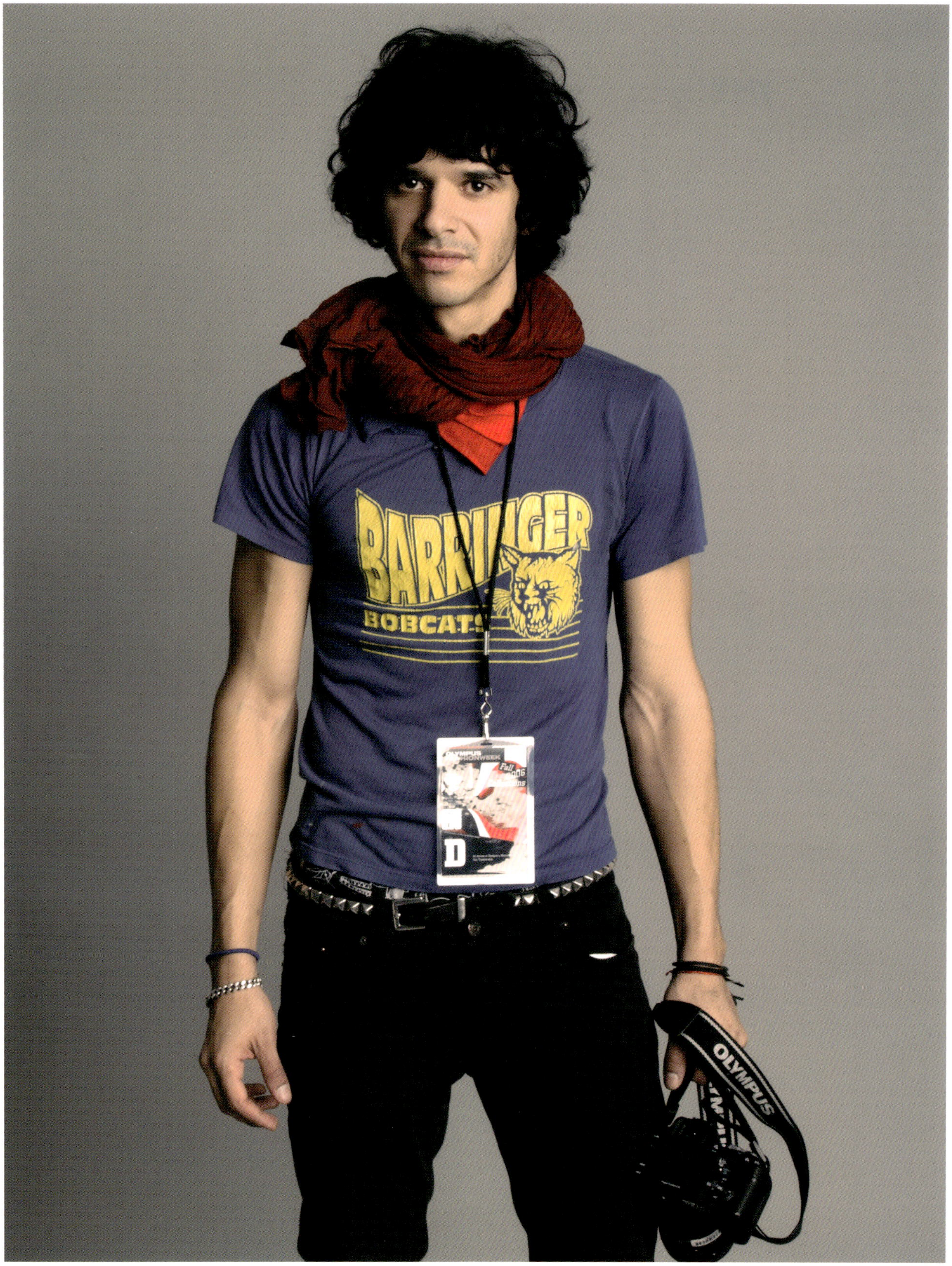

MIGUEL VILLALOBOS Photographer

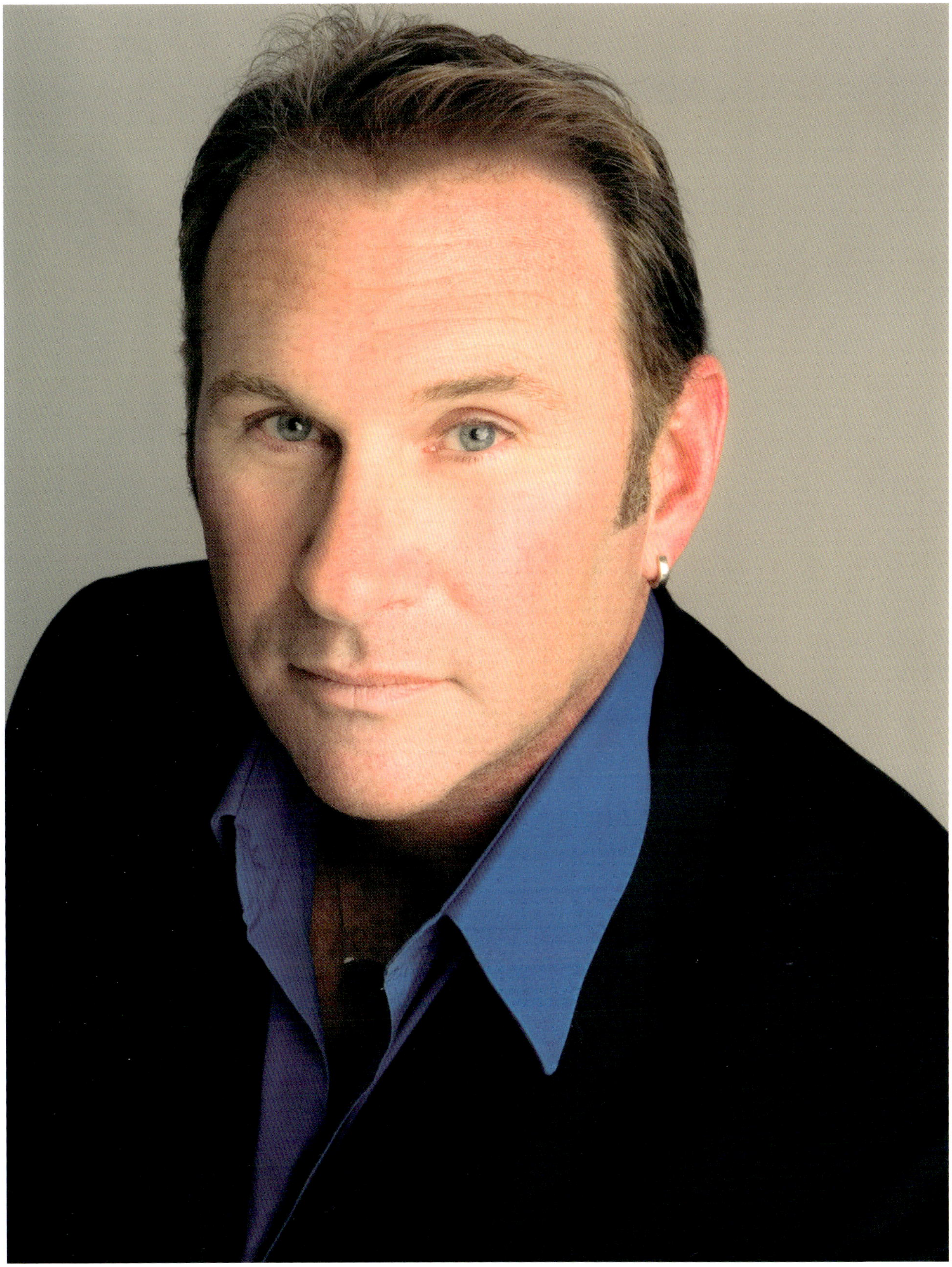

HAL RUBENSTEIN Fashion Director, *In Style*

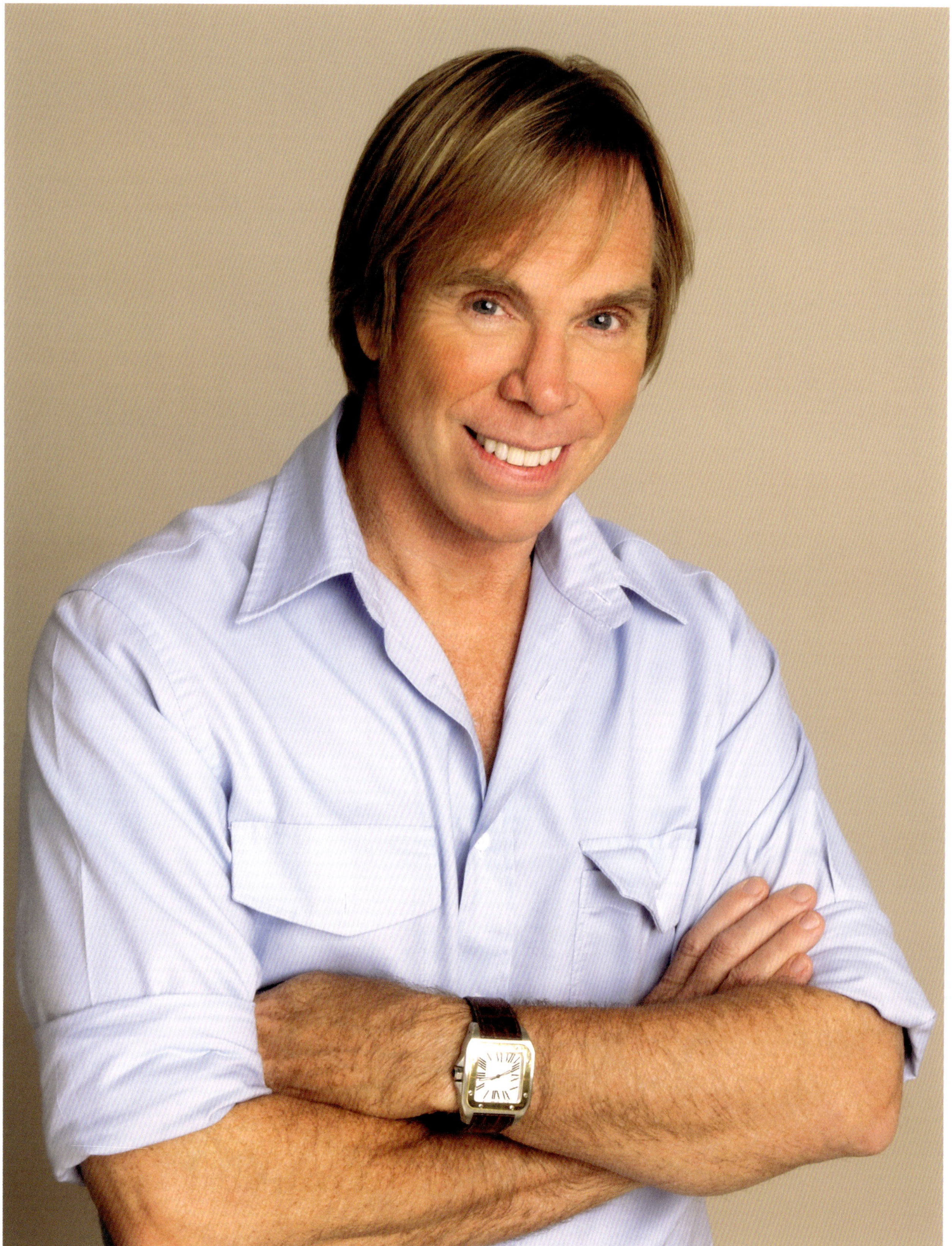

TOMMY HILFIGER Designer

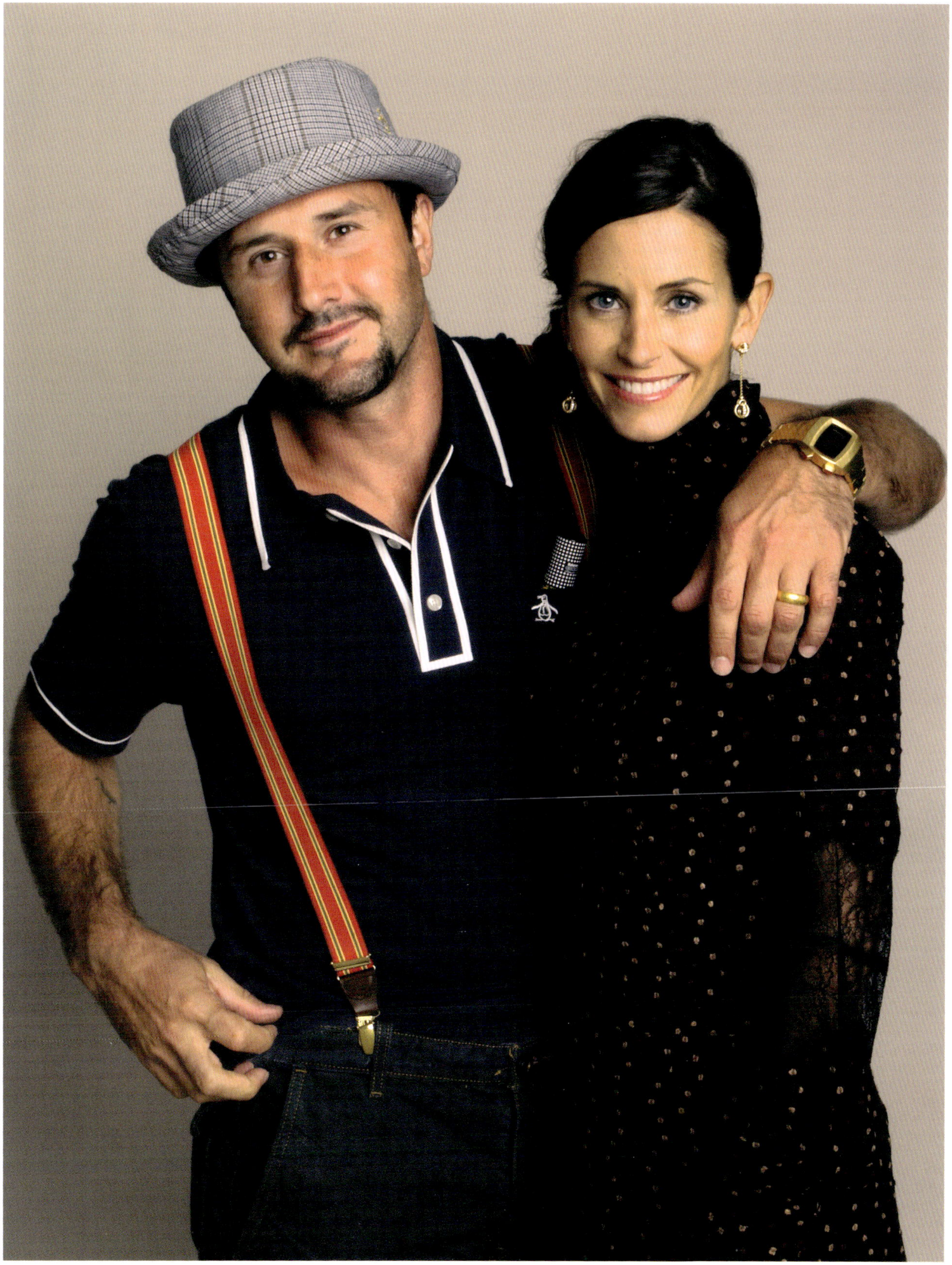

DAVID ARQUETTE & COURTENEY COX ARQUETTE Actors

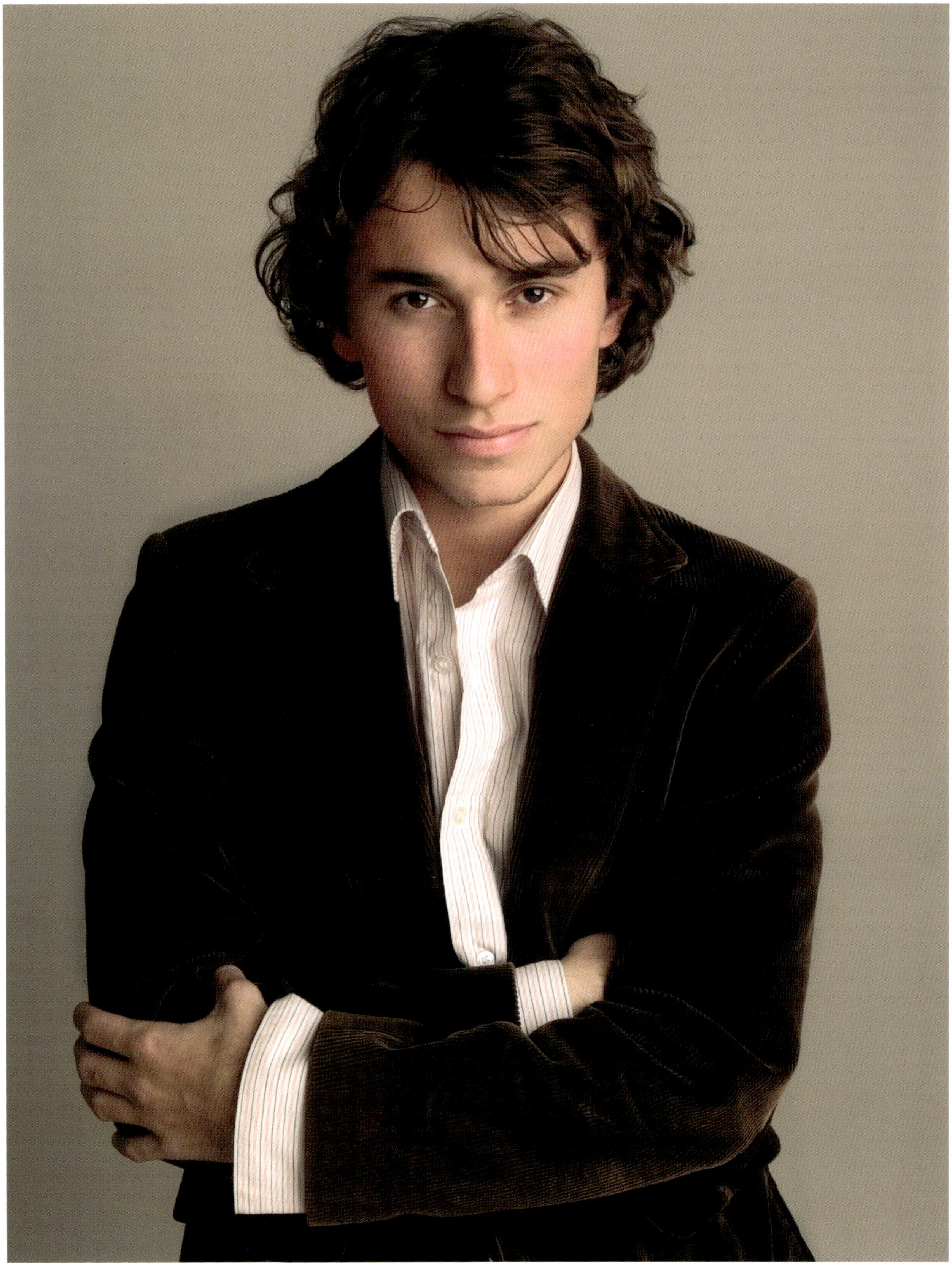

ESTEBAN CORTAZAR Designer

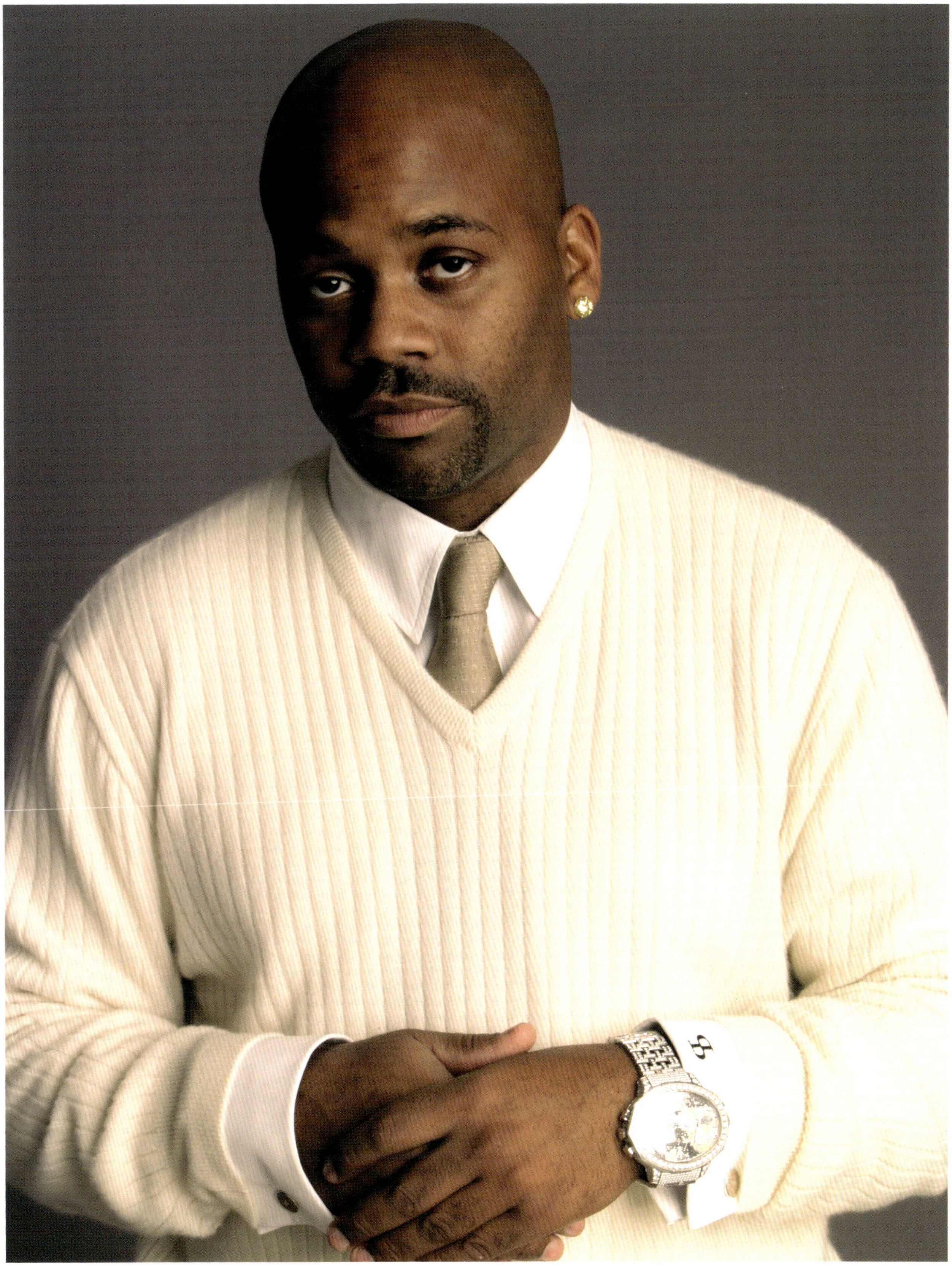

DAMON DASH Hip Hop Impresario

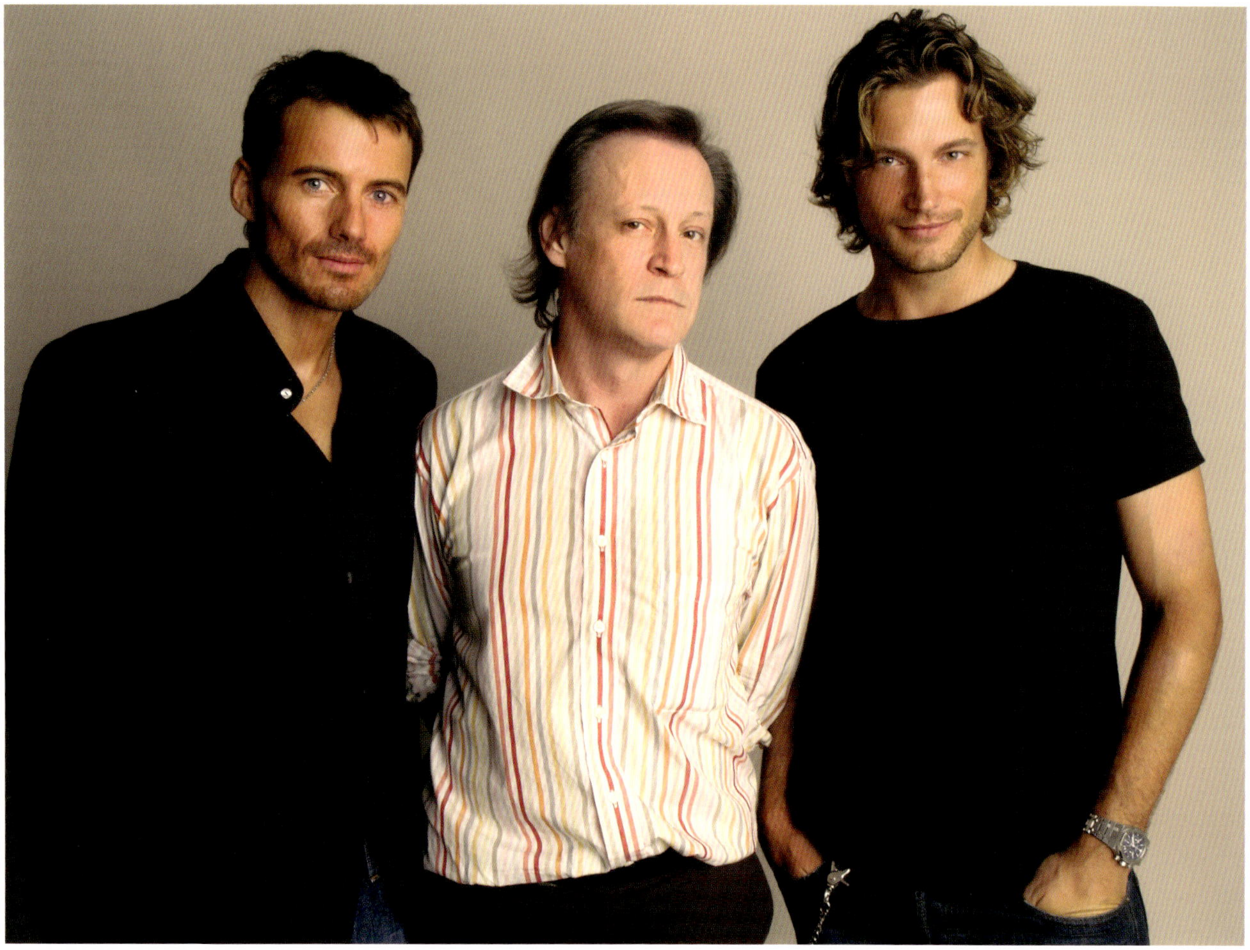

PATRICK MCMULLAN Photographer
ALEX LUNDQVIST & GABRIEL AUBRY Models

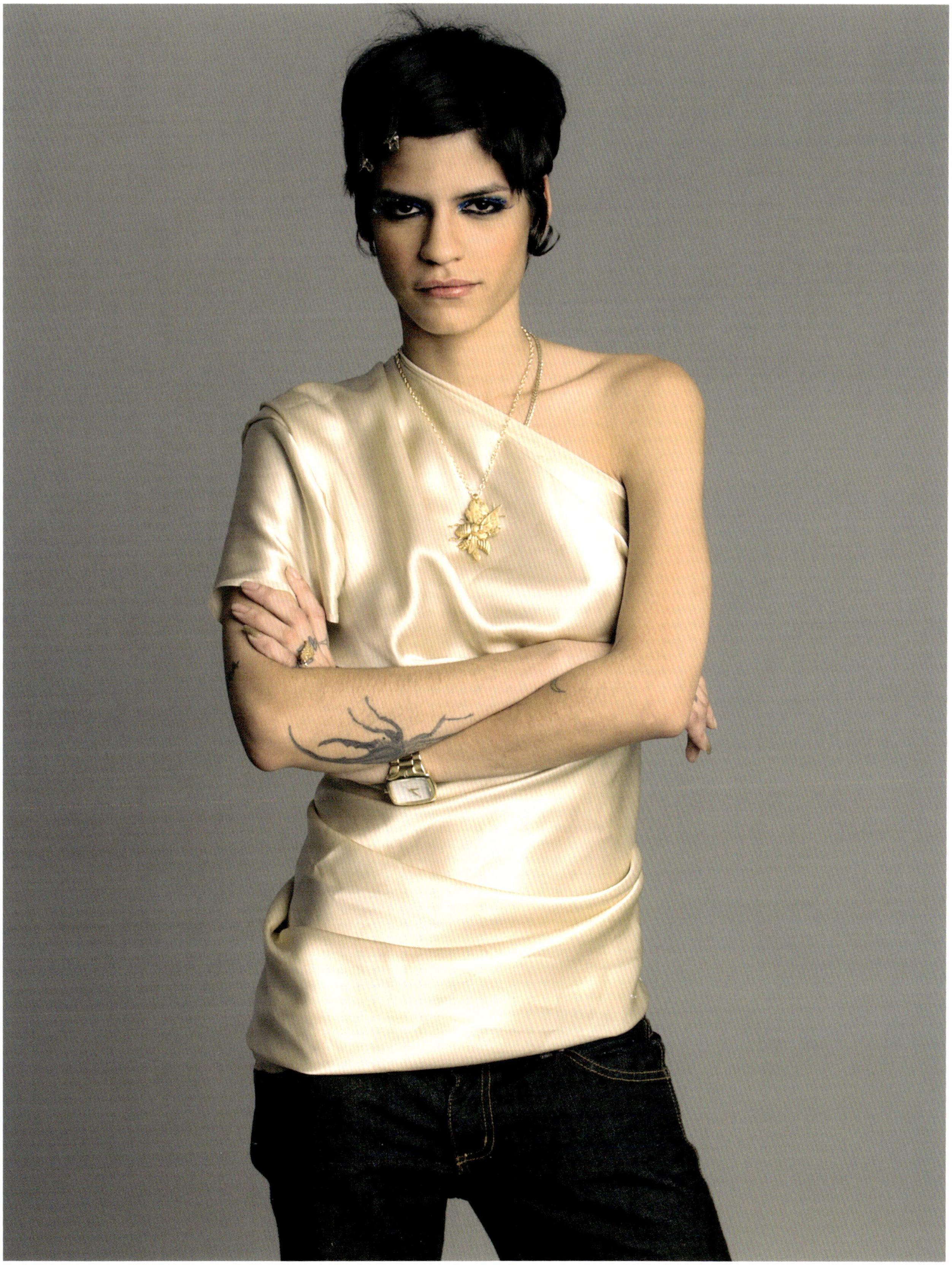

OMAHYRA MOTA Model

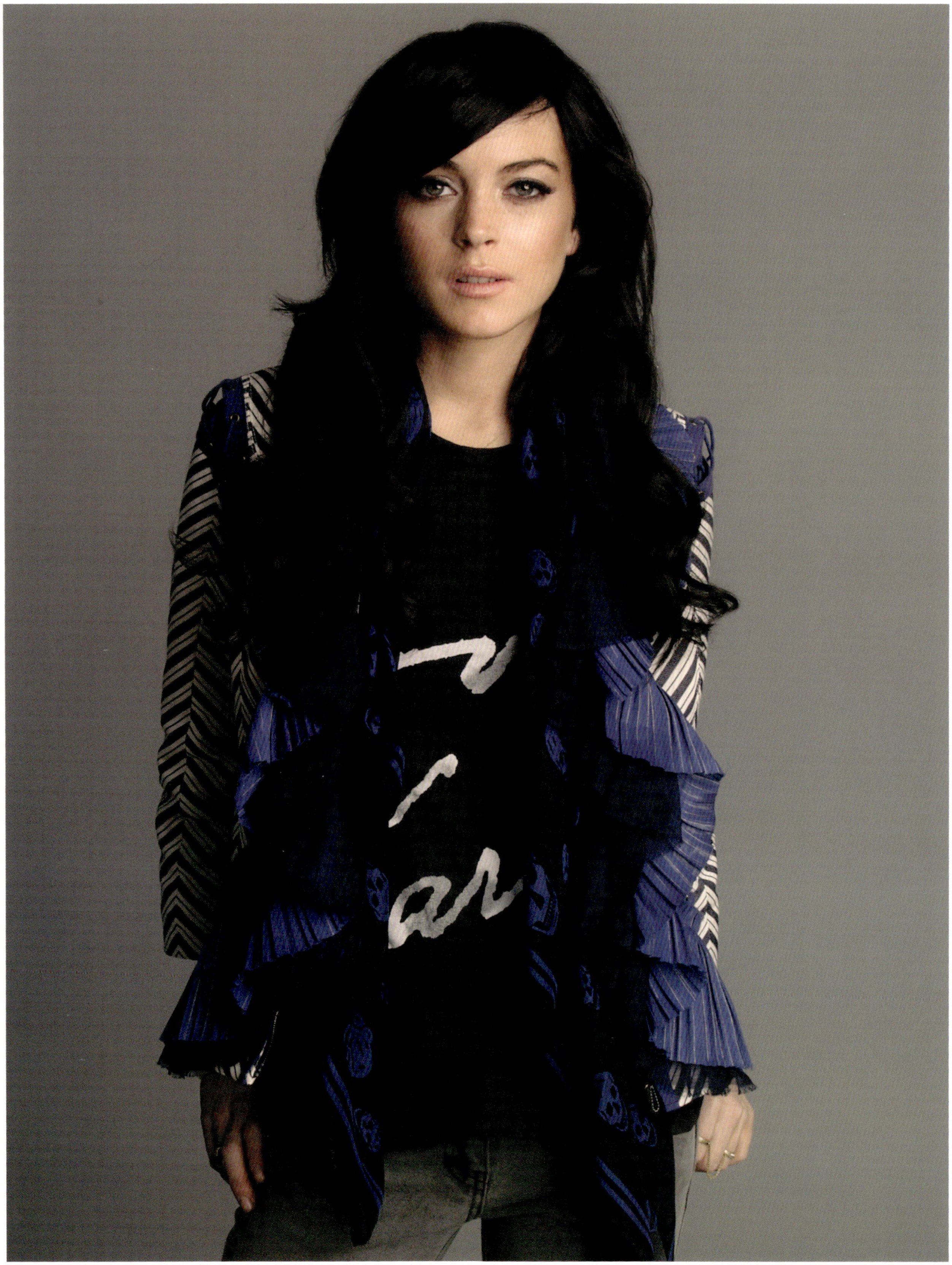

LINDSAY LOHAN Actor/Singer

Designers are the real stars of Fashion Week, and their collections are the reason people flock to the tents at all hours, in all weather. But no one can deny that celebrities do help to make a fashion show sizzle. Like the perfect necklace with a strapless gown, a handful of stars flung across the front row can make a runway sparkle.

Celebrities pop up at fashion shows for all kinds of reasons—some out of curiosity, to see what all the excitement is about. (Where else do actresses have the opportunity to see women who are thinner and better dressed than they are?) Others go because they enjoy the reflected glamour or because they're ready for some very high-end shopping. And some—let's be honest—are there because they are paid. That's why industry insiders treasure the few purists who simply love fashion and revere great design—and wear clothes very, very well.

Whatever attracts them, celebrities at the shows can count on being photographed nonstop. From the moment they step out of the car at Bryant Park, they are virtually surrounded by paparazzi, wire-service shooters, and magazine photographers. Every season hundreds of thousands of photographs are taken. But most images from Fashion Week—of celebrities, models, or designers—have a very short life. They trumpet the new looks, spotlight the trendsetters, and then disappear like last season's hot shoe.

How remarkable, then, that Timothy Greenfield-Sanders, in a small alcove, his personal backstage studio, has created such quiet, absorbing, and almost formal portraits from the collections. He turns Fashion Week on its head. Inside the shows, all eyes, all minds, and all focus are on the fashion. But inside his oasis of calm, and in the portraits he takes there, the power isn't in the clothes, it is in the personality. Yes, it is a treat to study these photographs and take apart the outfits everyone chooses to wear to Fashion Week—why that jacket? that fur? those earrings?—but these particular fashion photographs are ultimately about people.

That's what makes them appealing to *People* magazine and why for the last three seasons we have published them as a part of our fashion coverage. In the fizzy, frenetic atmosphere of the shows, they offer one of the few intimate moments, a chance to get closer to the creators of fashion, their admirers, and their muses.

MARTHA NELSON Editor, PEOPLE Group

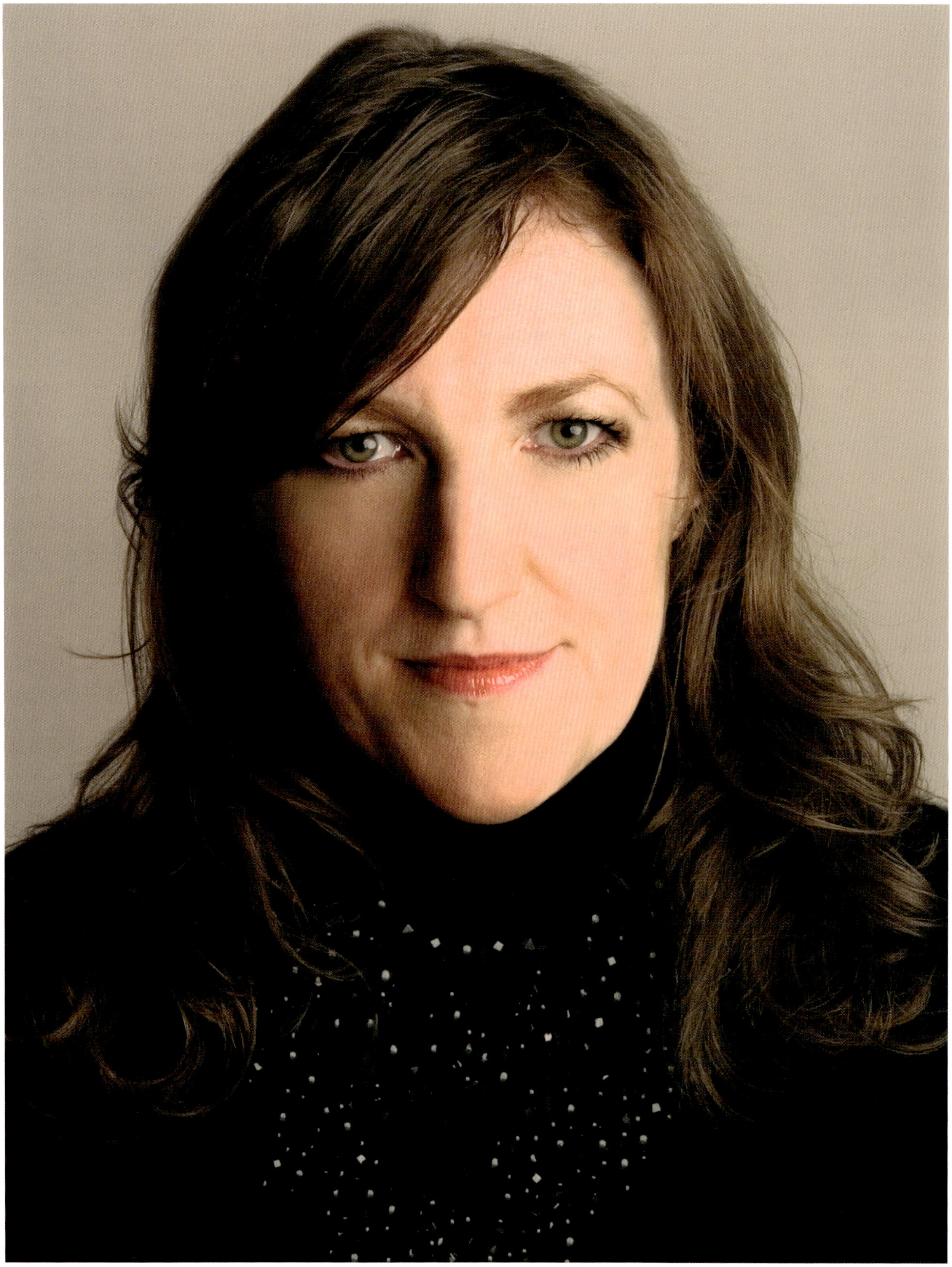

GLENDA BAILEY Editor in Chief, *Harper's Bazaar*

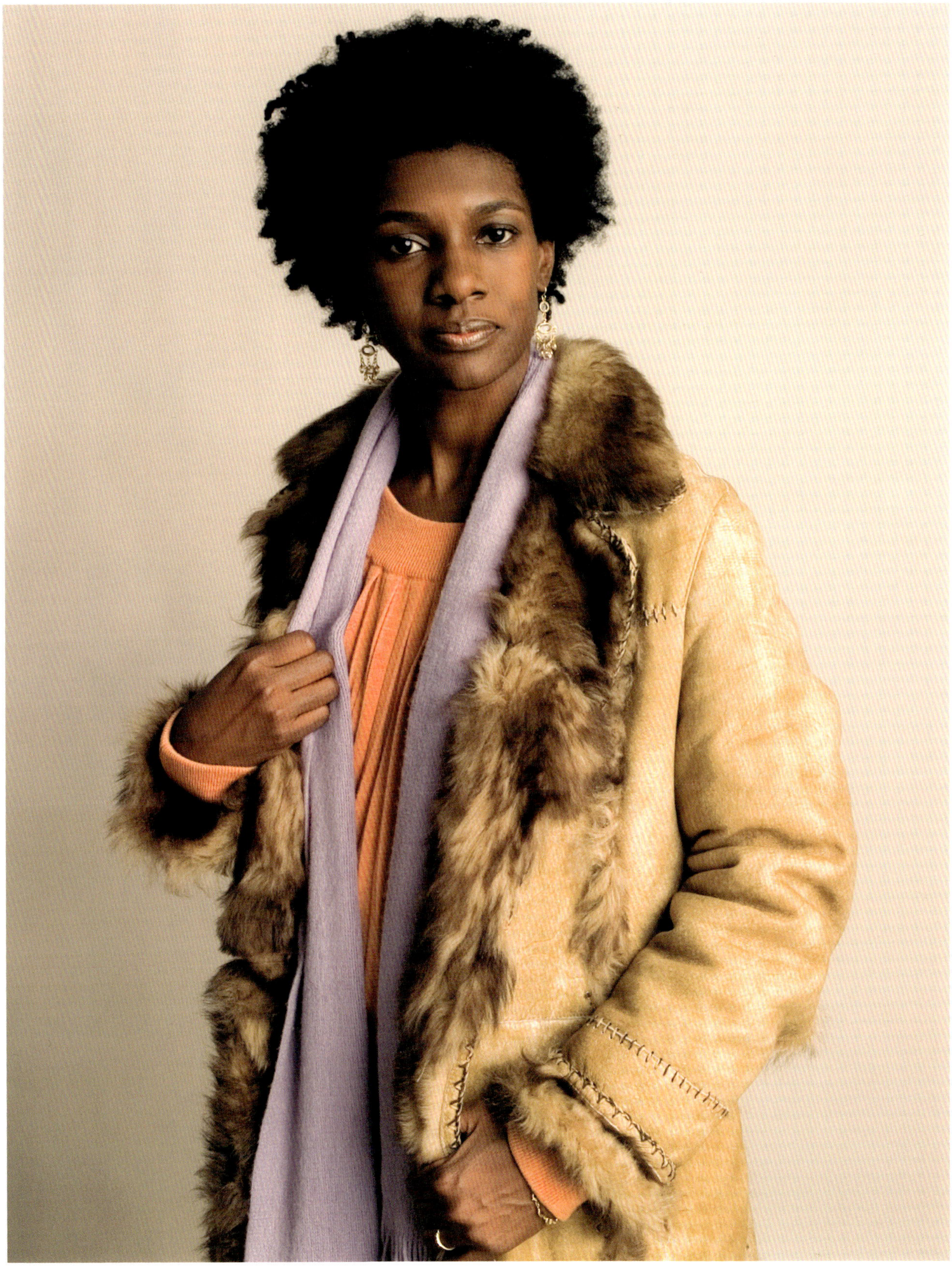

CONSTANCE WHITE Style Director, eBay

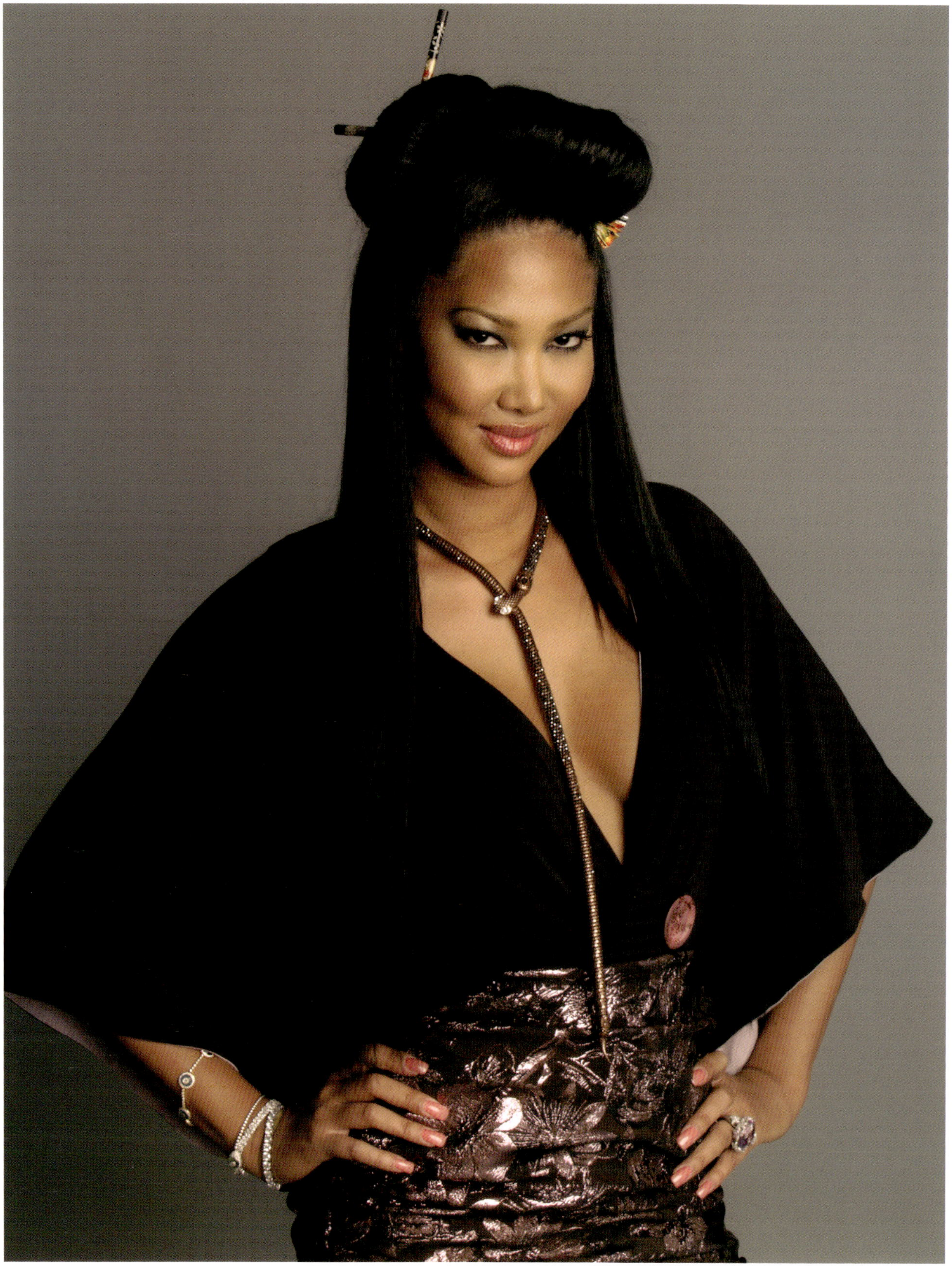

KIMORA LEE SIMMONS Designer, Baby Phat

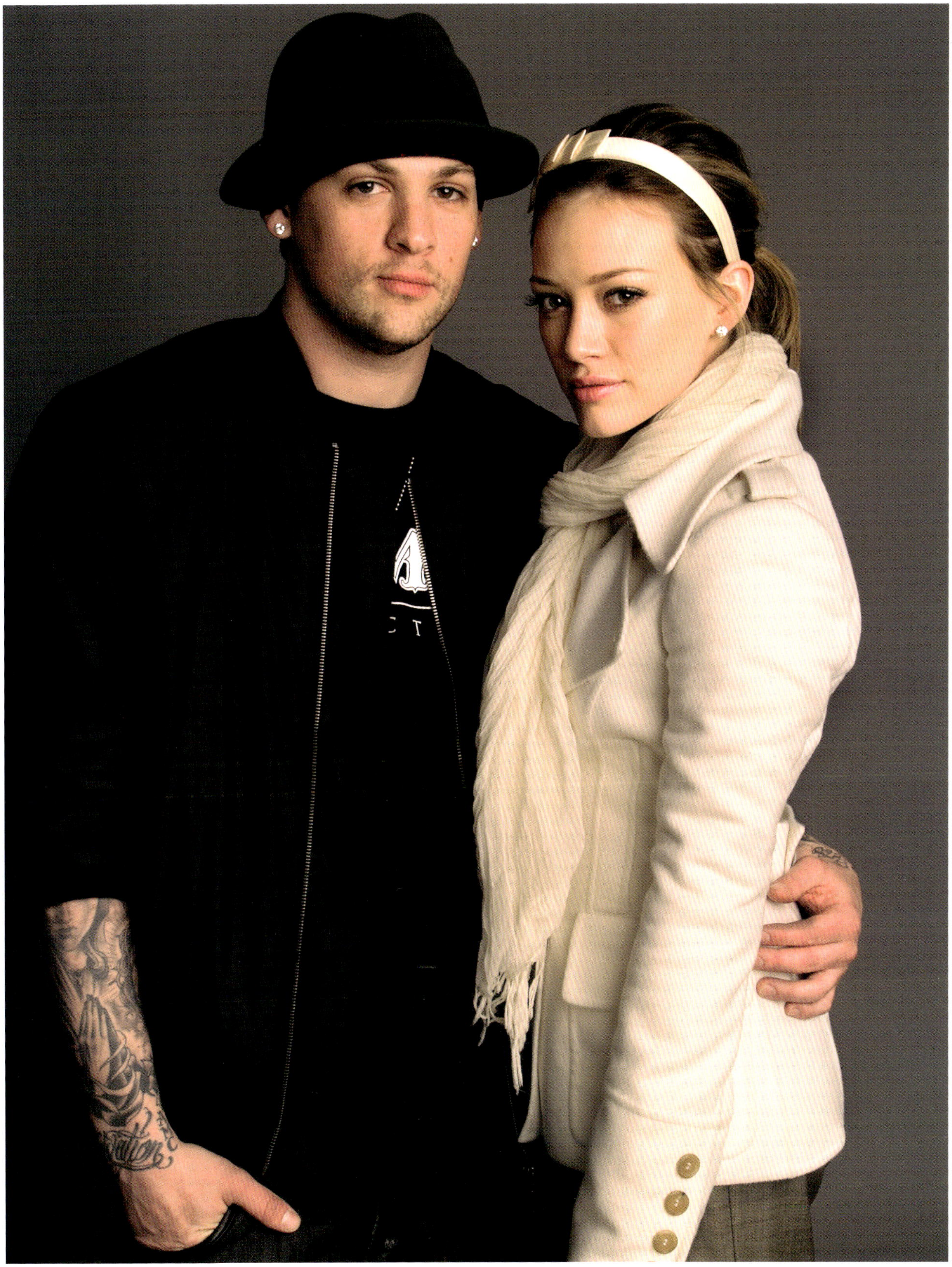

JOEL MADDEN Lead Singer, Good Charlotte
HILARY DUFF Singer/Actor

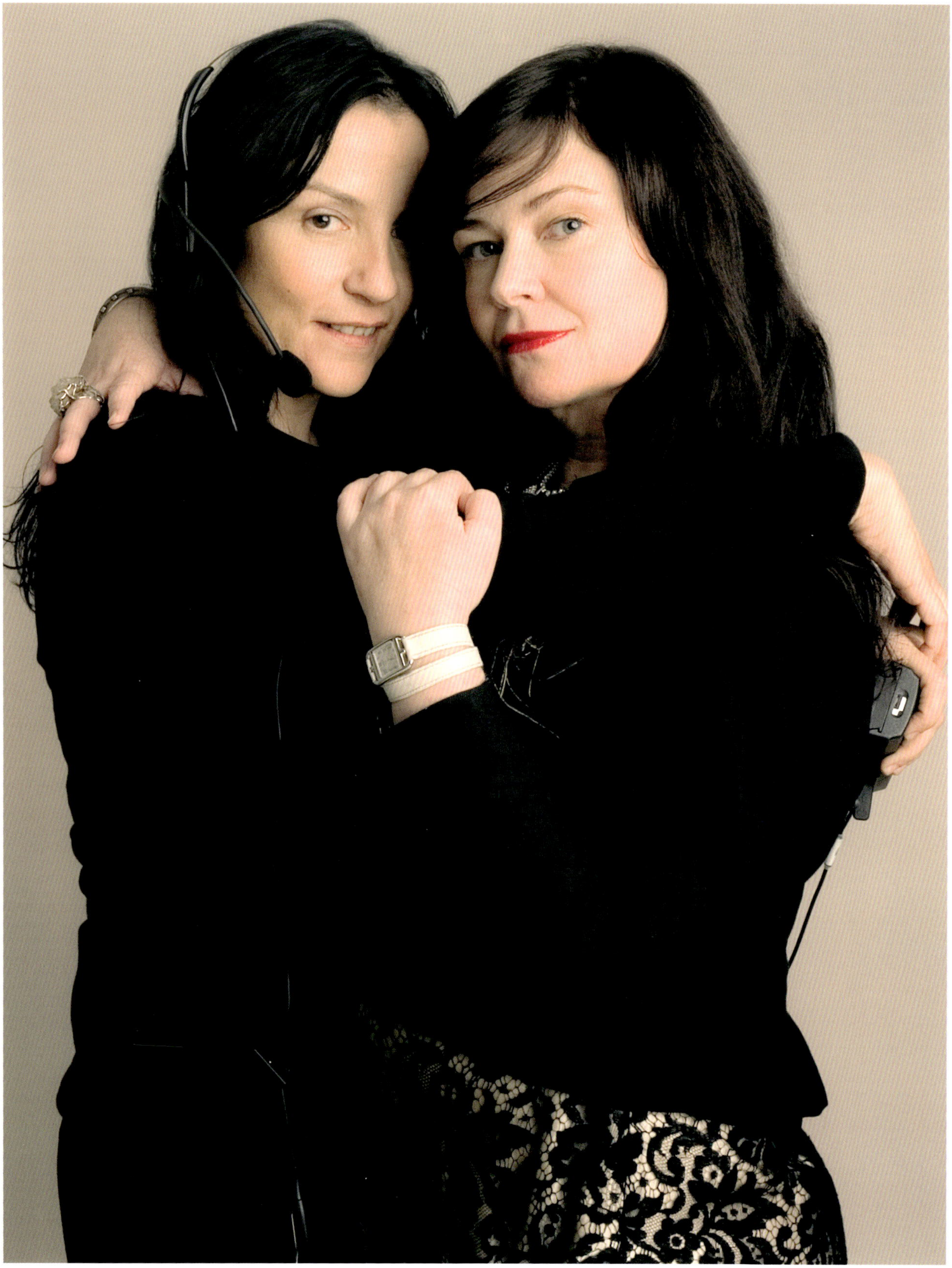

KELLY CUTRONE PR Powerhouse
JENNIFER NICHOLSON Designer

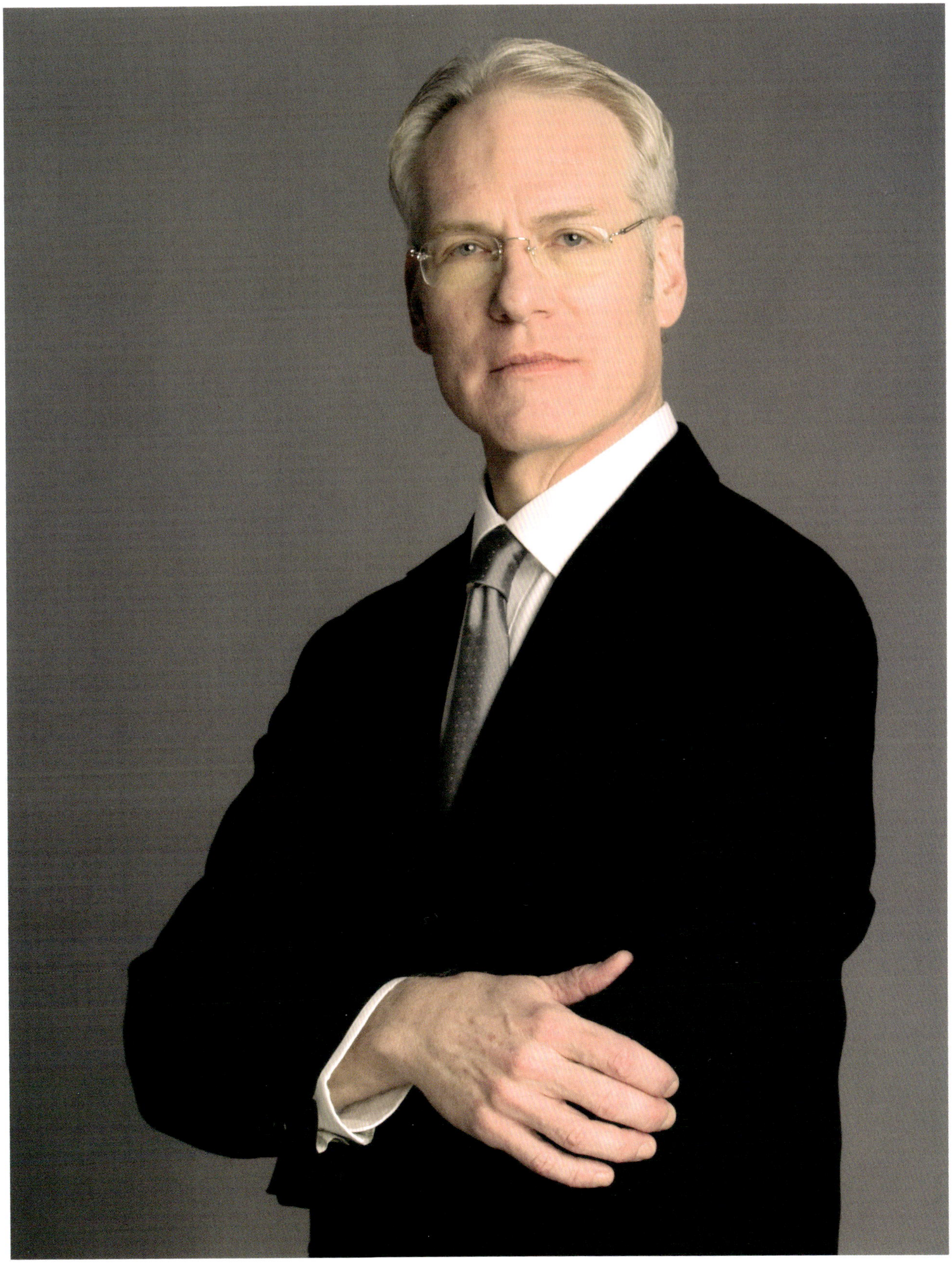

TIM GUNN Chair, Department of Fashion Design, Parsons School of Design

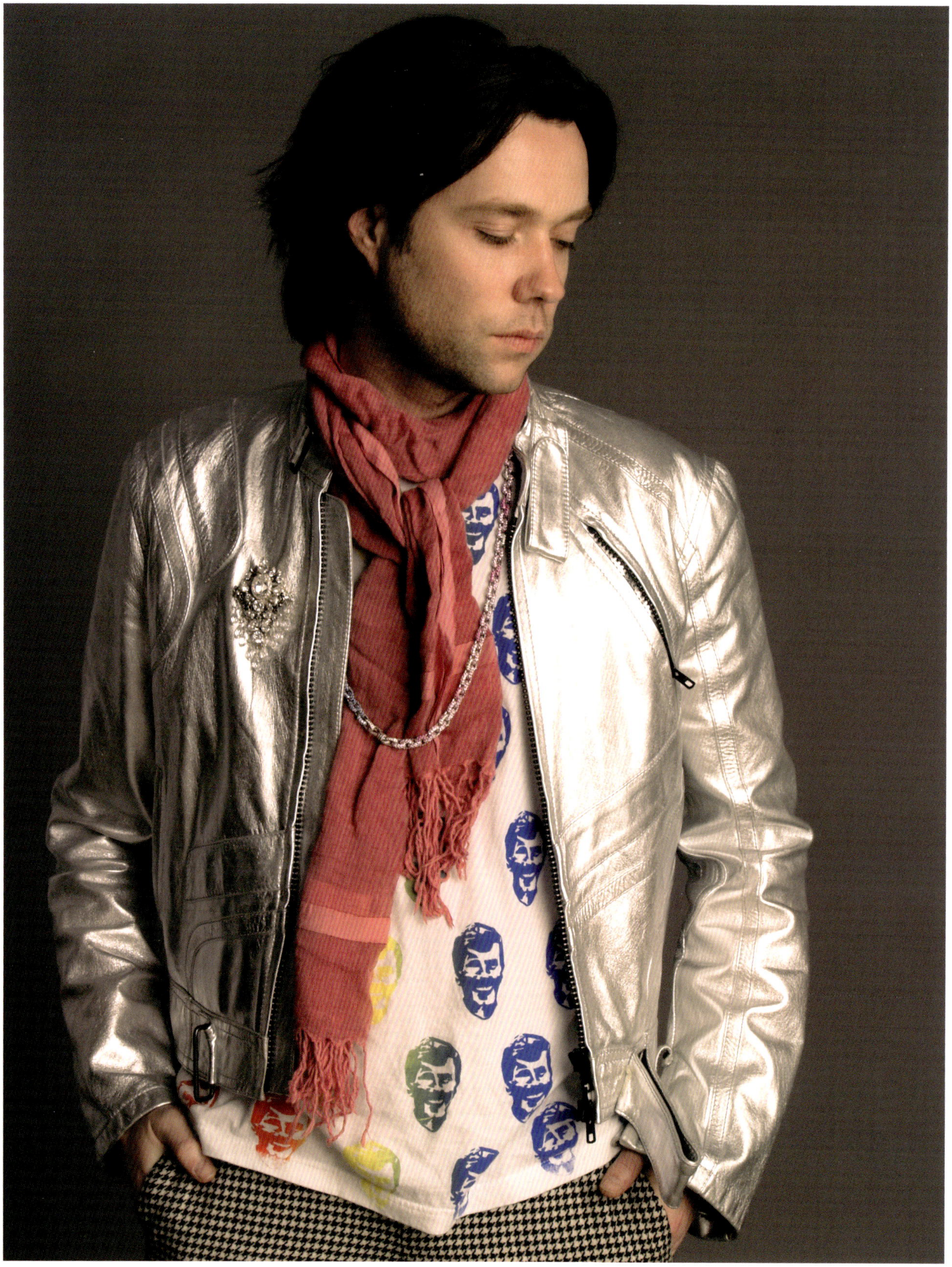

RUFUS WAINWRIGHT Singer-songwriter

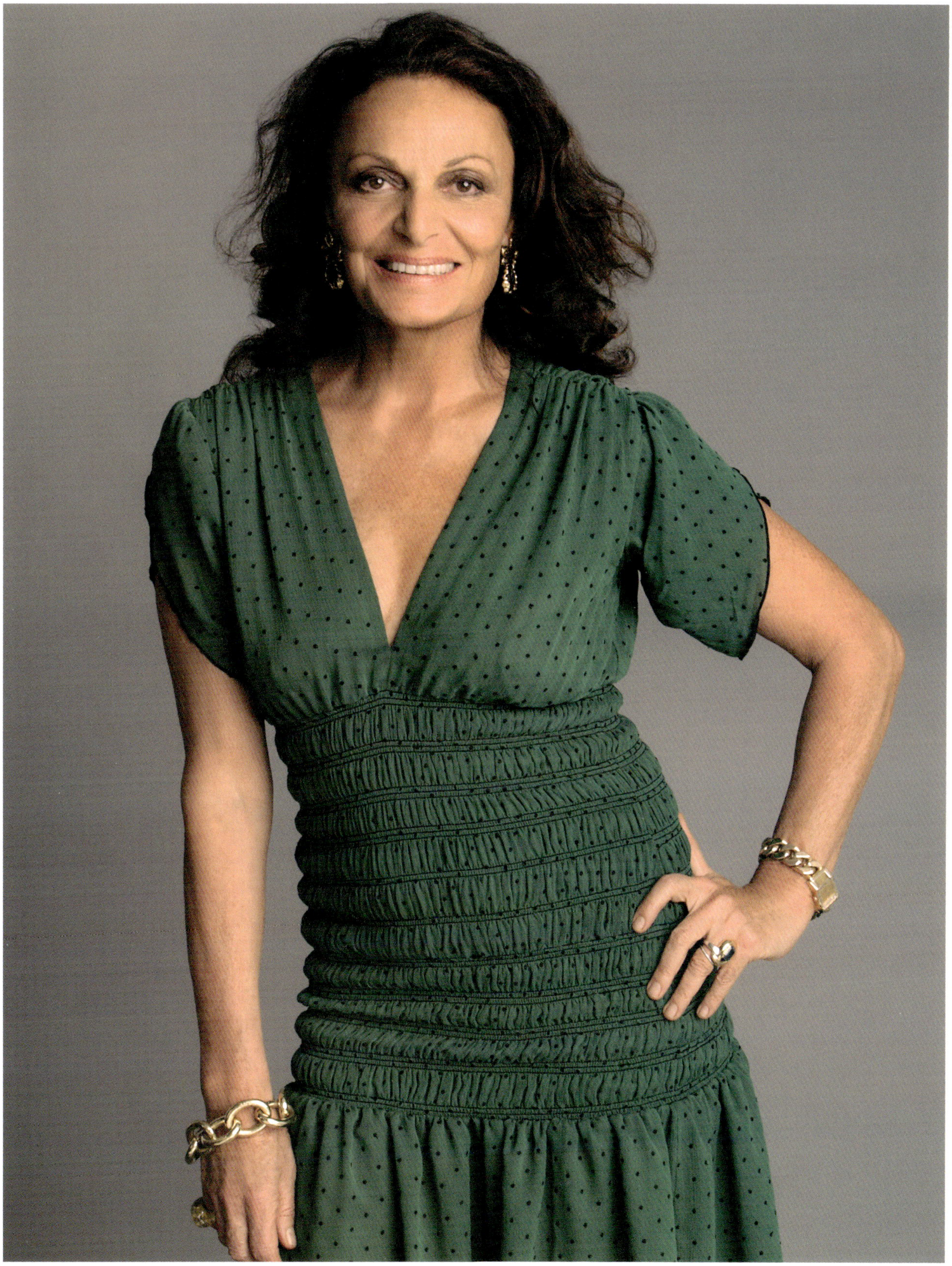

DIANE VON FURSTENBERG Designer

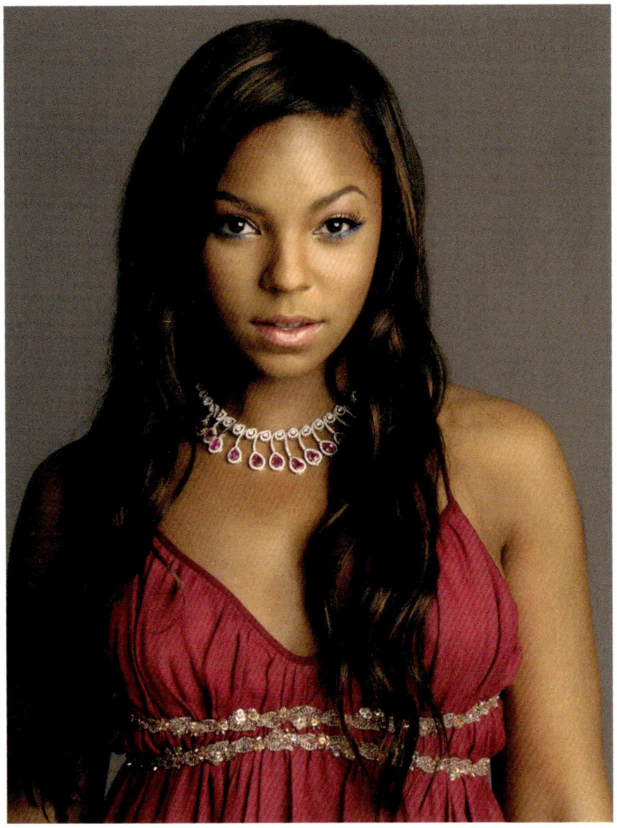

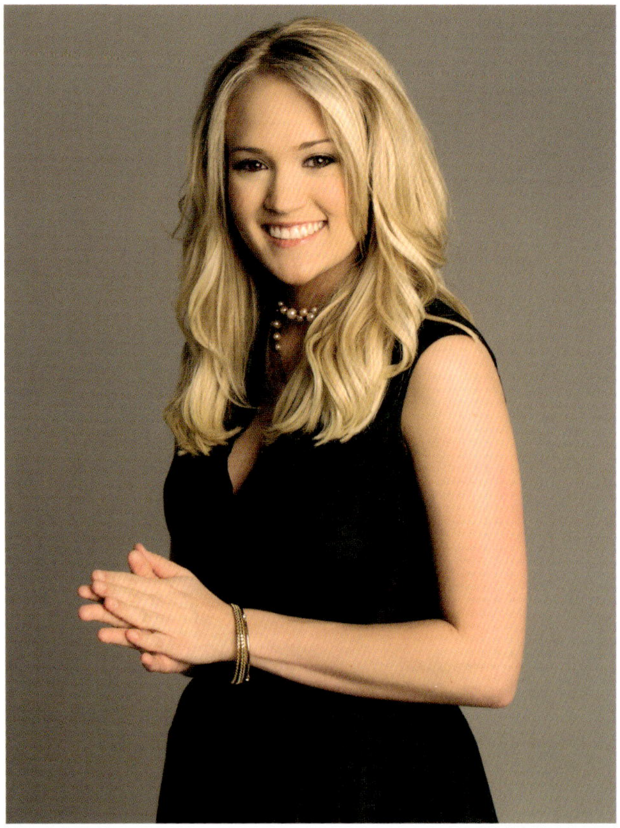

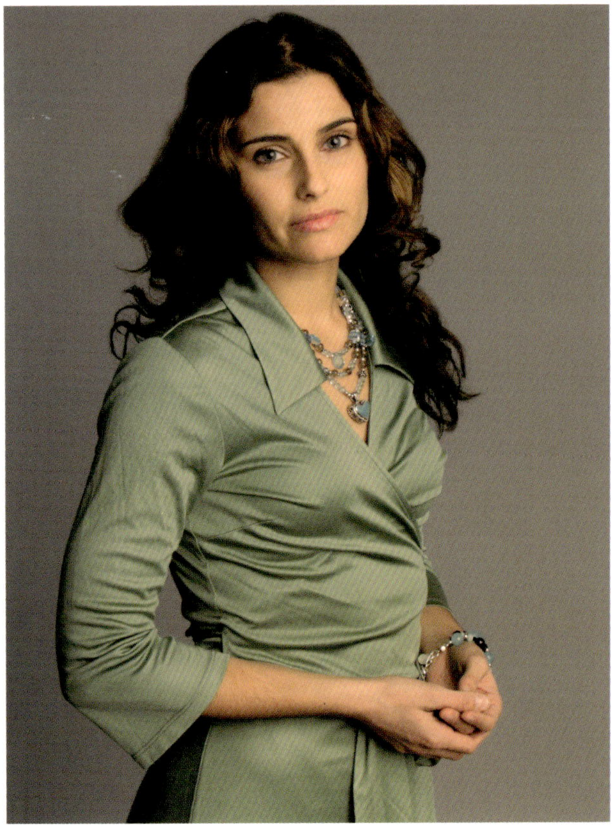

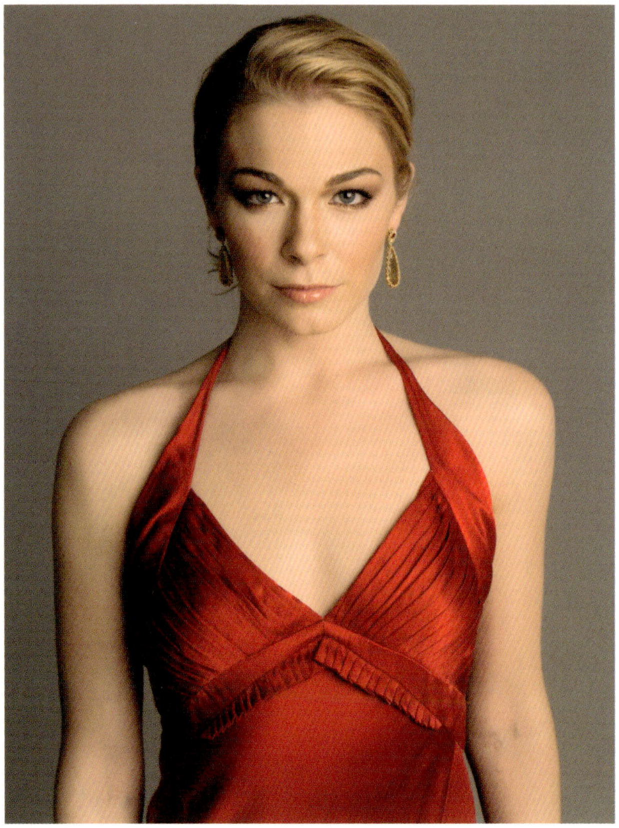

ASHANTI
NELLY FURTADO

CARRIE UNDERWOOD
LEANN RIMES

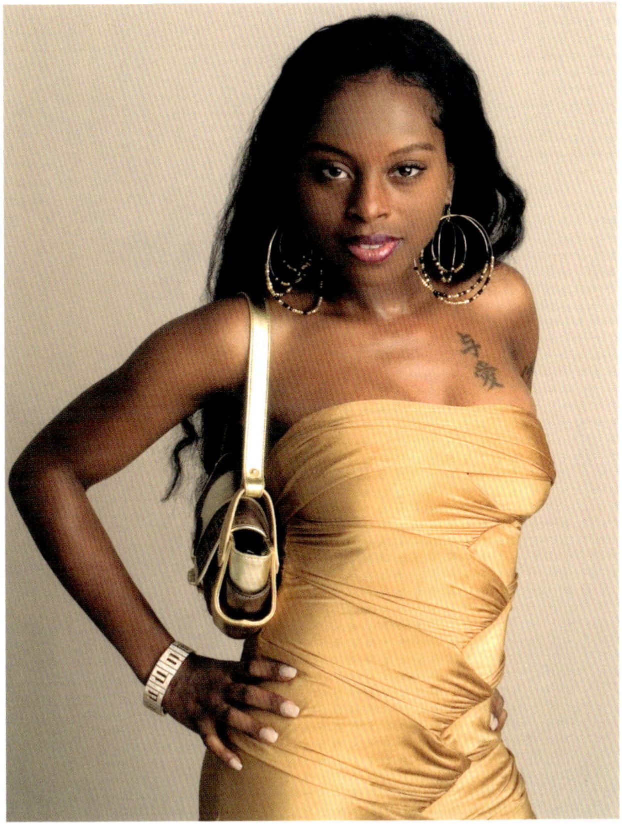

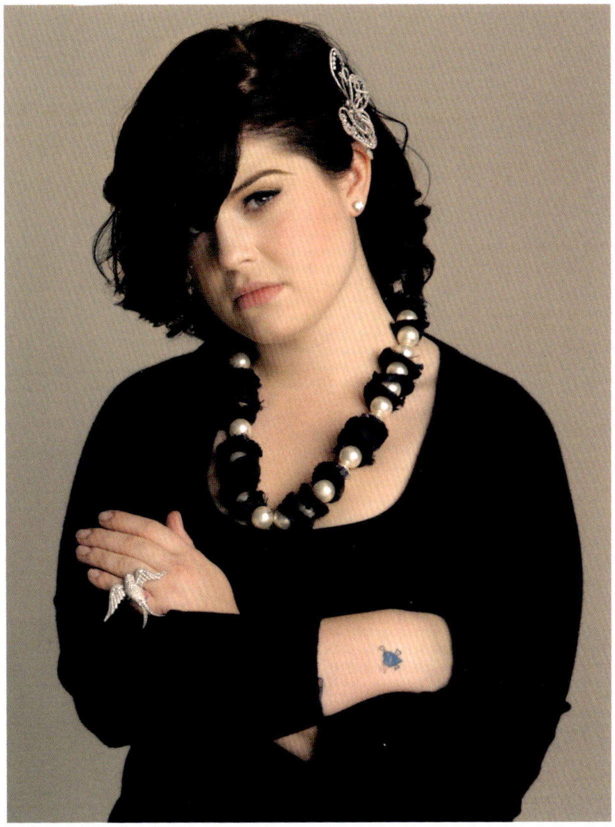

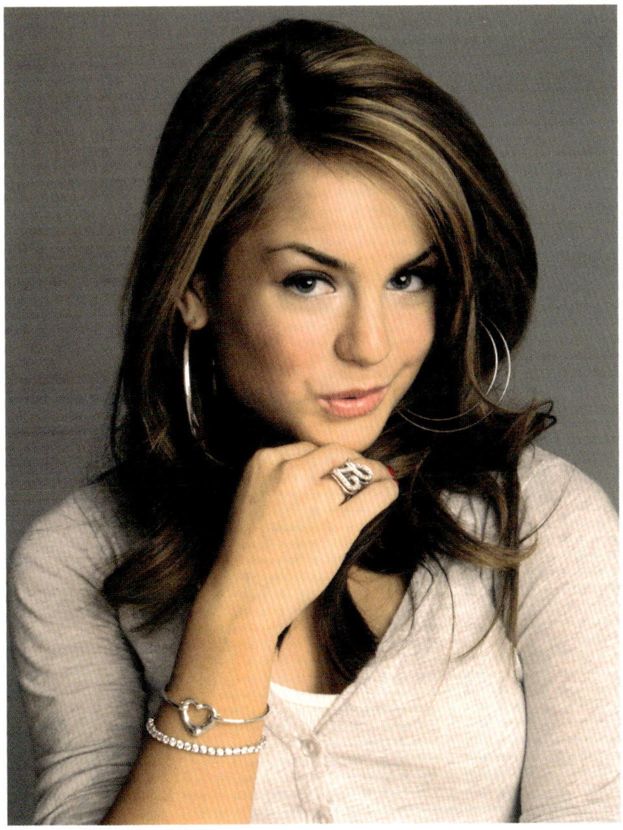

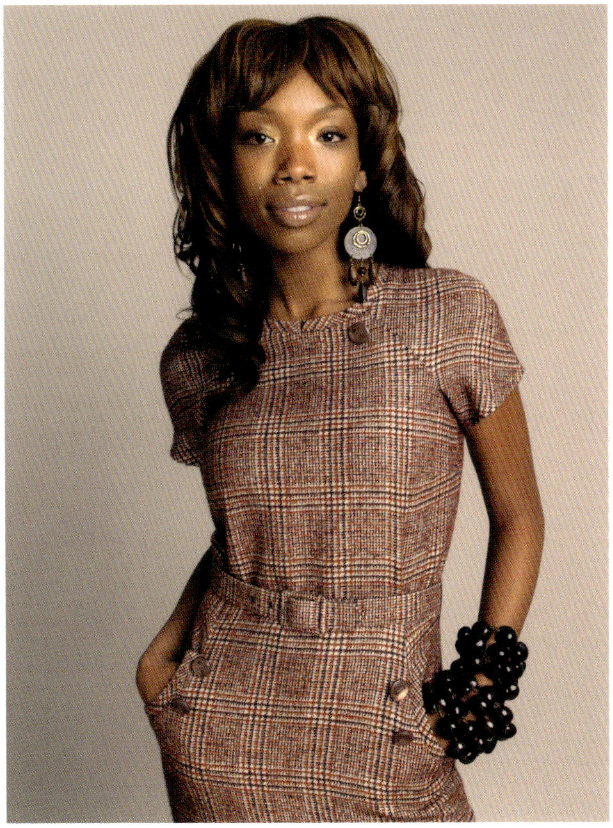

FOXY BROWN
JOJO

KELLY OSBOURNE
BRANDY Songbirds

First time I ever encountered the 7th on Sixth phenomenon? Like all New Yorkers, it was when I mistakenly tried to make my way up Sixth Avenue in a cab, only to get bottlenecked by all the paparazzi, the limos, the hair, the publicists, the jewelry, the bona fide designers, the attitude.

You would drive past that entrance on Bryant Park and you could feel the hum and pulse of High Fashion/Couture New York in the throes of its biannual rite. A mating season, if you will. It's spring (or fall) in New York and the world's most celebrated designers are finding out if they will get the fashion world pregnant with the seeds of their imaginations.

I had never been inside that tent, to my recollection, until this year. It was like a womb. Somewhat dark. Warm. Female energy washing over everything. Even the men emitted a kind of feminine frequency. Initially, I thought only of the chemicals that were used to dye all of the fabric. I didn't recognize anyone. In any way. The women slinked by, impossibly slinky. I thought that if Kate Moss snorted an eightball of cocaine a day, who could blame her? How else could one fit into these clothes? This tent? This idea itself?

I was there with Scott Ellis. He is the boyfriend of Chaiken designer Jeff Mahshie while inside the tent. A brilliant theater director outside of it. Scott and I sat through Jeff's show. You could hold your breath during the entire thing, it goes by so quickly. I was wedged between Julianna Margulies, Kyra Sedgwick, and Martha Plimpton. I resigned myself that this was for the girls. I was there simply to carry some famous actresses' swag bags to their cars.

Now I have been inside the tent. The womb. The Temple of Fashion. I'm glad my girlfriend or my daughter wasn't there. It would have cost me a fortune.

ALEC BALDWIN

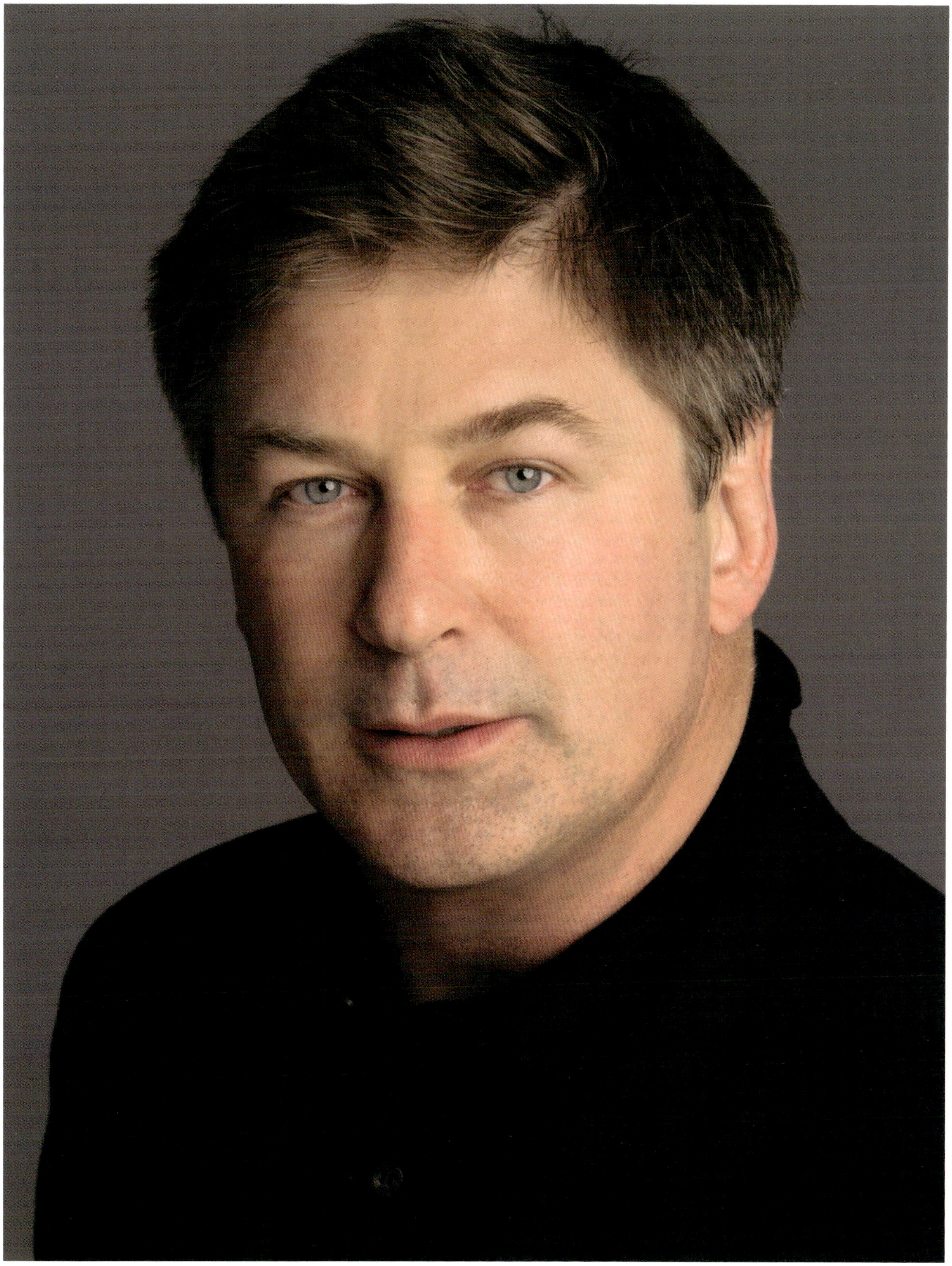

ALEC BALDWIN Actor

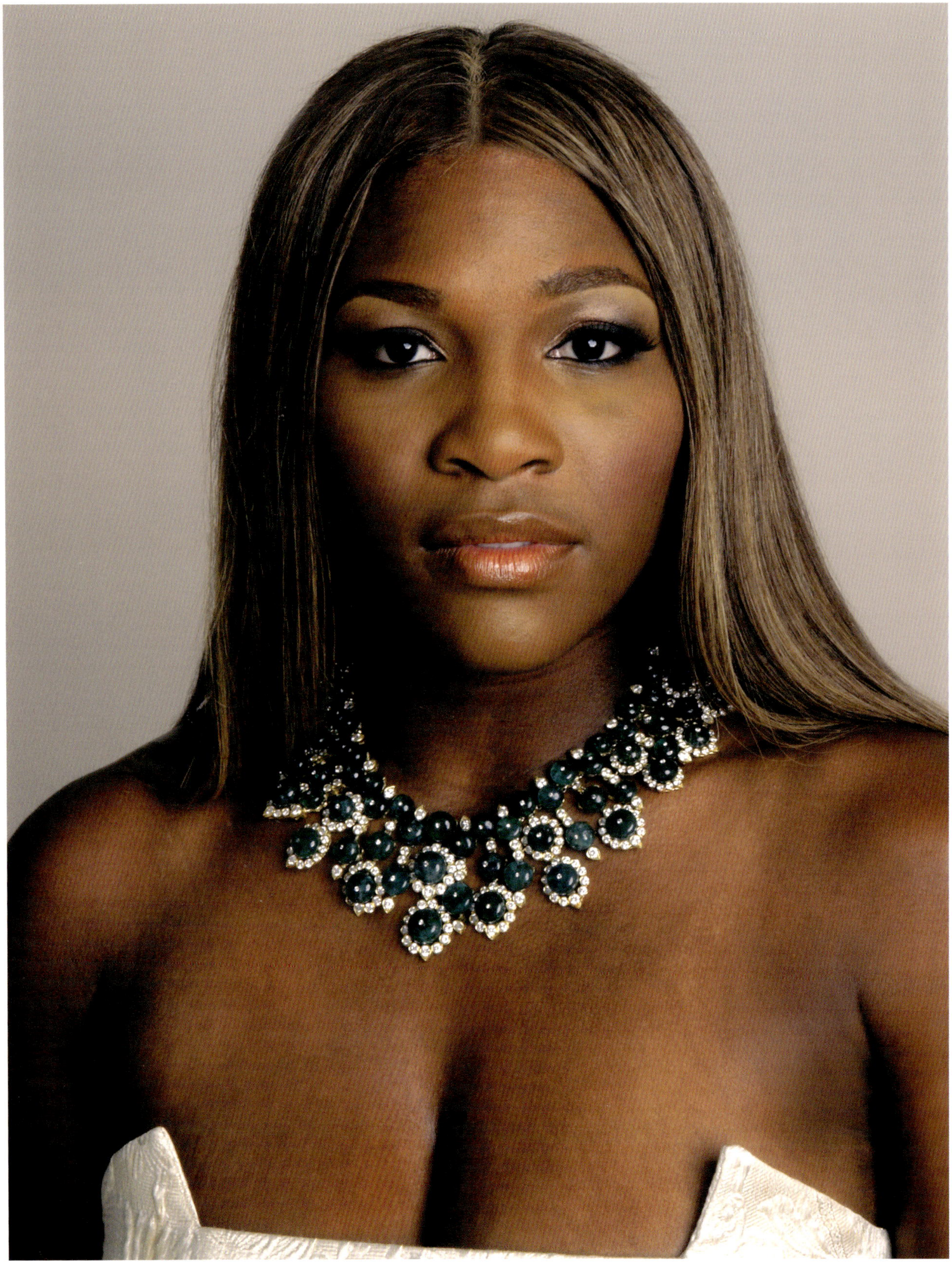

SERENA WILLIAMS Queen of the Court

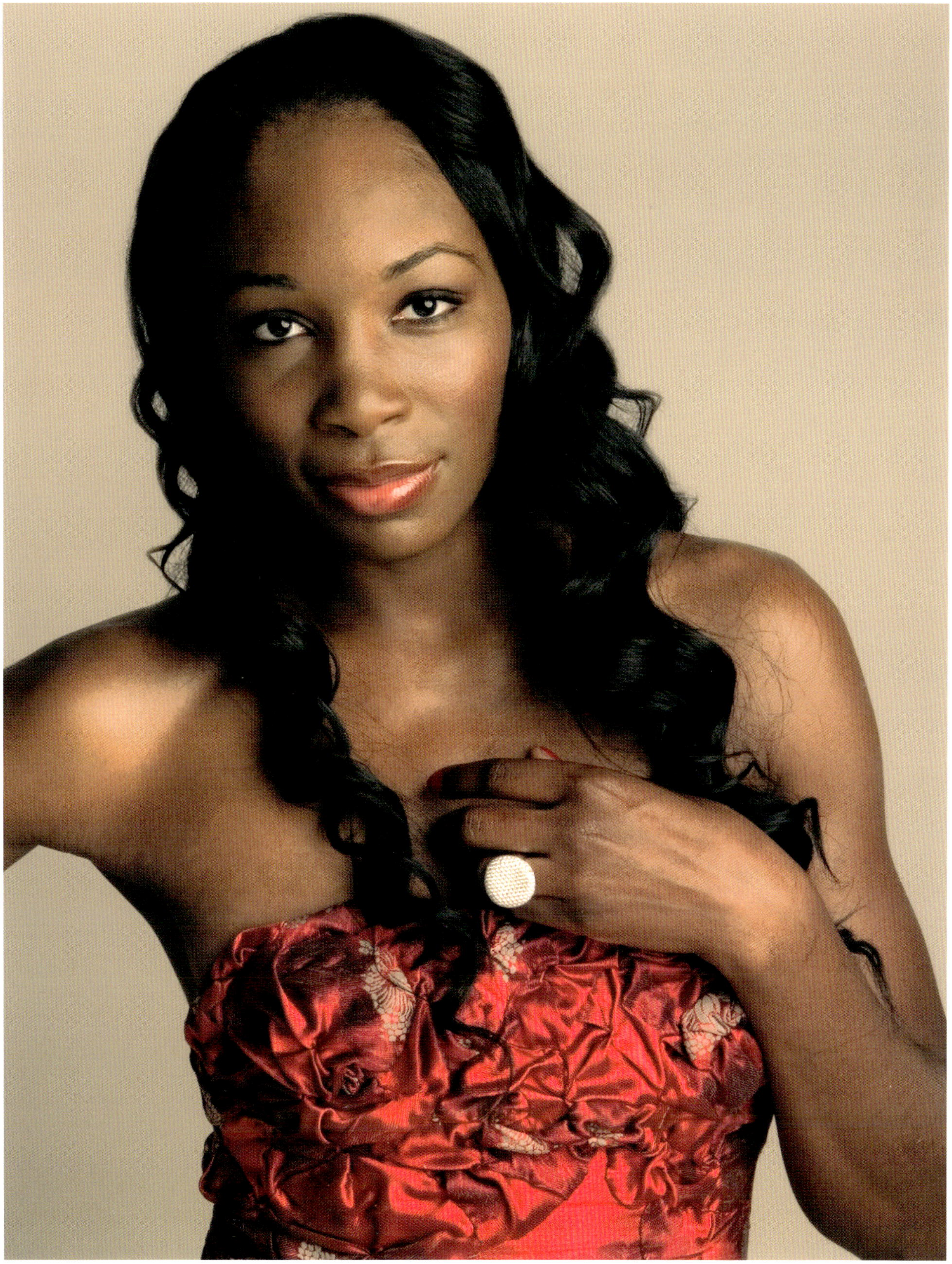

VENUS WILLIAMS Grand Slam Goddess

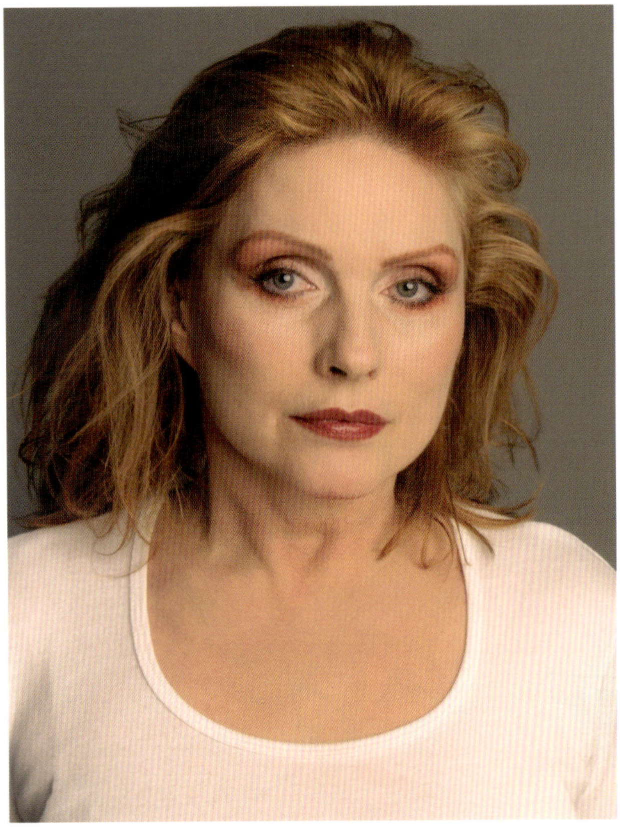

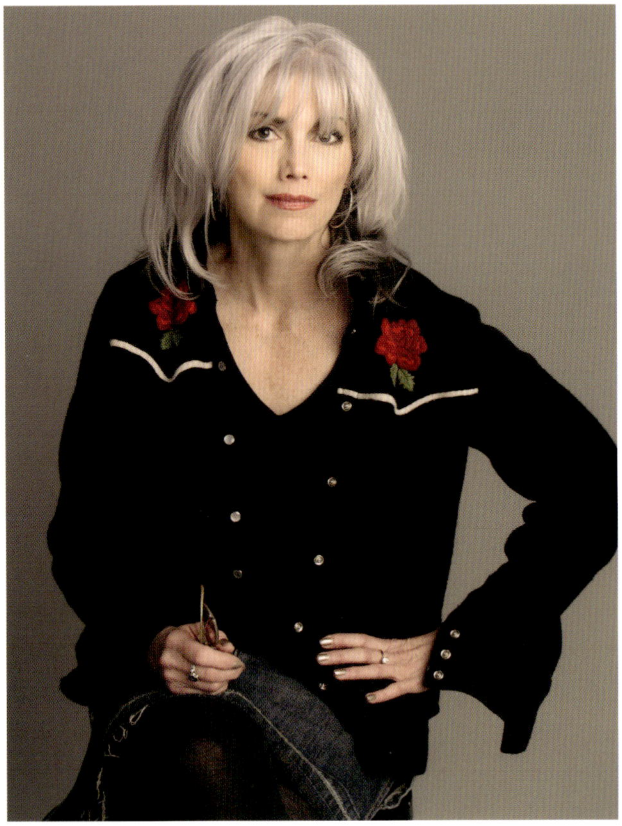

DEBBIE HARRY Lead Singer, Blondie

EMMYLOU HARRIS Singer-songwriter

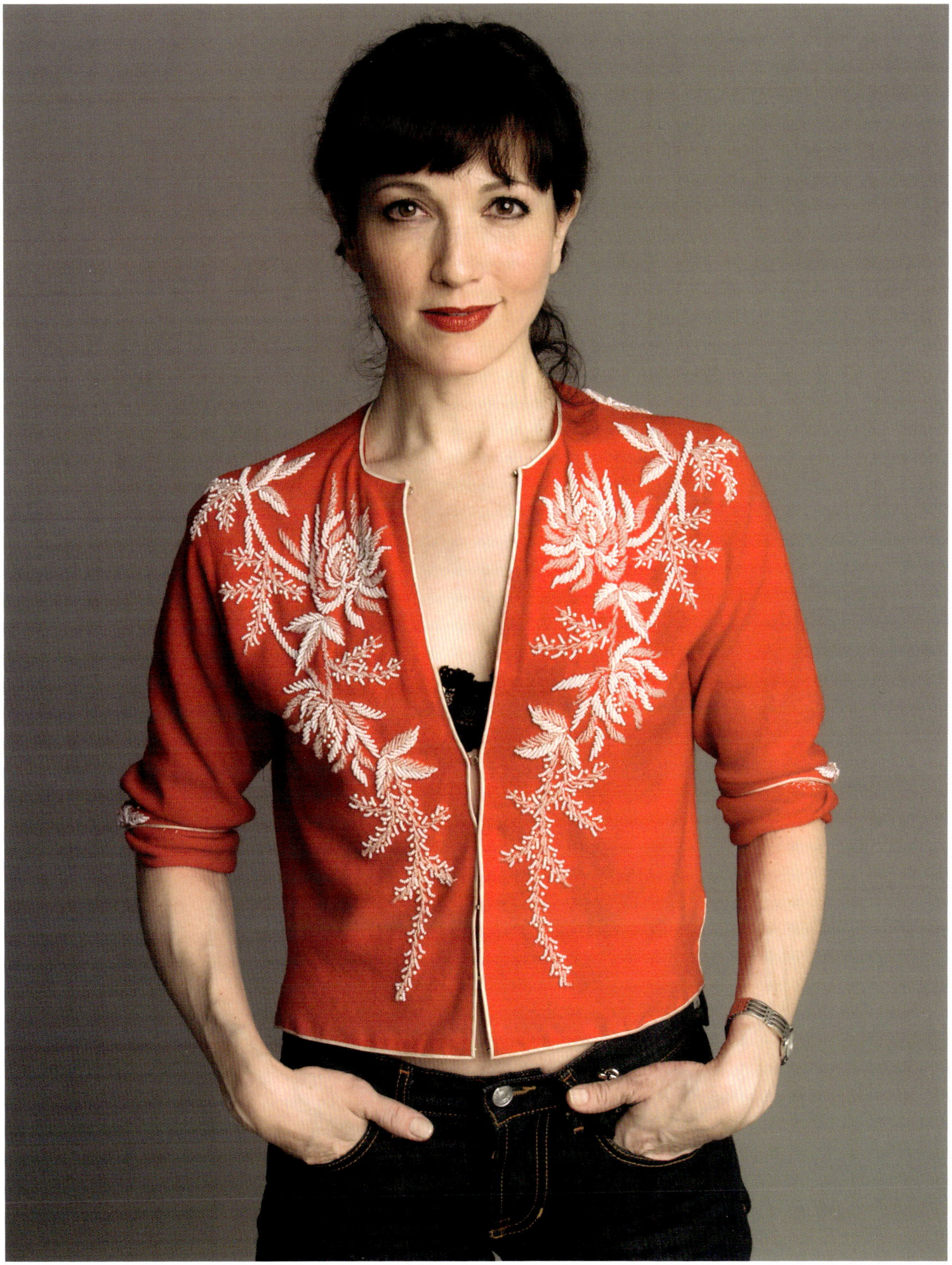

BEBE NEUWIRTH Broadway Babe

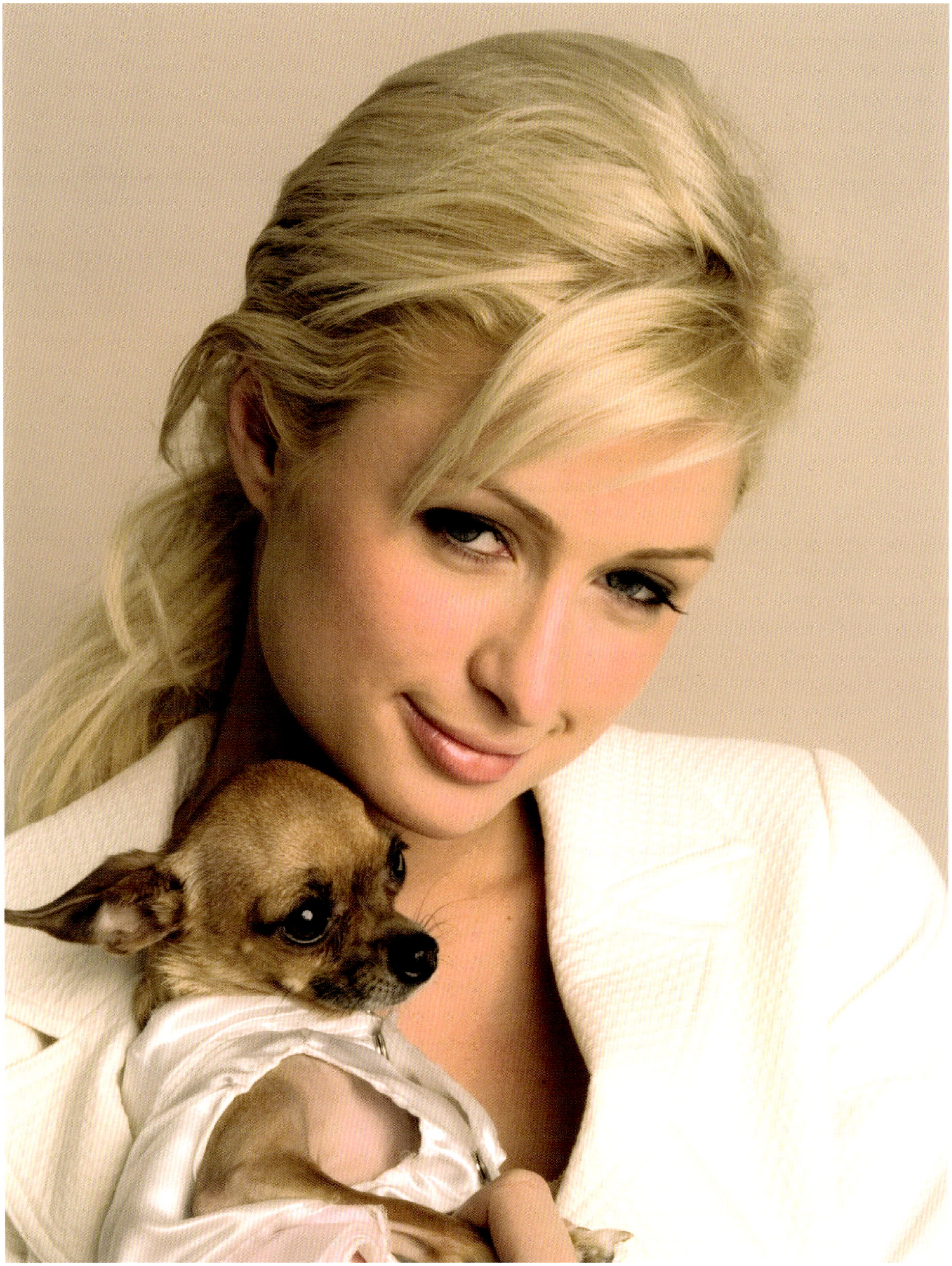

PARIS HILTON Heiress

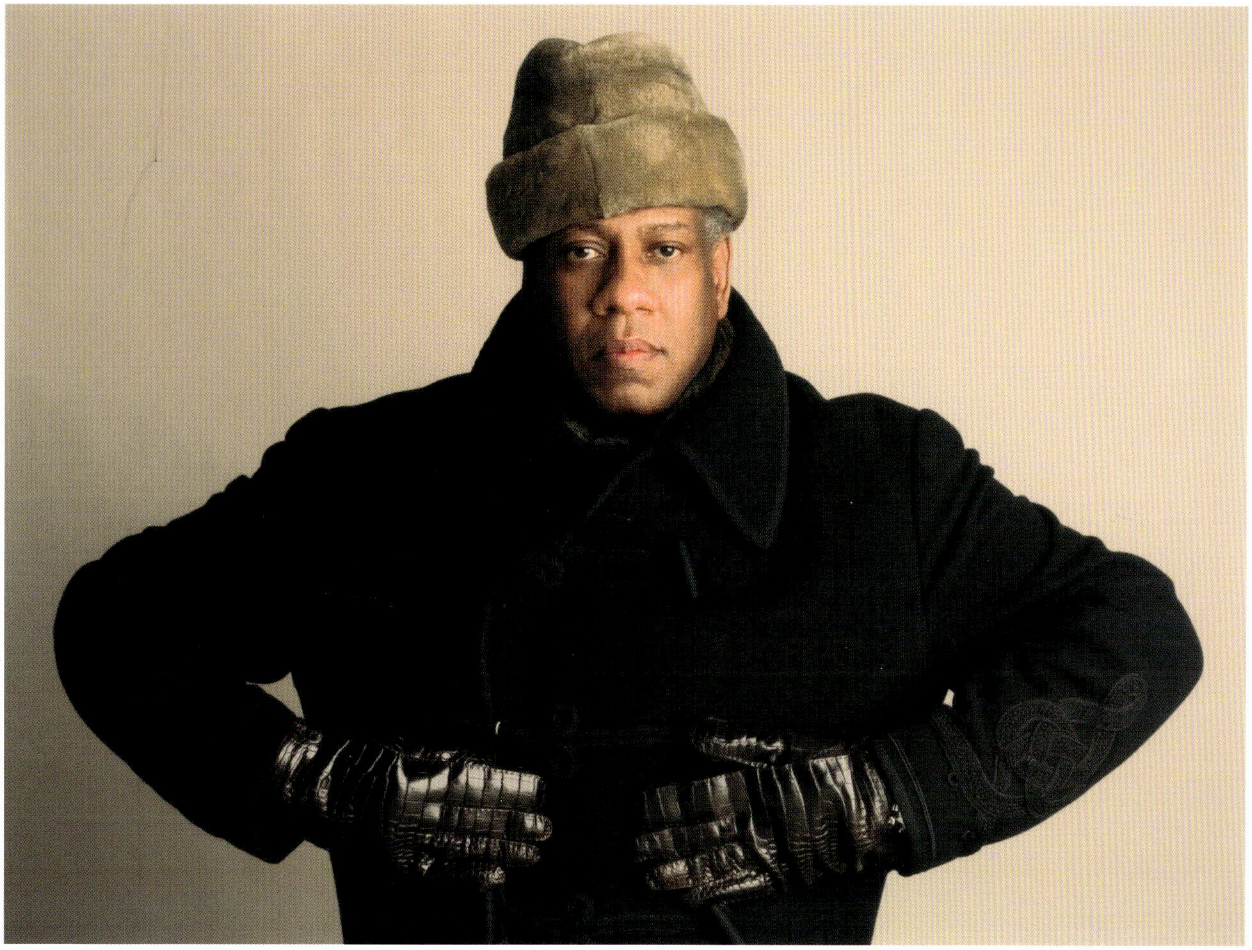

ANDRÉ LEON TALLEY Editor at Large, *Vogue*

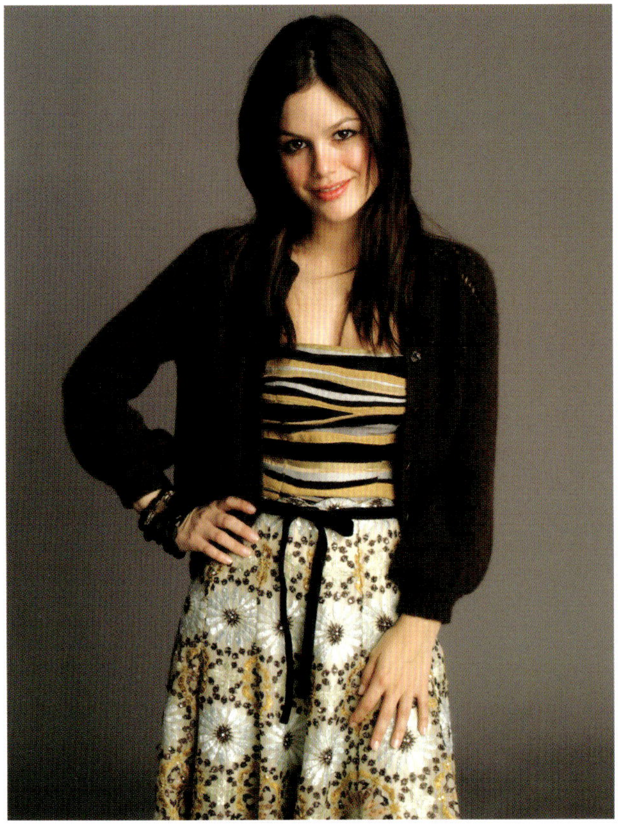

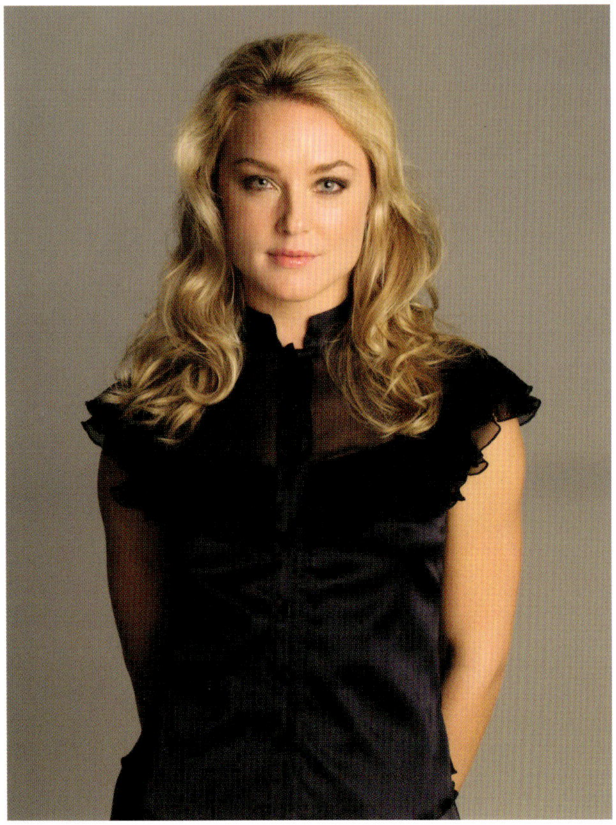

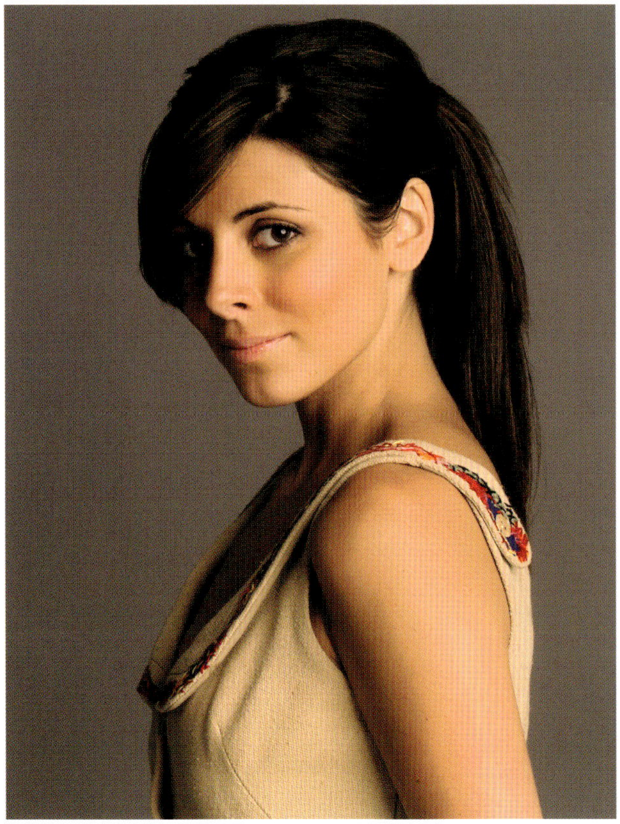

RACHEL BILSON
ELISABETH ROHM

JAMIE-LYNN SIGLER Actors

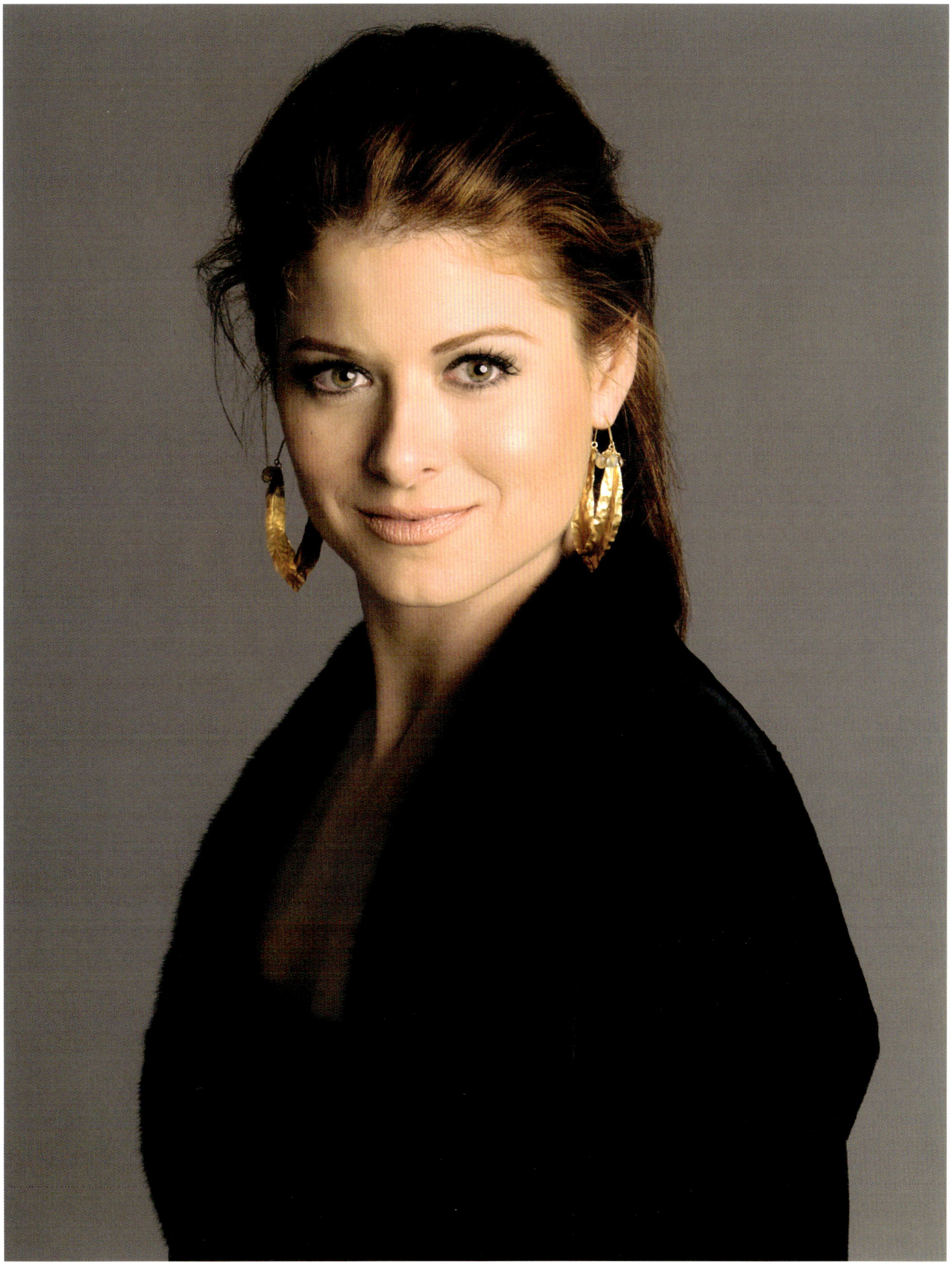

DEBRA MESSING Actor

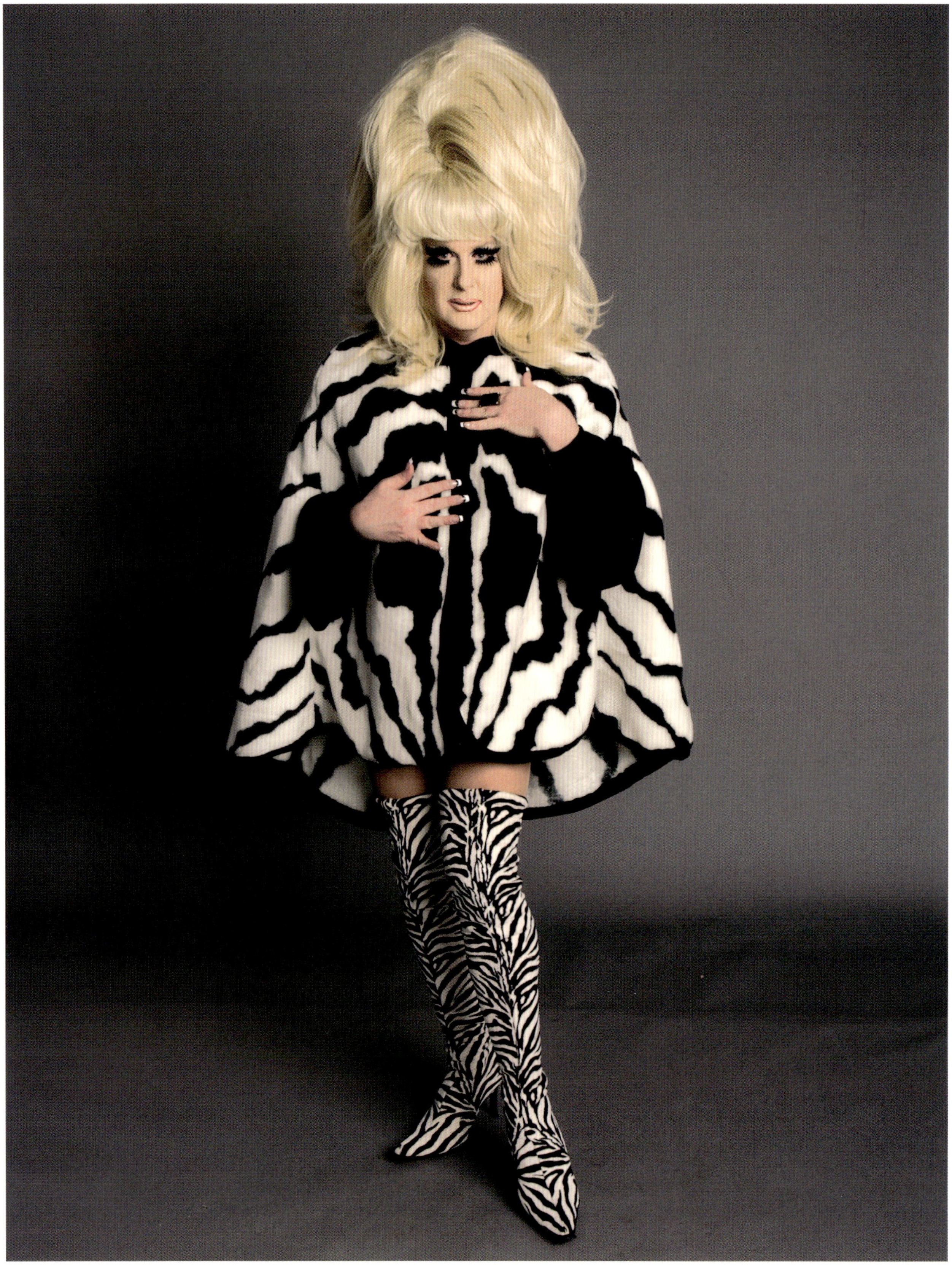

LADY BUNNY Blonde Bombshell

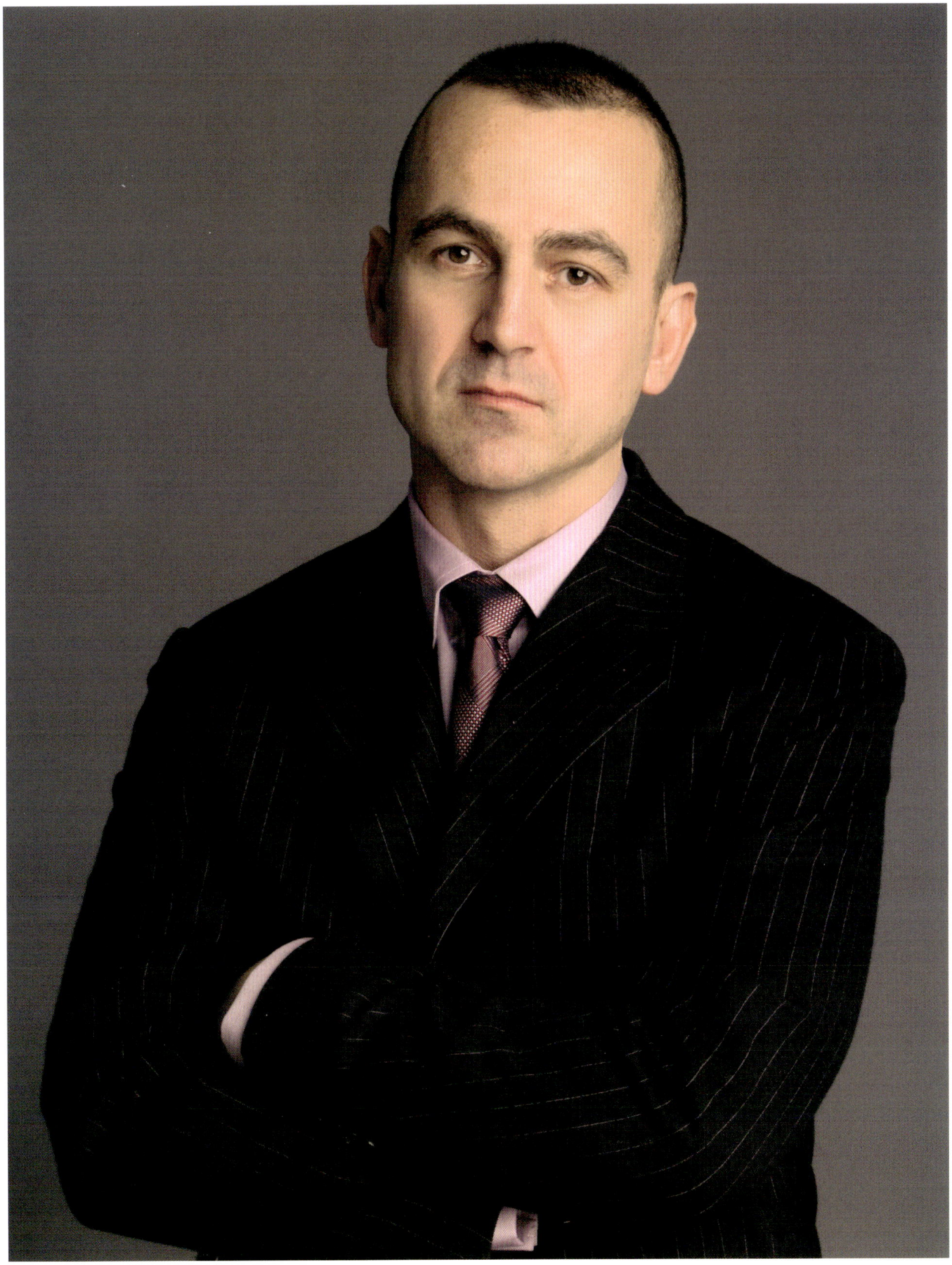

STEVEN KOLB Executive Director, Council of Fashion Designers of America

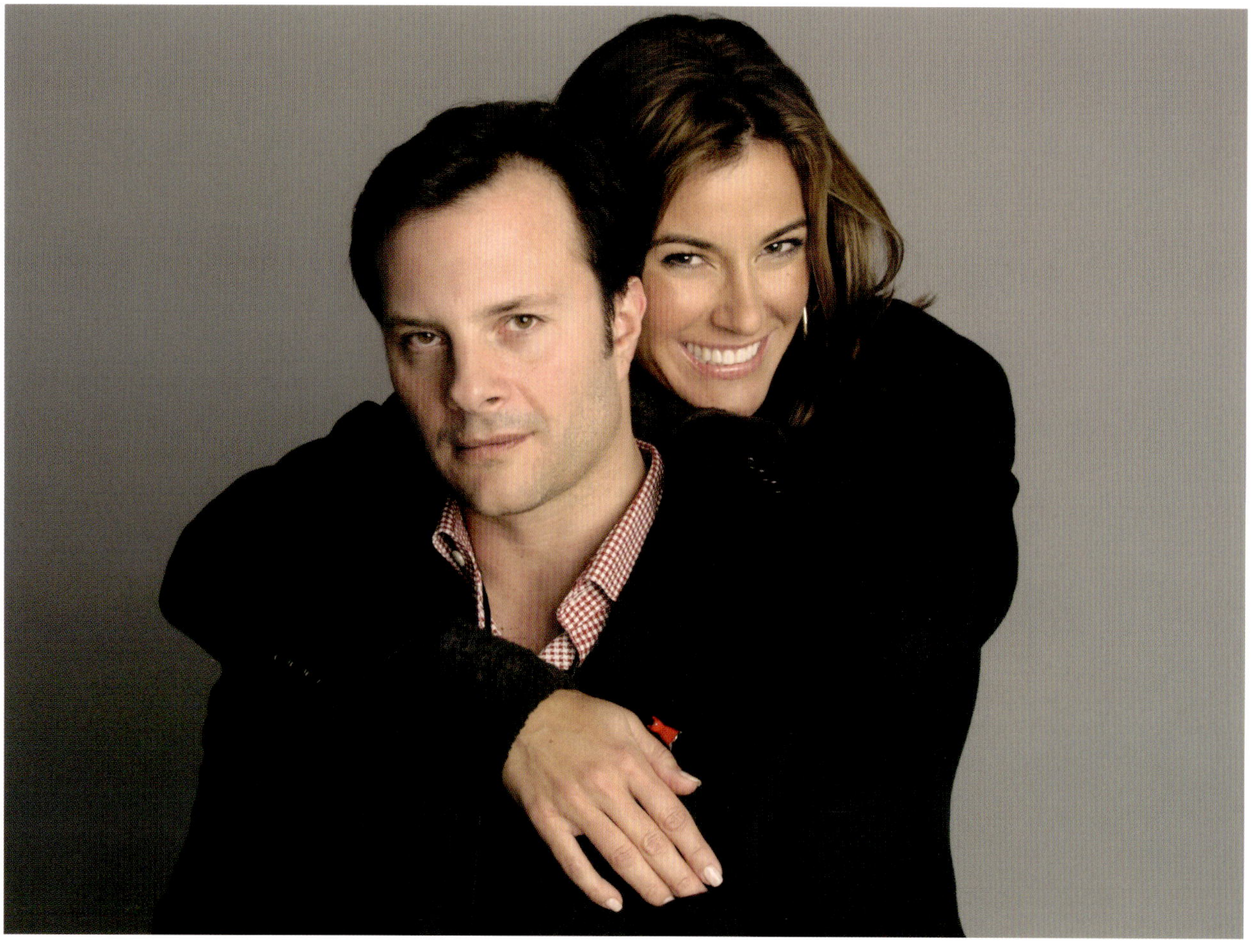

IVAN BART Model Maker
KELLY KILLOREN BENSIMON Author

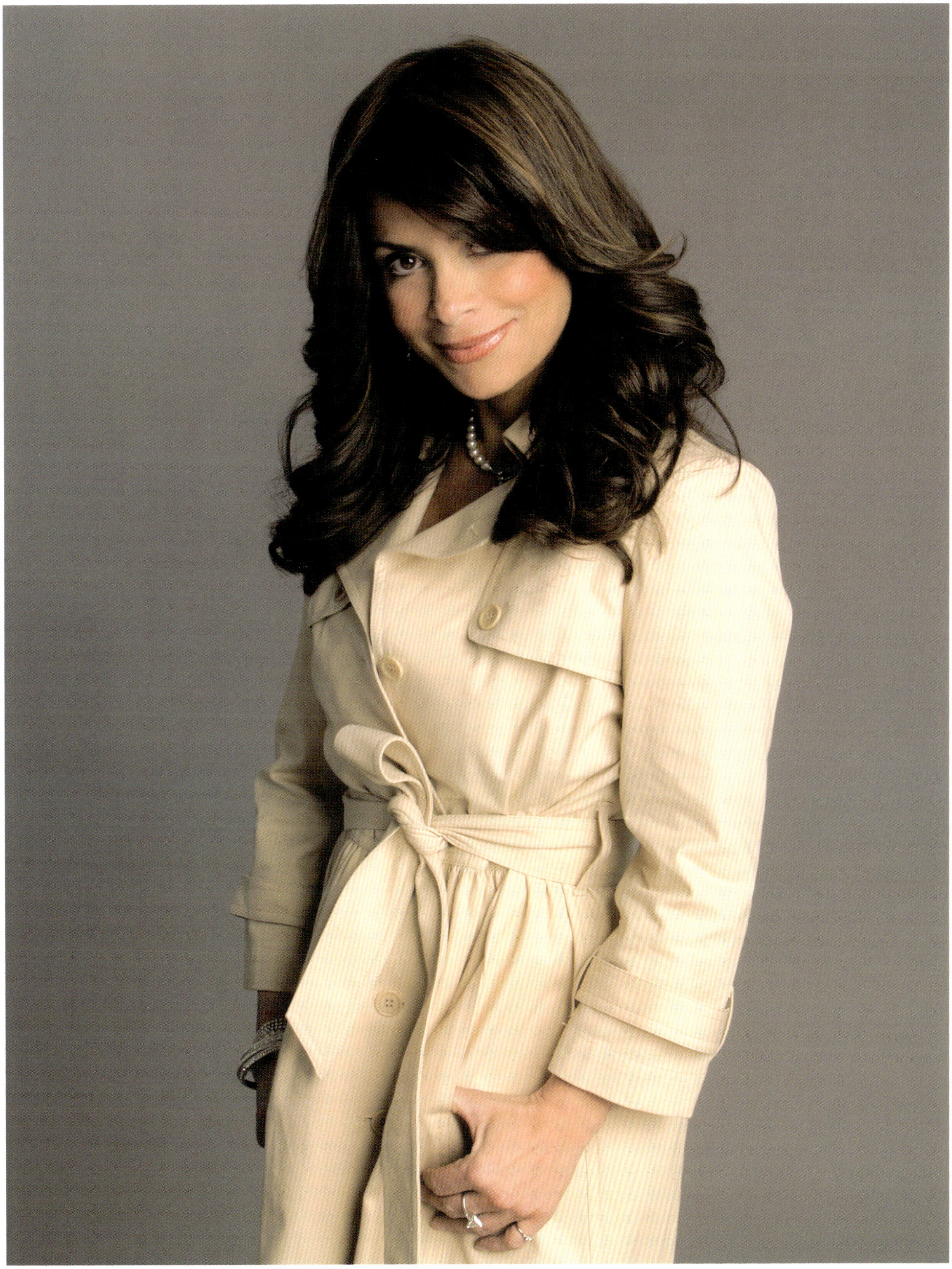

PAULA ABDUL Judge, *American Idol*

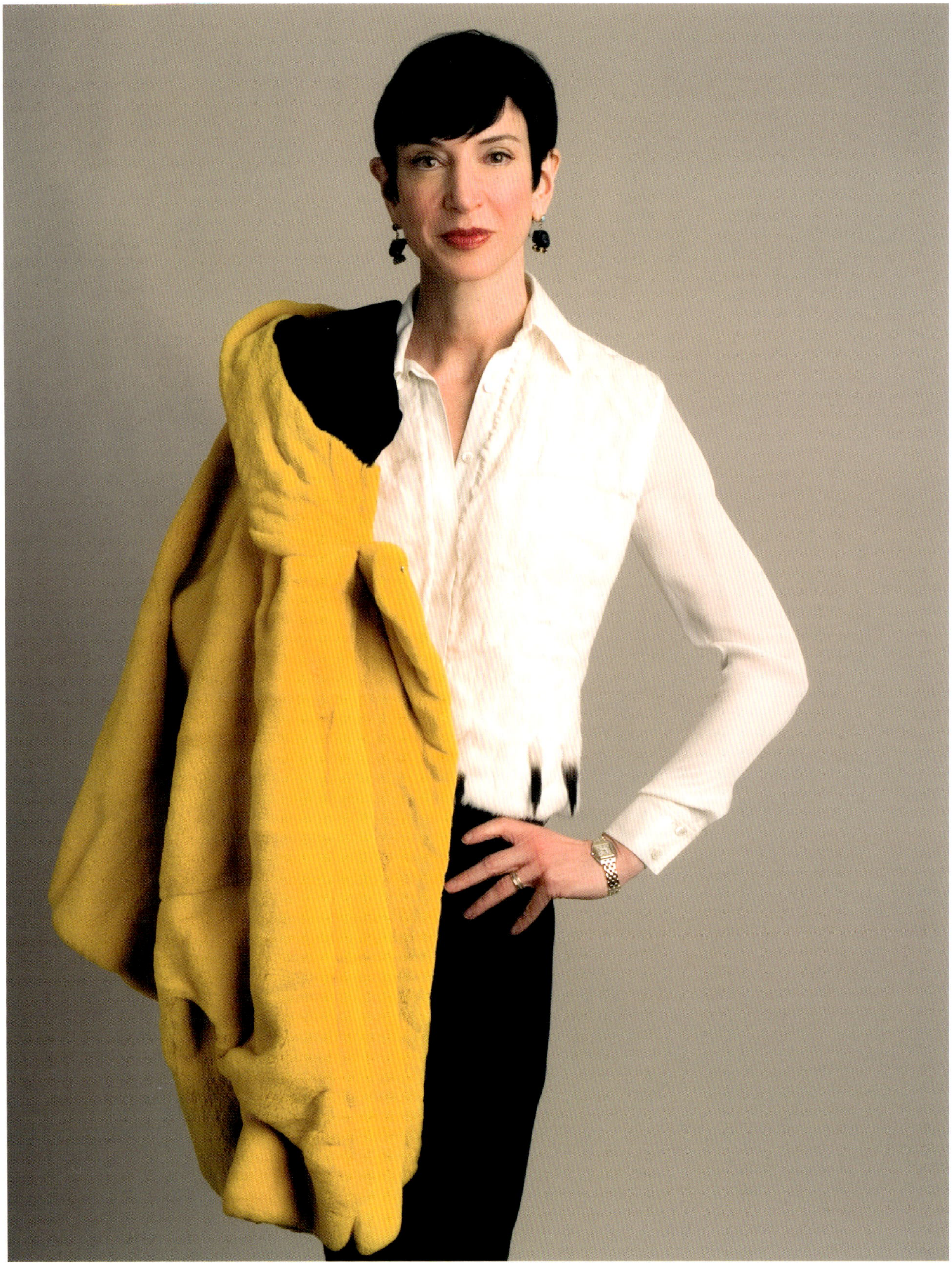

AMY FINE COLLINS Journalist

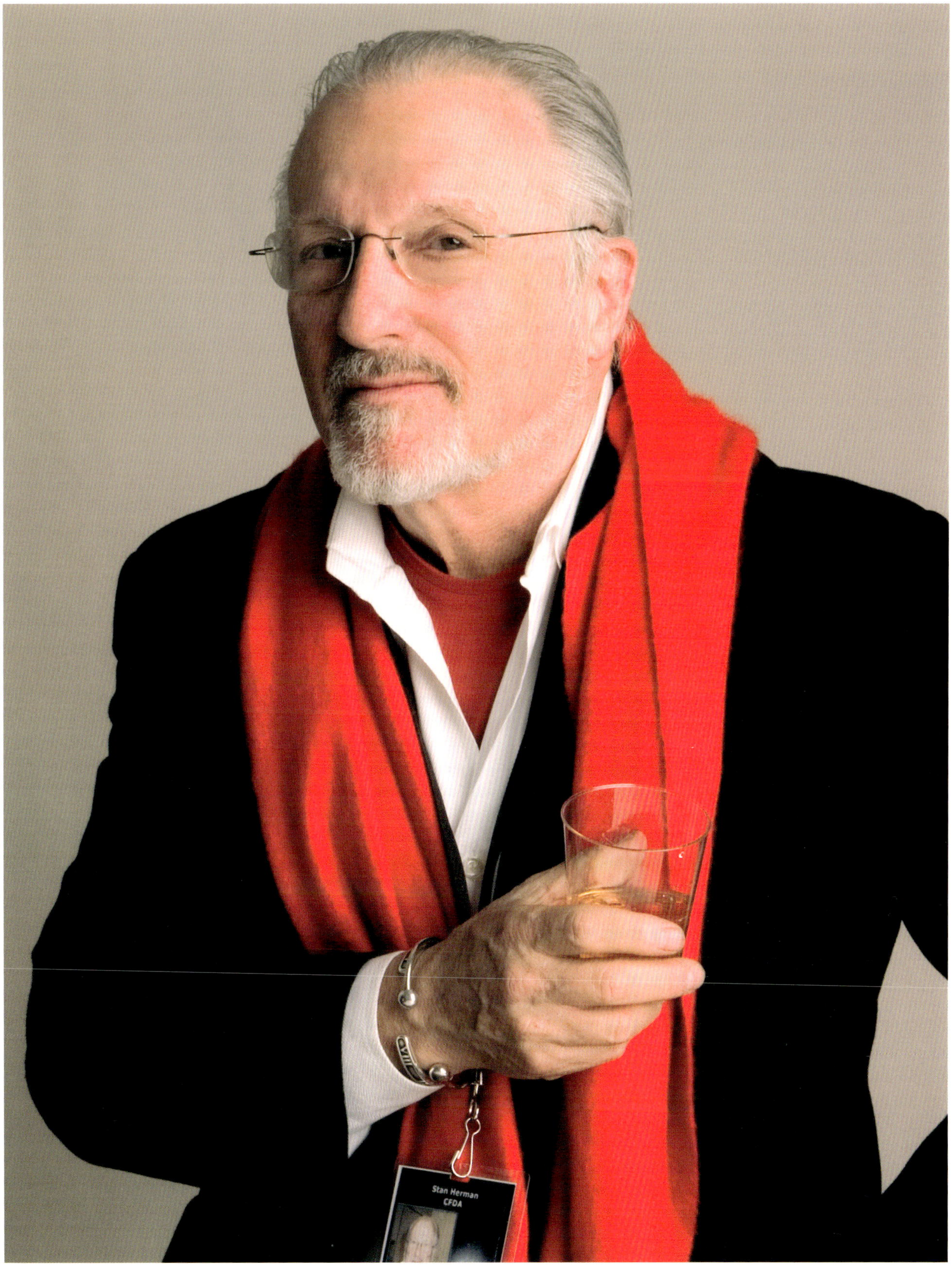

STAN HERMAN President, Council of Fashion Designers of America

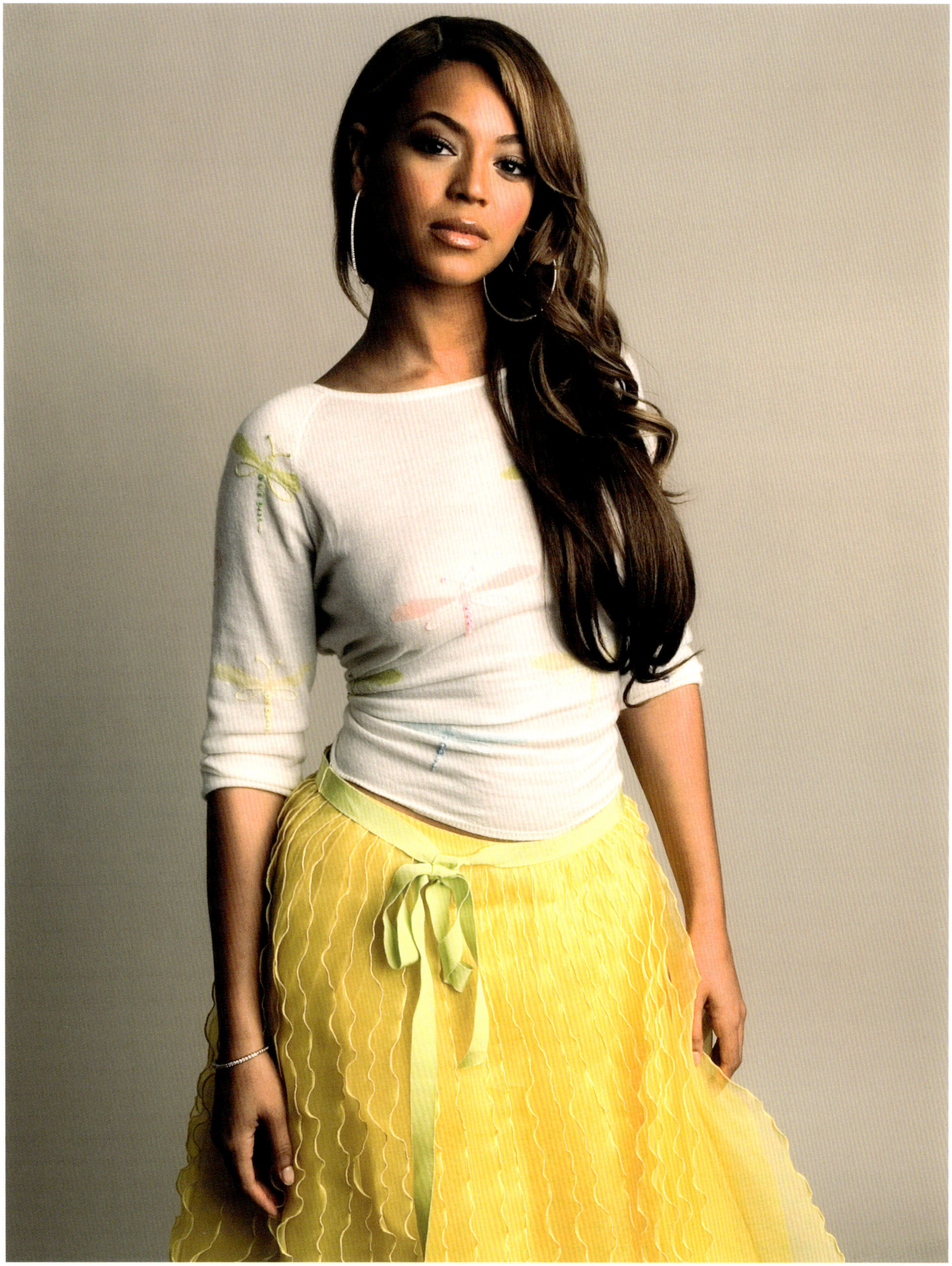

BEYONCÉ KNOWLES Dreamgirl

Mary J. Blige, Lindsay Lohan, Lou Reed, Eva Longoria, Beyoncé, Russell Simmons, Parker Posey, Venus Williams, Laura Bush, and so on (and on). The shock of seeing all of these grandees backstage during Olympus Fashion Week in Manhattan has a lot to do, of course, with the sheer incongruity of it all. (I mean, c'mon, Lou and…Laura?)

But the real shock is in seeing these icons of every possible persuasion not as rock or rap or pop stars, or as actors, or as athletes, or as politicians, but as fans. Fans of fashion. Fashionistas. Groupies.

It wasn't always like this, remember. Fashion in America was its own thing, had its own subculture, with its own internalized, hermetic star power. Sure, there was notable crossover now and then: Jackie Kennedy wearing Oleg Cassini's creations and making him a bona fide celebrity; Katharine Hepburn immortalizing Coco Chanel on the Broadway stage; Ralph Lauren landing the cover of *Time* ("Selling That Sporty Look") in 1986; assorted ripped male torsos and crotches (in ads and on billboards) making Calvin Klein a household name through the '80s and '90s. But for the most part fashion was regarded by creative types outside of fashion as either an afterthought or a means to an end. (And for most American consumers it was basically what was on sale at the mall.)

Fashion was subsidiary to pop culture. If various stars' fame was persistently intensified because of how they dressed (Bowie comes to mind; so, hilariously, does Cher), it was because they were eccentrics.

Today, quite simply, pop culture is subsidiary to fashion.

It's hard to imagine, even ten years ago, stars lining up to serve fashion instead of merely being served by fashion. Now the likes of Gwen Stefani and Sean Combs and Jennifer Lopez have made fashion—their own fashion sense, their proximity to fashion, their power within the fashion world—absolutely central to their identities.

It's like this now: Sean Combs (a.k.a. Diddy) is a fashion designer—and also, by the way, a music mogul and rap star. Not the other way around.

My friend Timothy Greenfield-Sanders has had a better-than-front-row seat for this transformation, this peculiar role reversal. At the invitation of Fashion Week's lead sponsor, Olympus, he's set up an ad hoc photo studio backstage at the Bryant Park tents each of the past three seasons.

Look closely at the cast of characters who have graciously posed for him—not only musicians, actors, athletes, and politicians but designers, models, socialites, journalists, and assorted hangers-on—and you'll see that they're all aiming for the exact same thing: their moment.

Their fashion moment.

SIMON DUMENCO 'Media Guy' Columnist

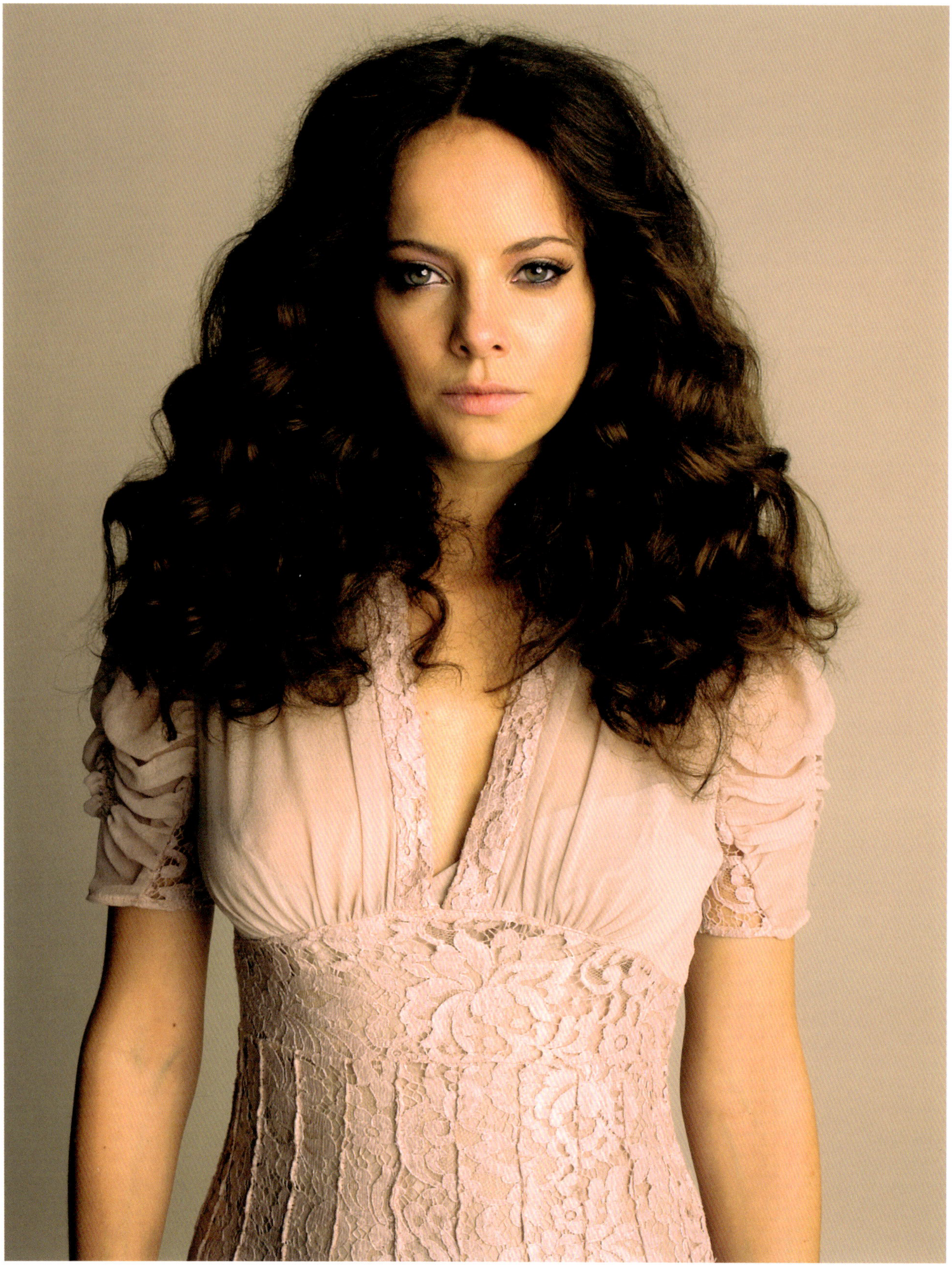

BIJOU PHILLIPS Actor

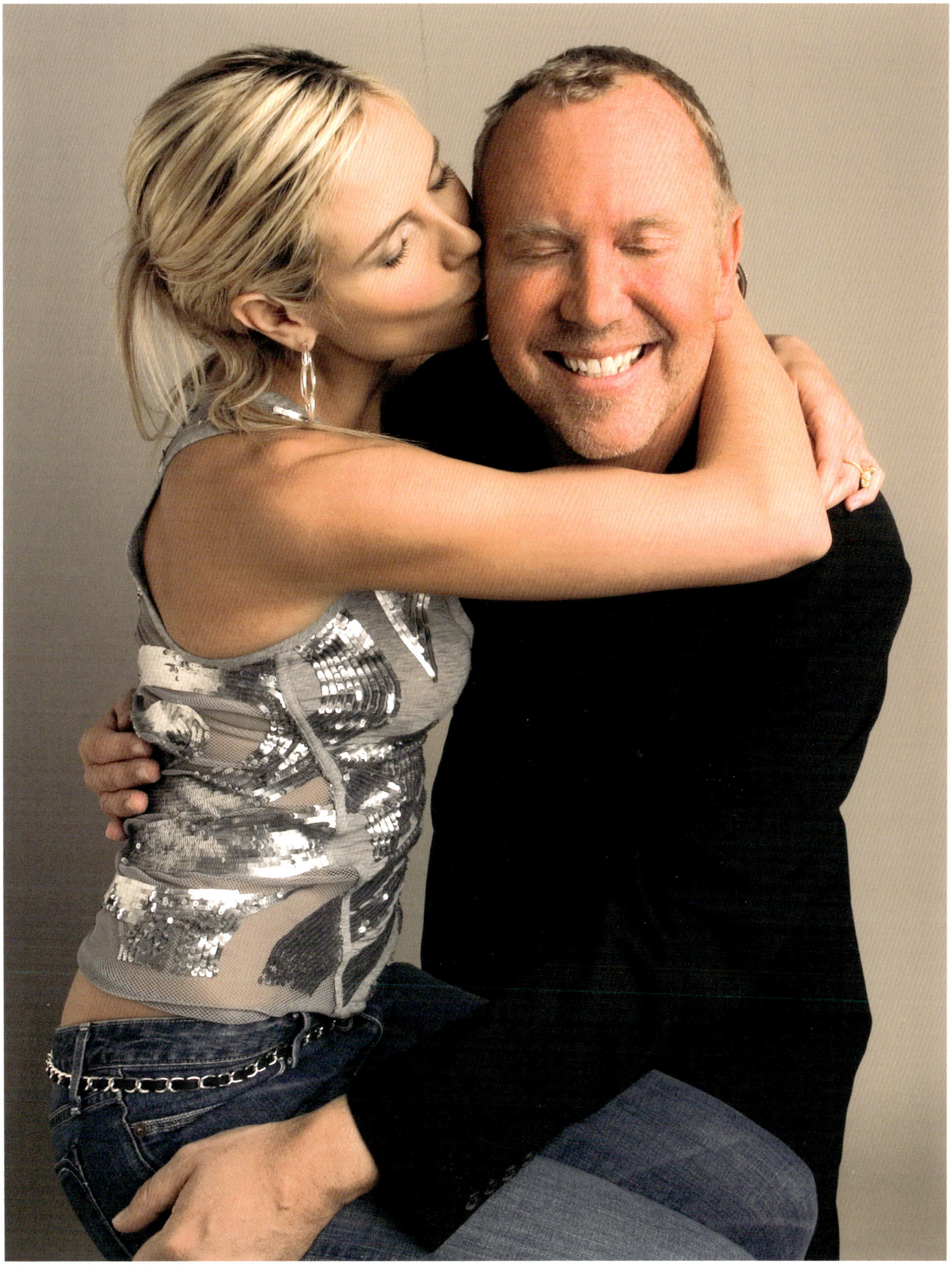

HEIDI KLUM Supermodel
MICHAEL KORS Designer

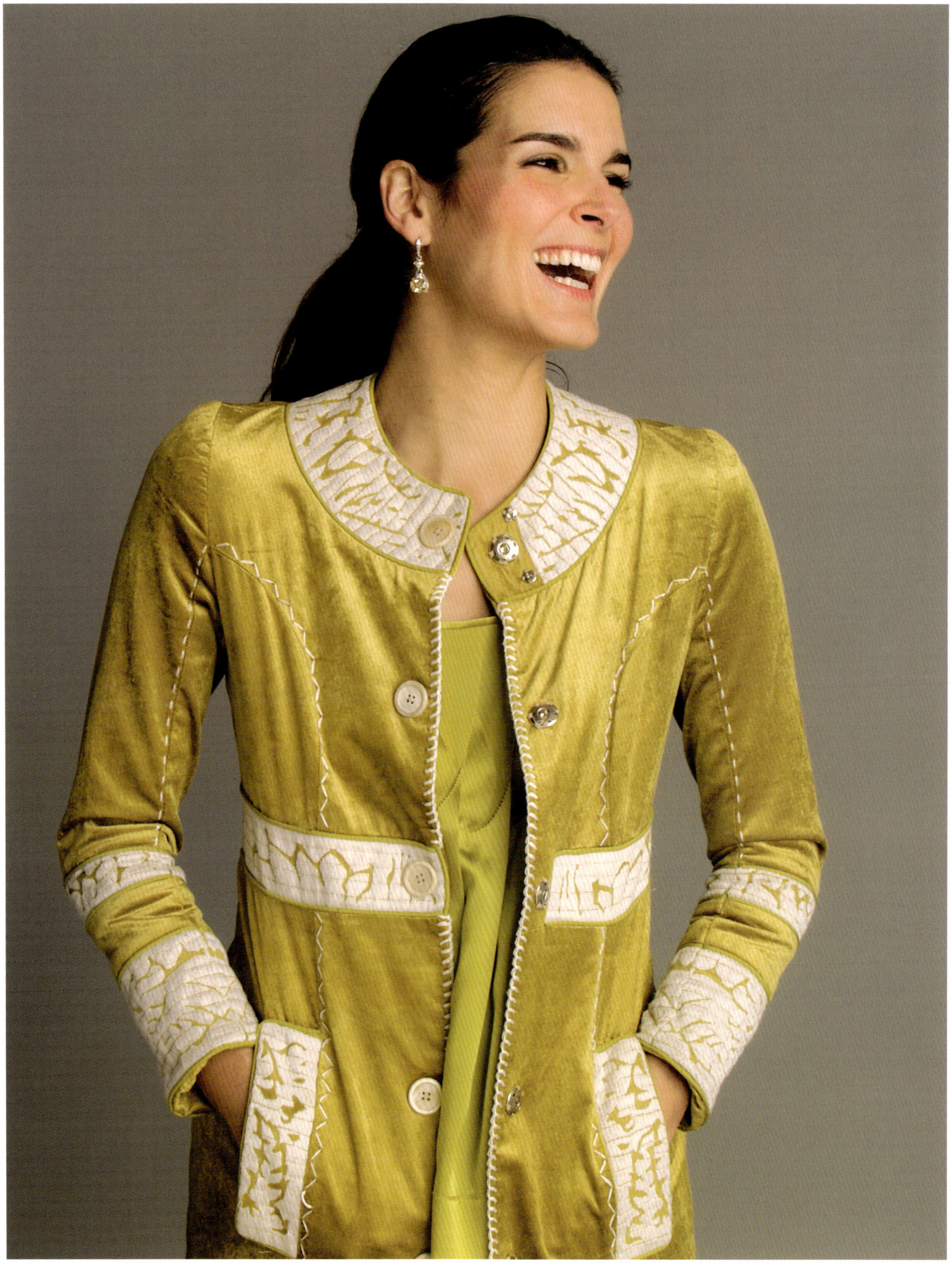

ANGIE HARMON Actor

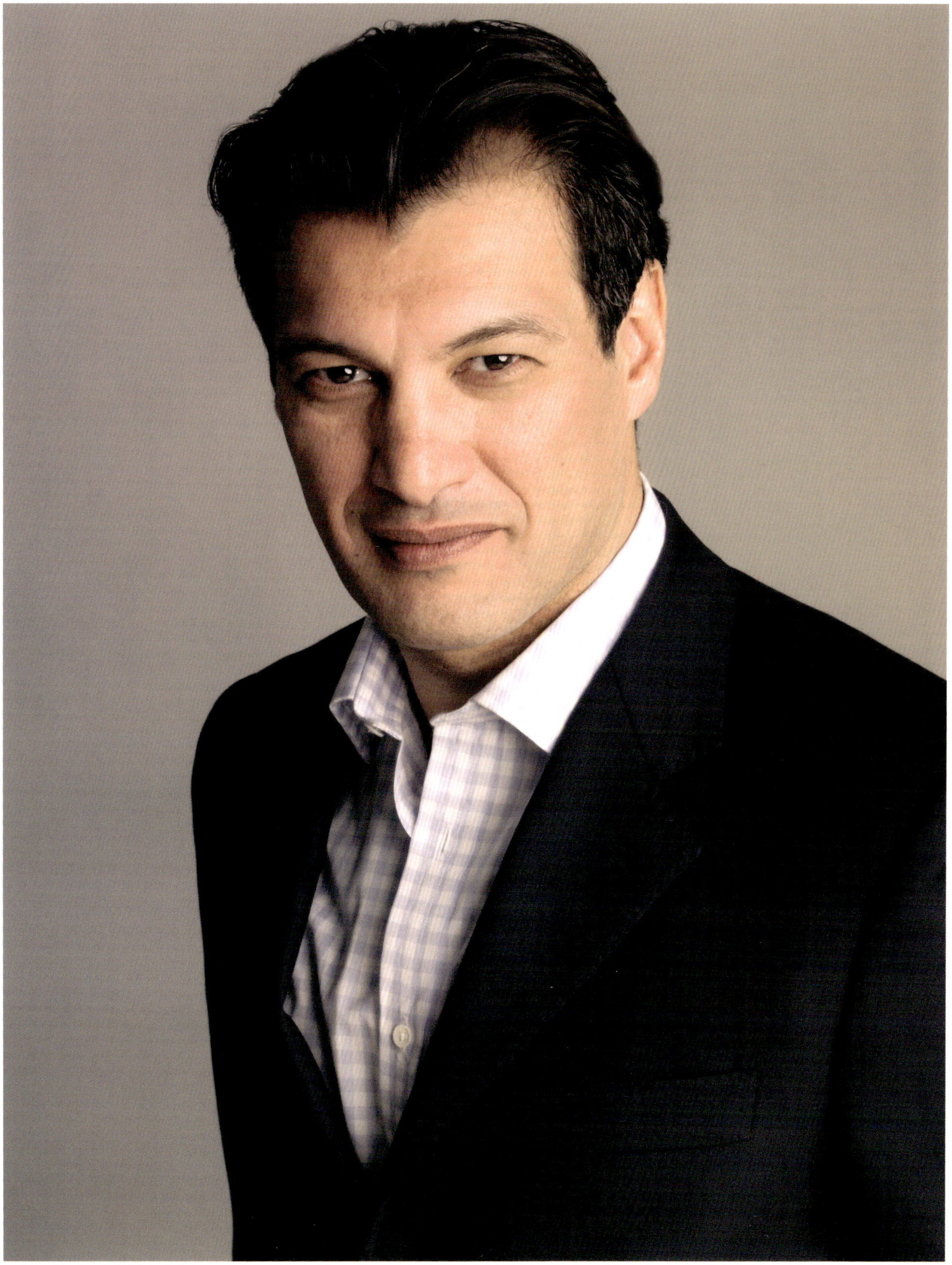

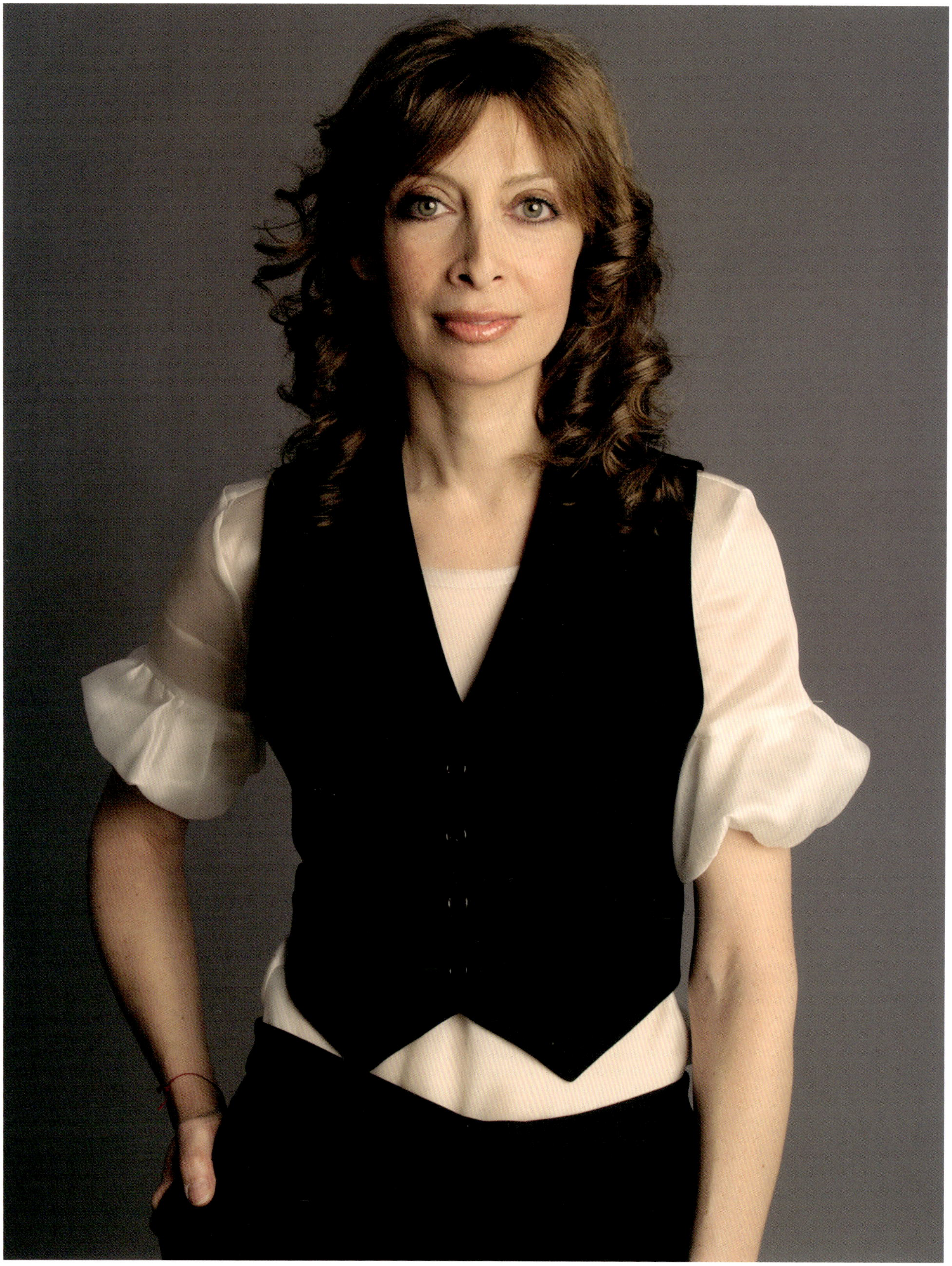

ILLEANA DOUGLAS Actor

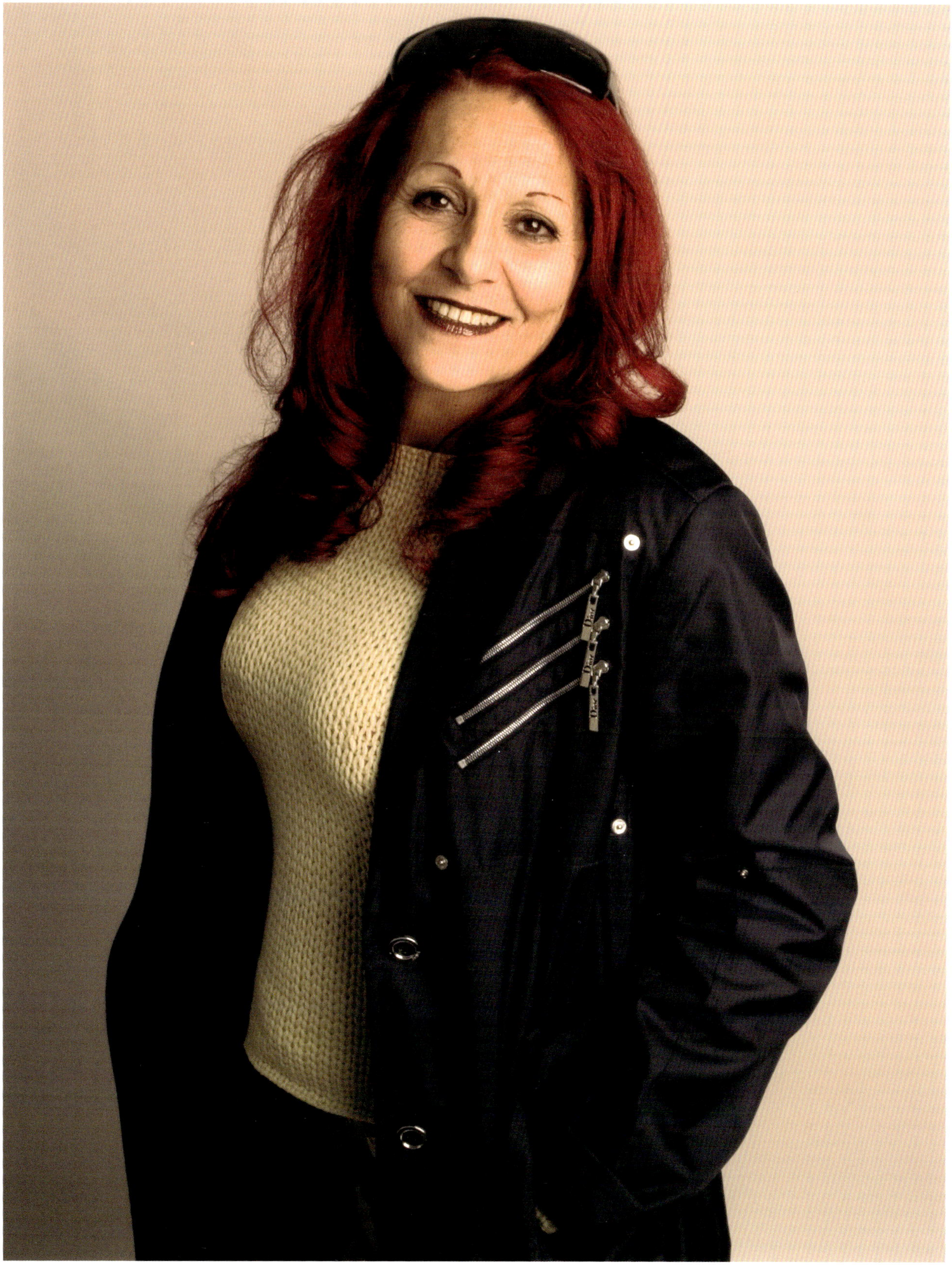

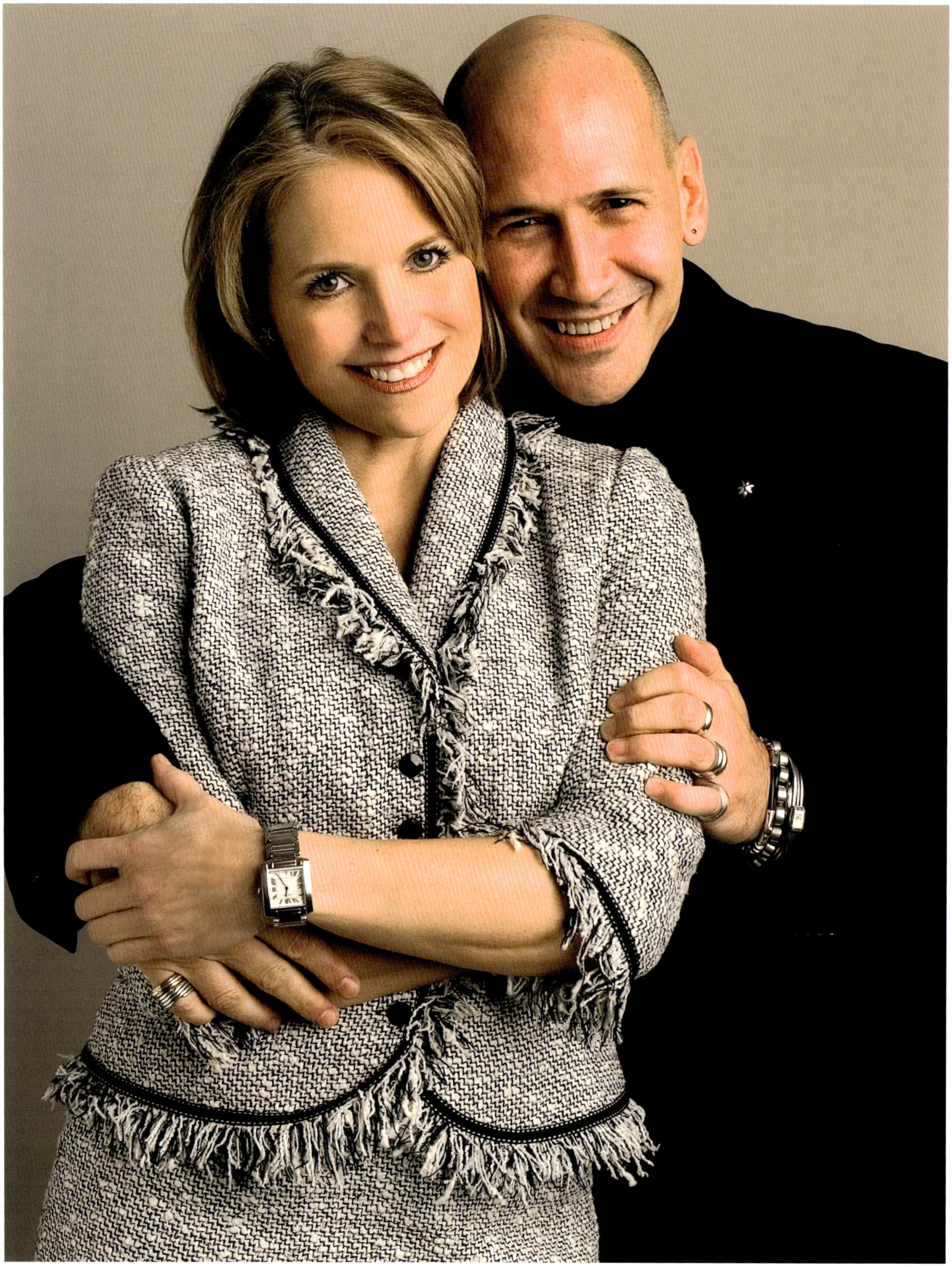

KATIE COURIC Co-founder, National Colorectal Cancer Research Alliance
CARMEN MARC VALVO Designer

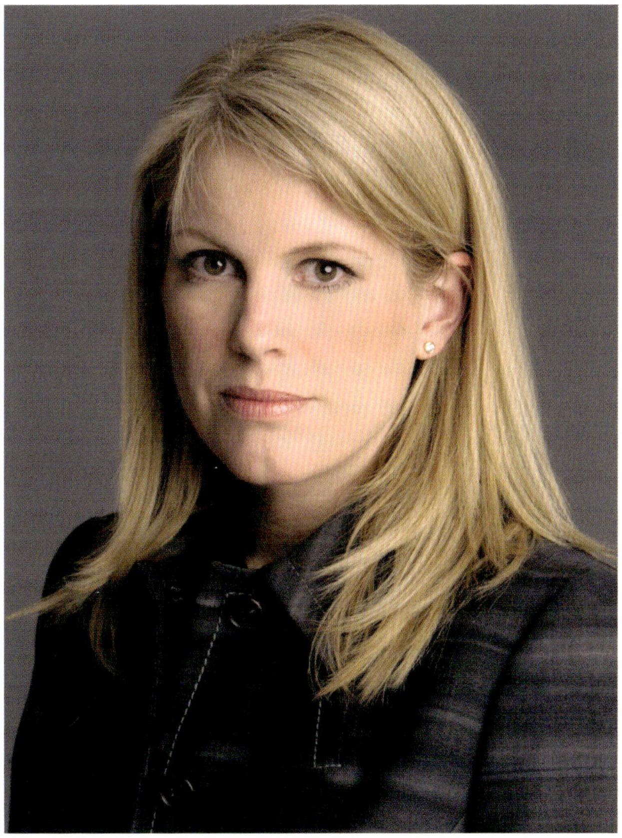

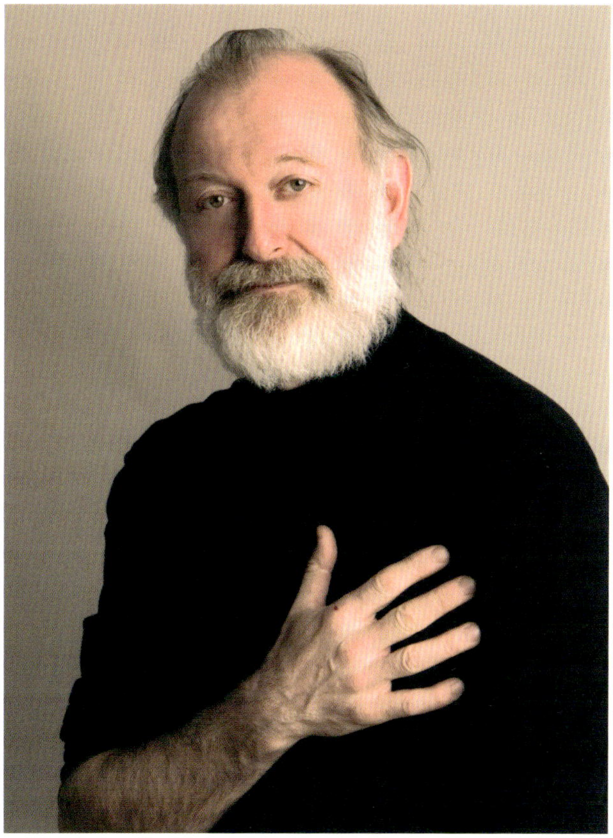

KATE BETTS Editor, *TIME Style & Design*

DAN LECCA Photographer

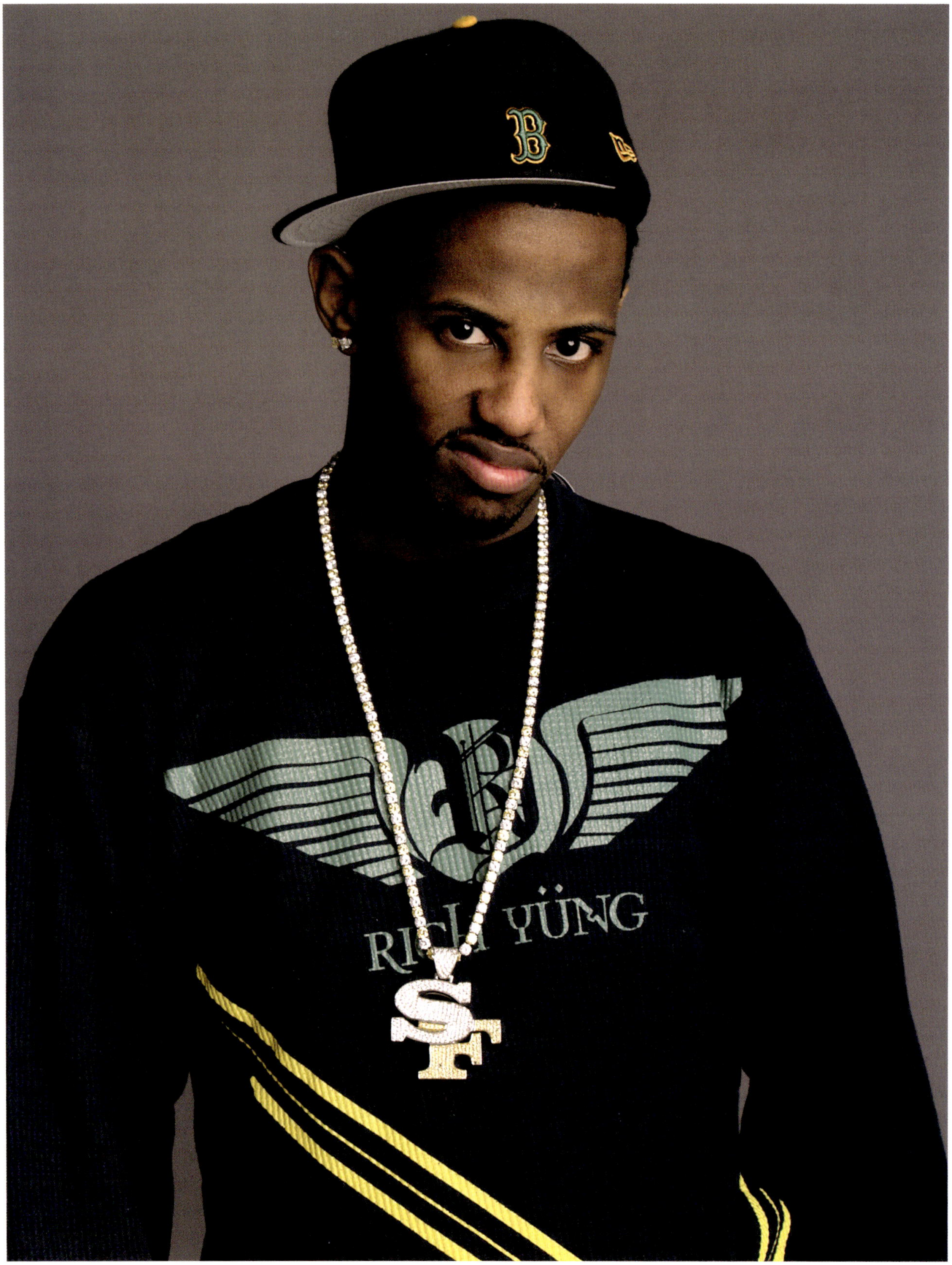

FABOLOUS Rapper

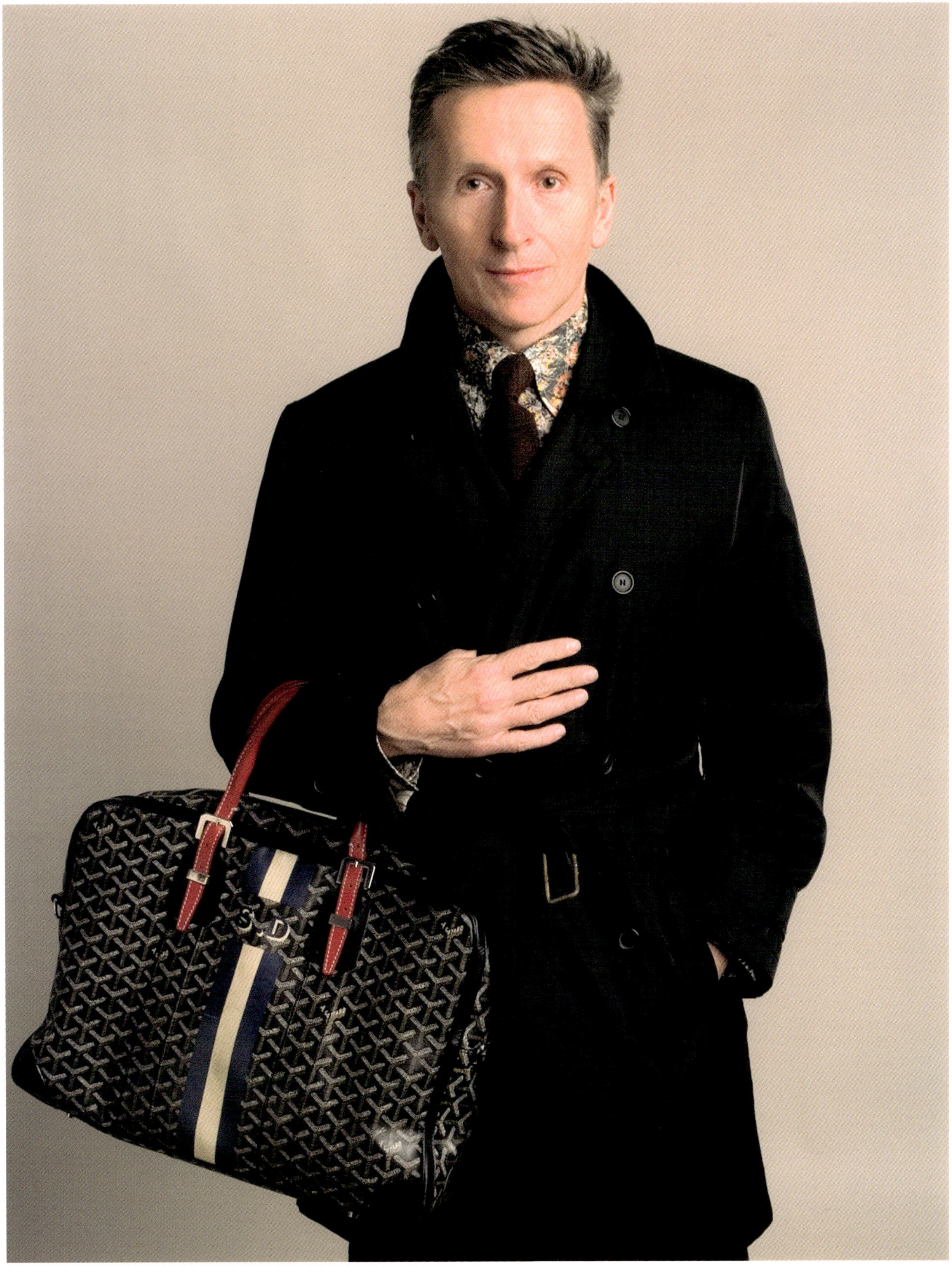

SIMON DOONAN Creative Director, Barneys New York

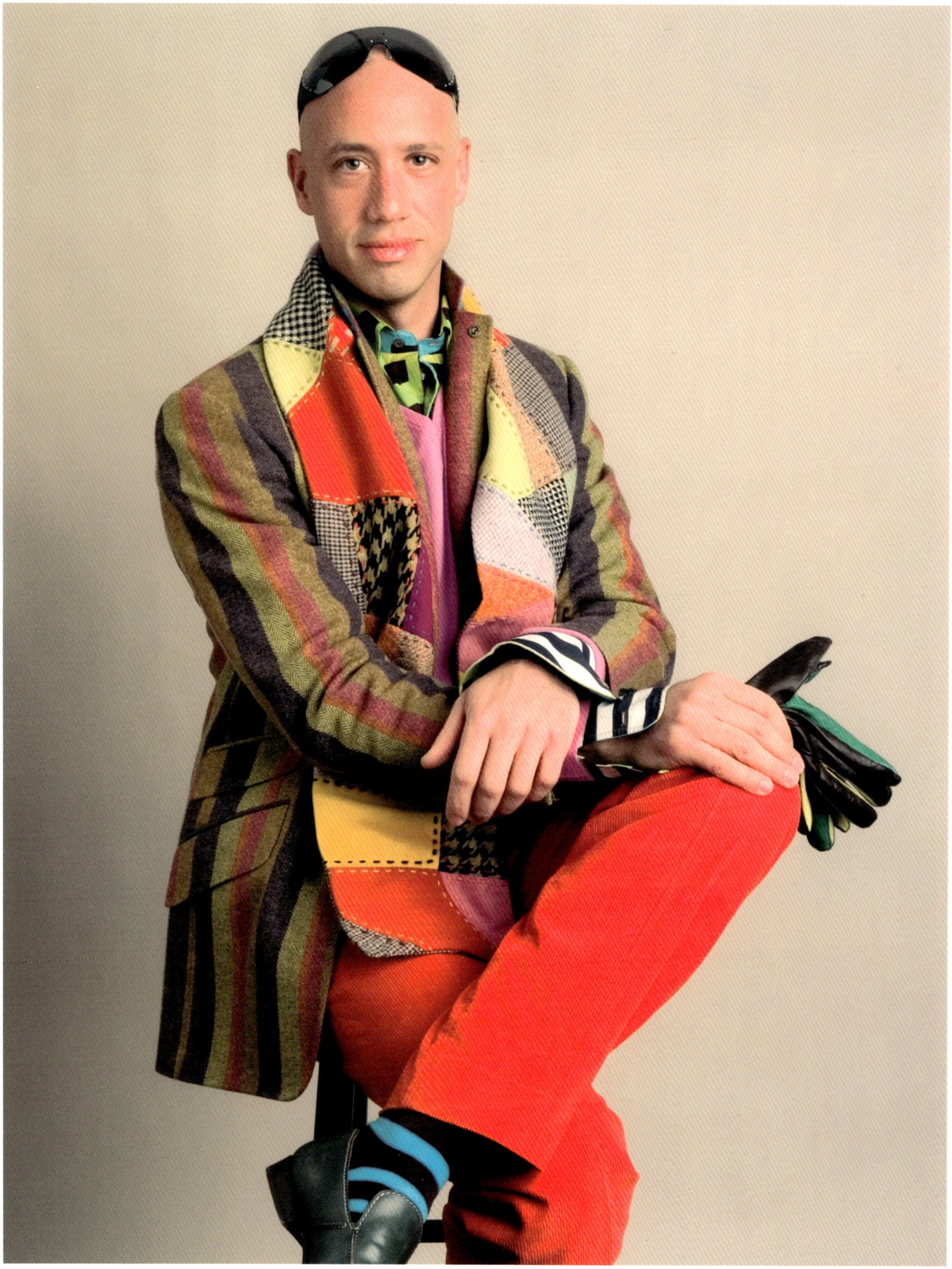

ROBERT VERDI Style Guru

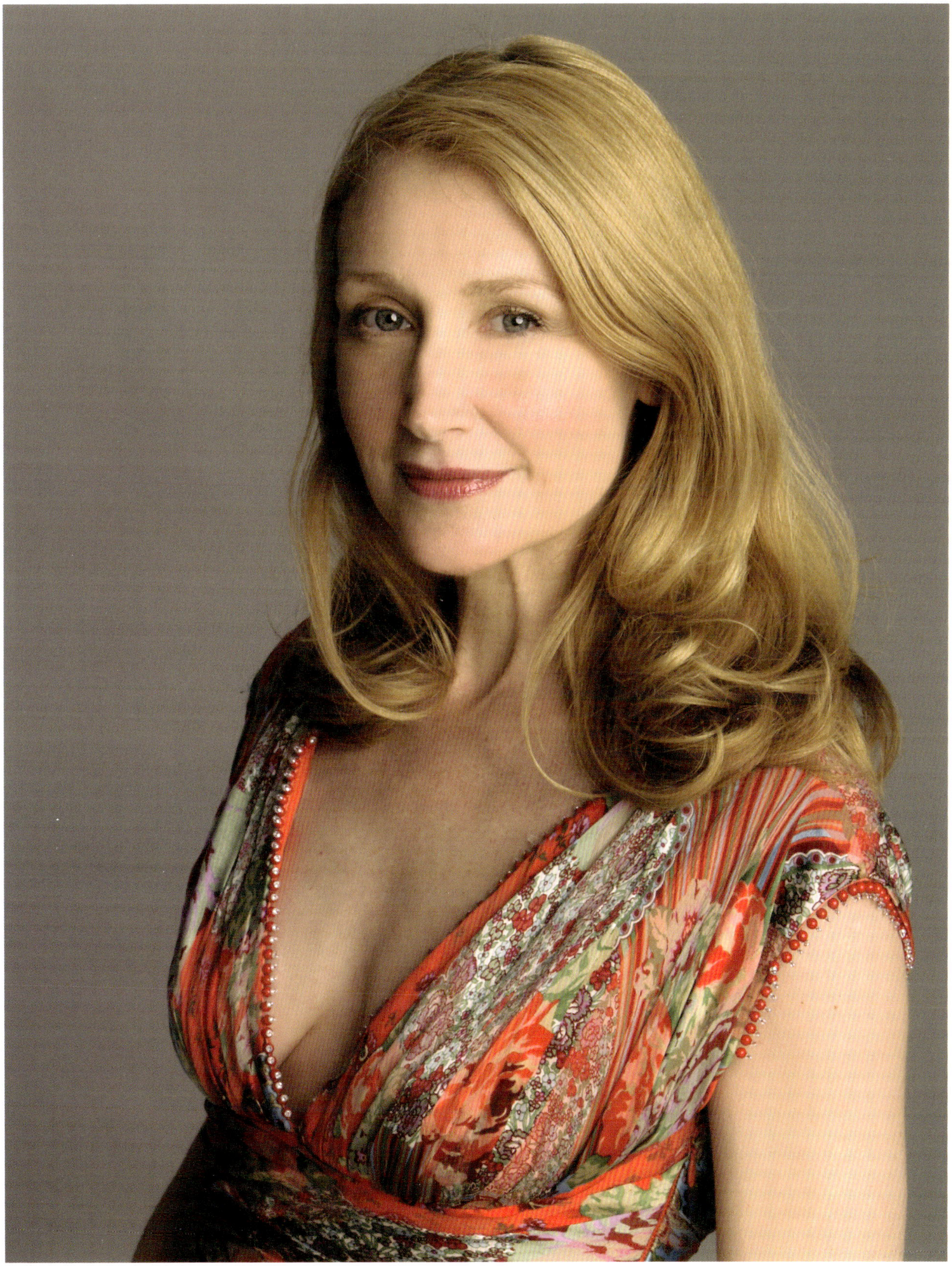

PATRICIA CLARKSON Actor

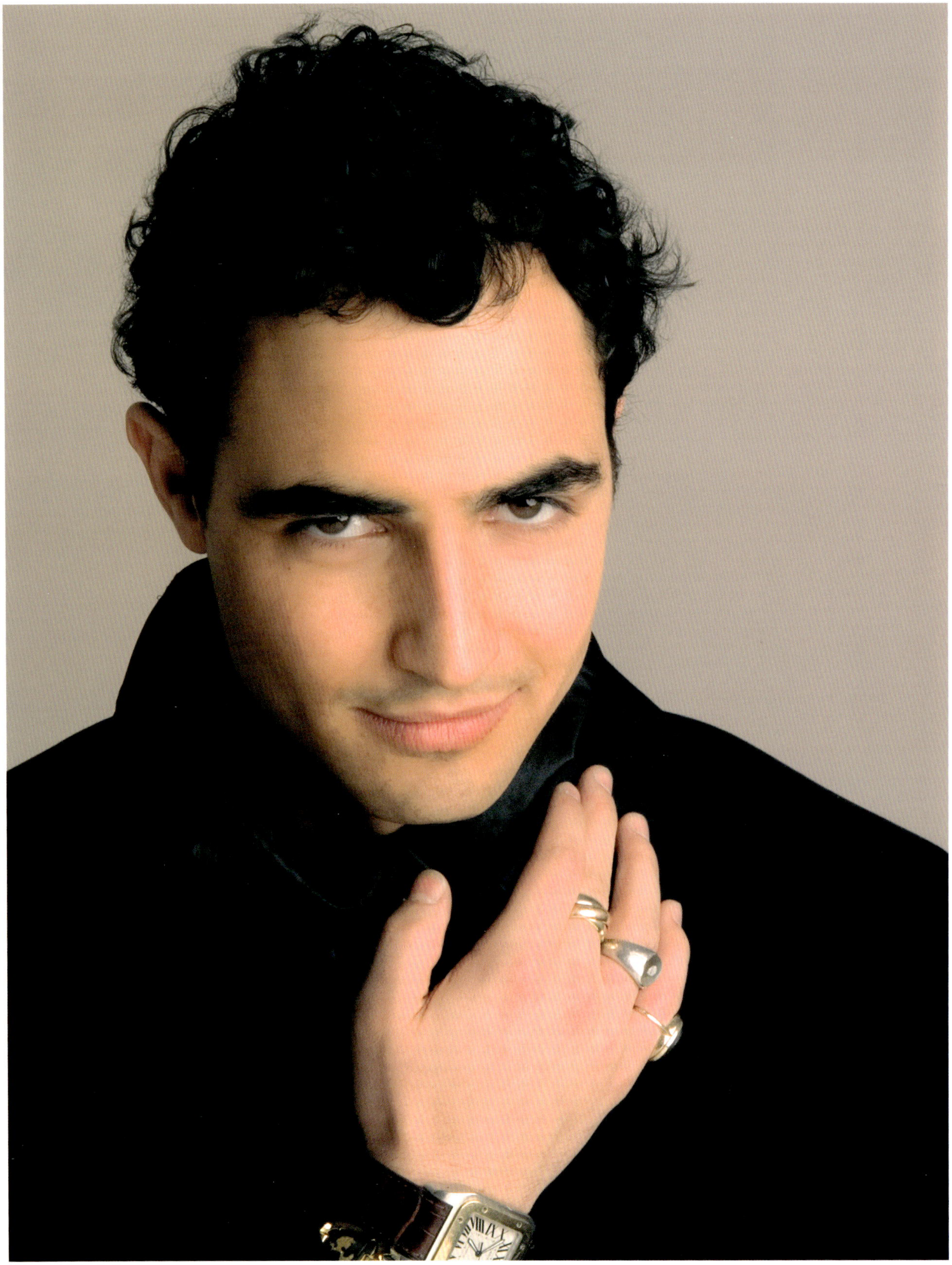

ZAC POSEN Designer

Creating a collection, of course, begins months before the looks go down the runway. It is always a delicate and complicated process, requiring the skill and passion of my team. We research and explore various fabrics and carefully consider every decision—the hour of the show, the makeup, the shoes. As showtime approaches, everyone is working feverishly to ensure that each piece looks right, fits well, and feels good.

There is a spectacular amount of energy backstage—jammed with models, makeup artists, hairstylists, and celebrities—before a show. It's a time that I love. Oddly enough, I never get to see the live runway show, because I'm backstage working the entire time. It's only later, when I get back to my house and am able to kick off my shoes and relax, that I can watch the show on tape.

When the show is over, I always ask myself whether I accomplished what I had intended. Was I able to deliver my message for that season?

It has been a luxury to have my family involved in my work, as I trust their opinions and can rely on their honesty. When a new collection launches, I feel very proud and hopeful that everyone will appreciate my work. Of course, it's important to set aside time to speak with the press and retailers to ensure that I have the opportunity to explain my inspiration, my vision, as well as my customer.

When I first showed at the Bryant Park tents after a few seasons of showing in independent venues, I was thrilled to come to the center of the U.S. fashion world. Olympus Fashion Week is a fleeting, magical moment when you have the eyes—and, hopefully, the hearts—of the retailers, editors, and others who are passionate about fashion.

And for that precious moment, it feels, at least to me, like the most important thing in the world.

ZAC POSEN

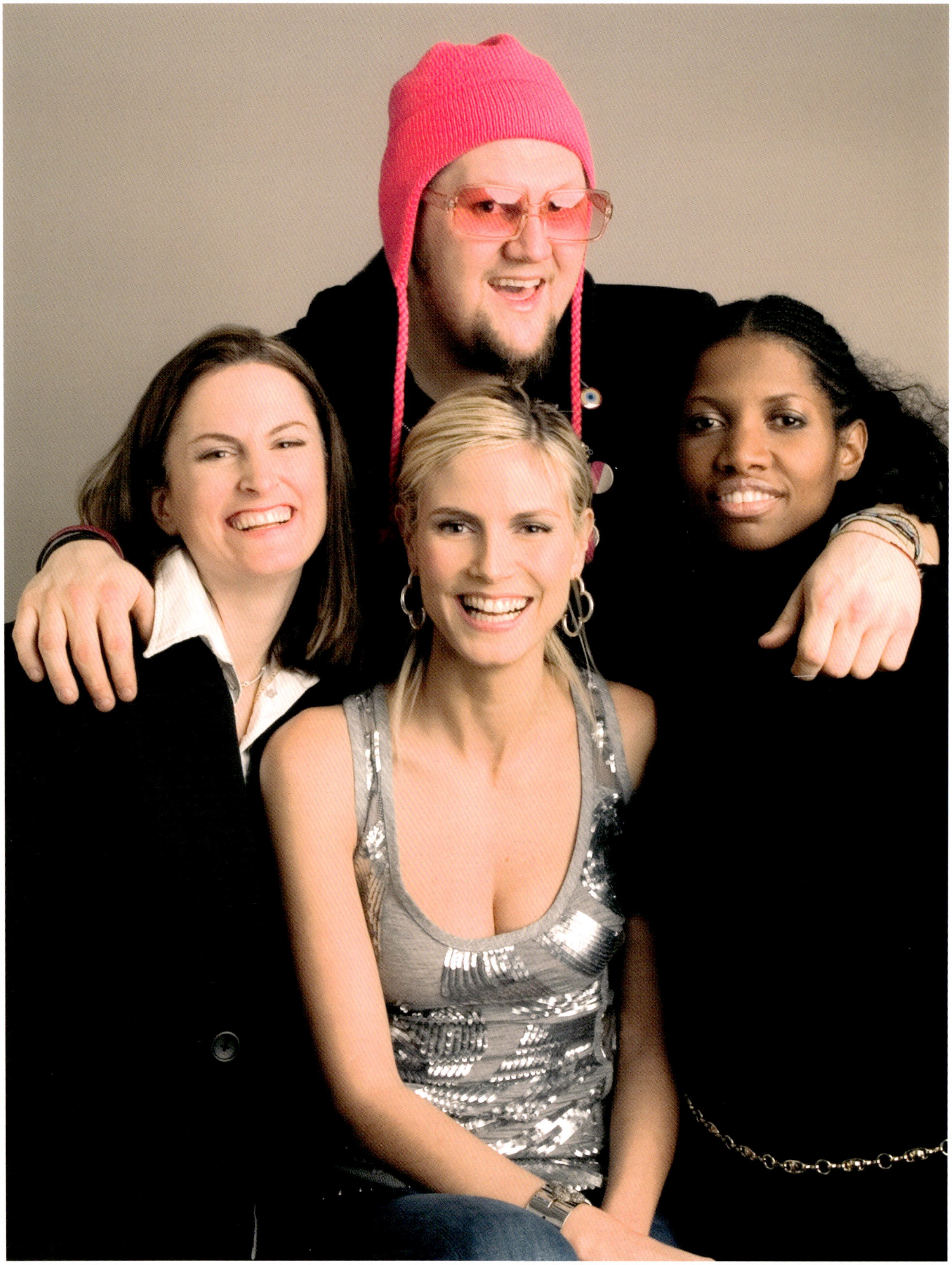

WENDY PEPPER, JAY MCCARROLL, HEIDI KLUM & KARA SAUN

Cast, *Project Runway*, Season 1

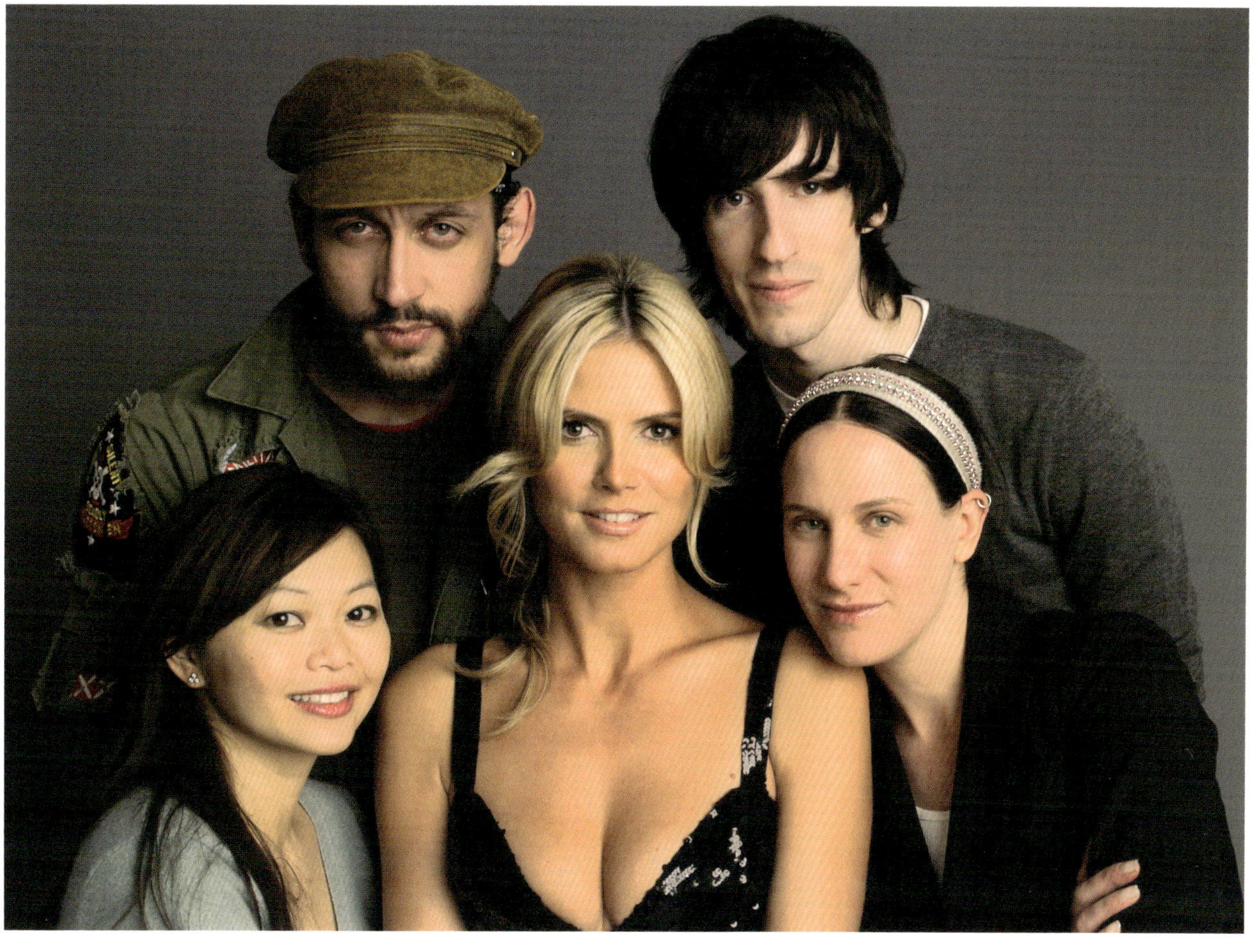

CHLOE DAO, SANTINO RICE, HEIDI KLUM, DANIEL VOSOVIC & KARA JANX
Cast, *Project Runway*, Season 2

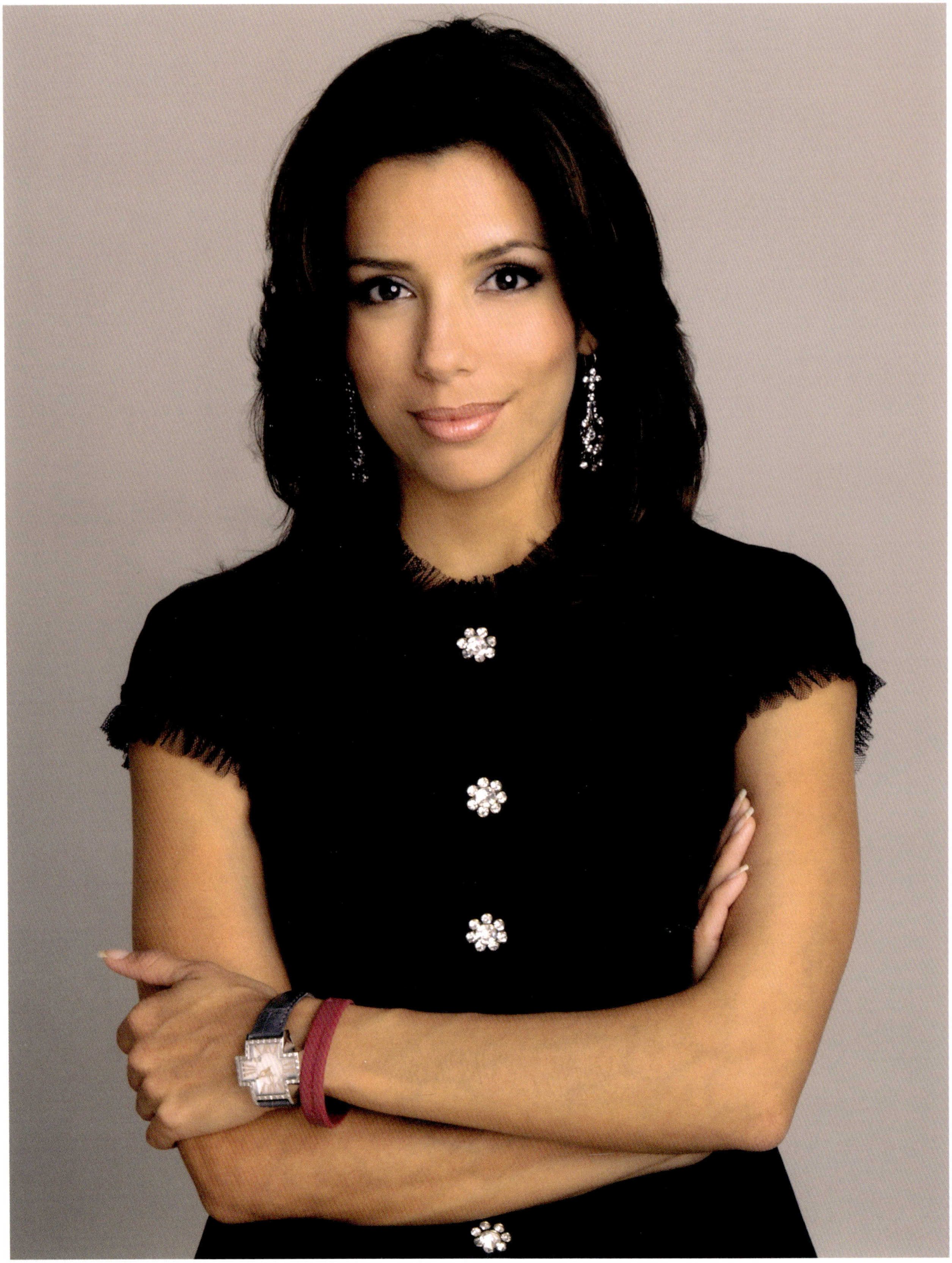

EVA LONGORIA Actor

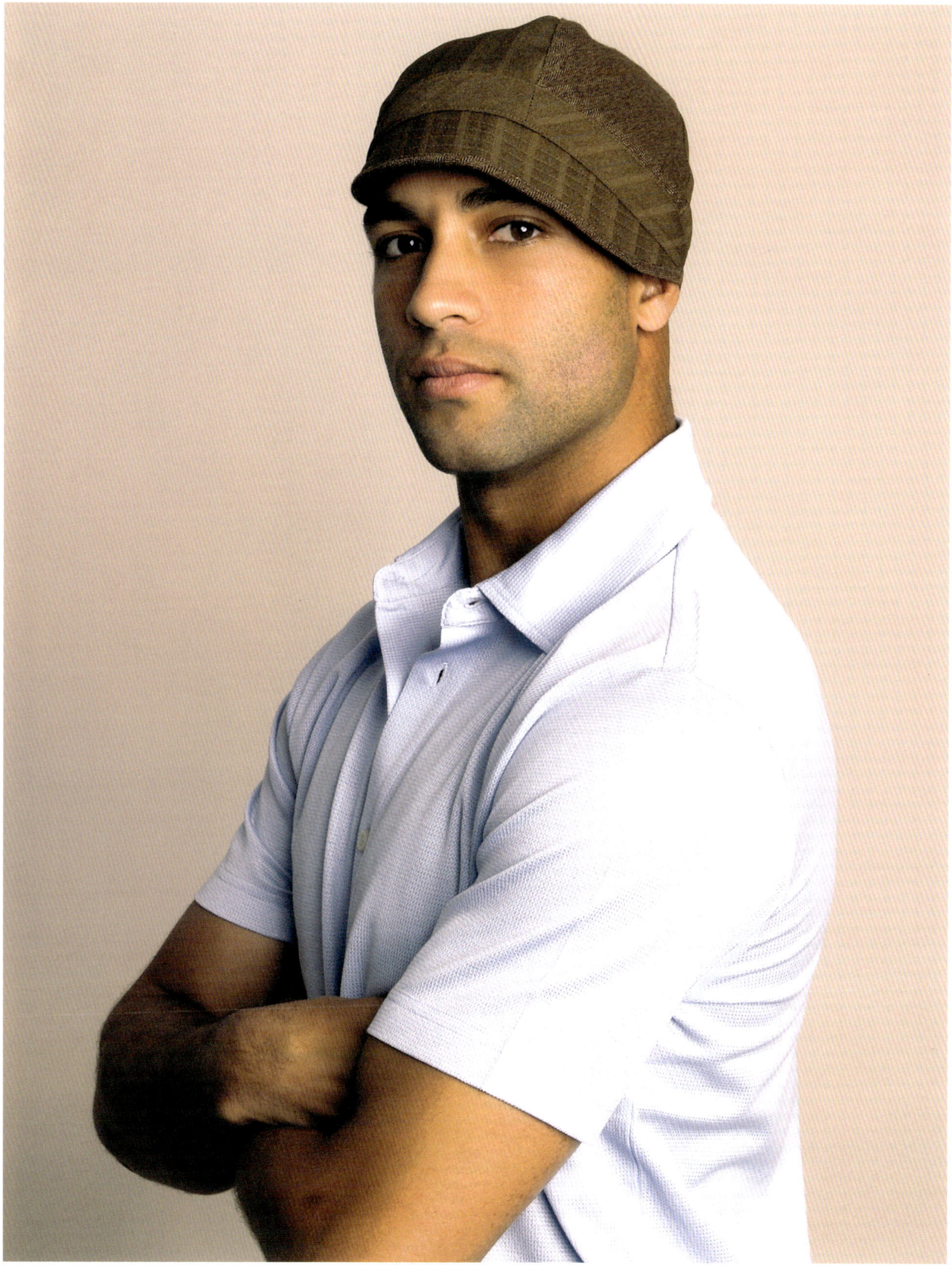

JAMES BLAKE Racquet Man

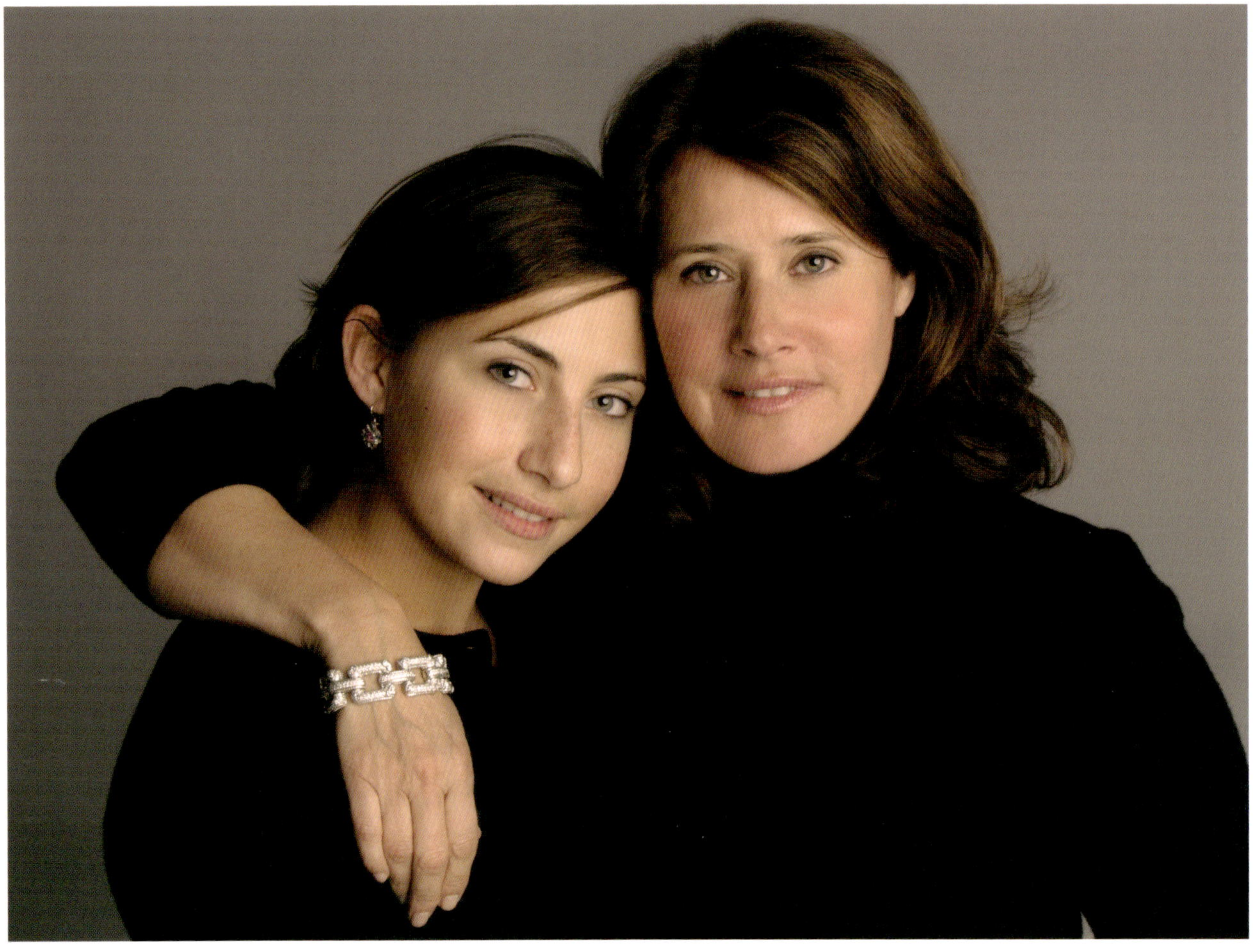

STELLA KEITEL & LORRAINE BRACCO Actor with Daughter (at left)

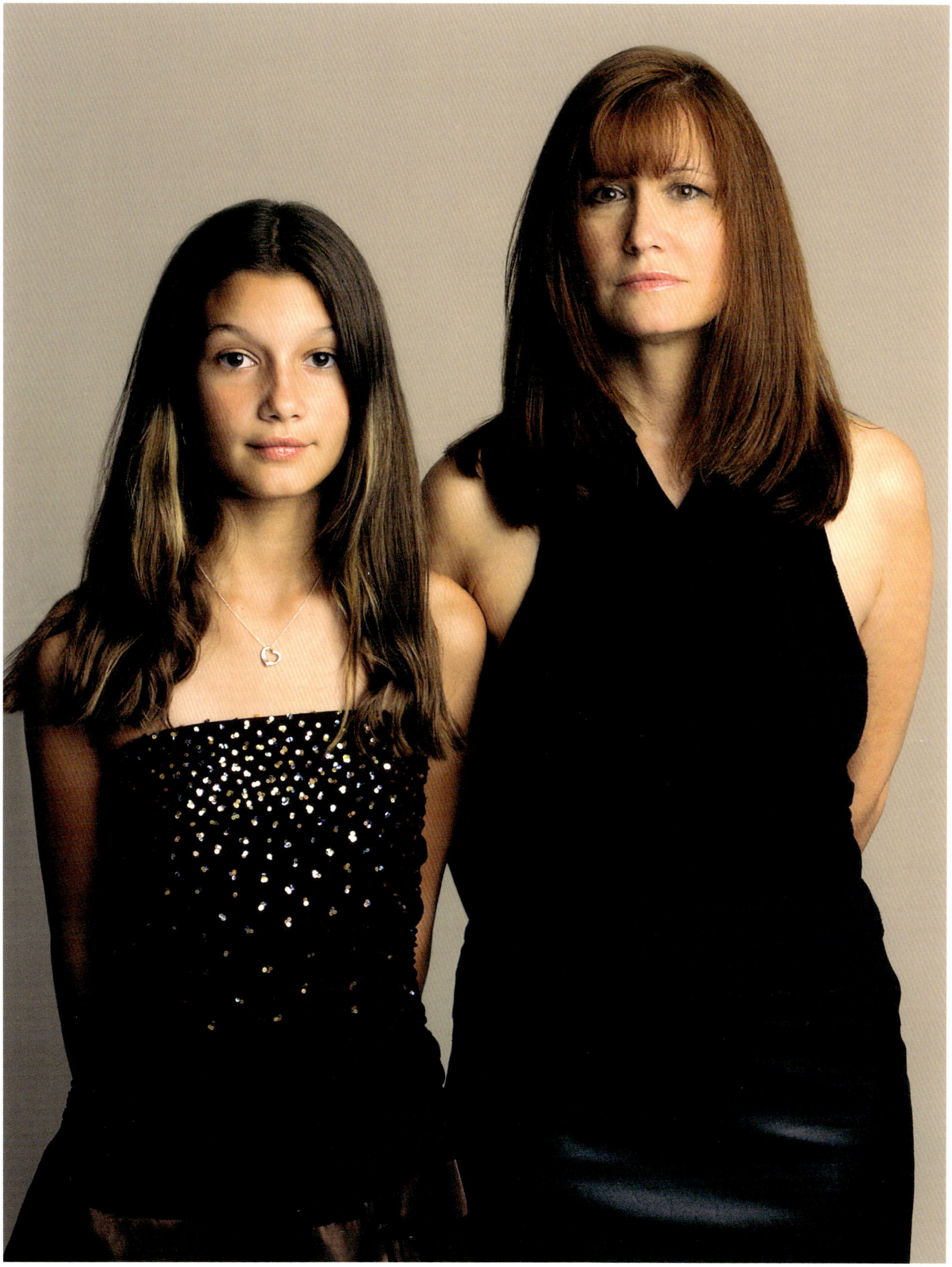

VIOLET OVERN & KAREN FINLEY Performance Artist with Daughter (at left)

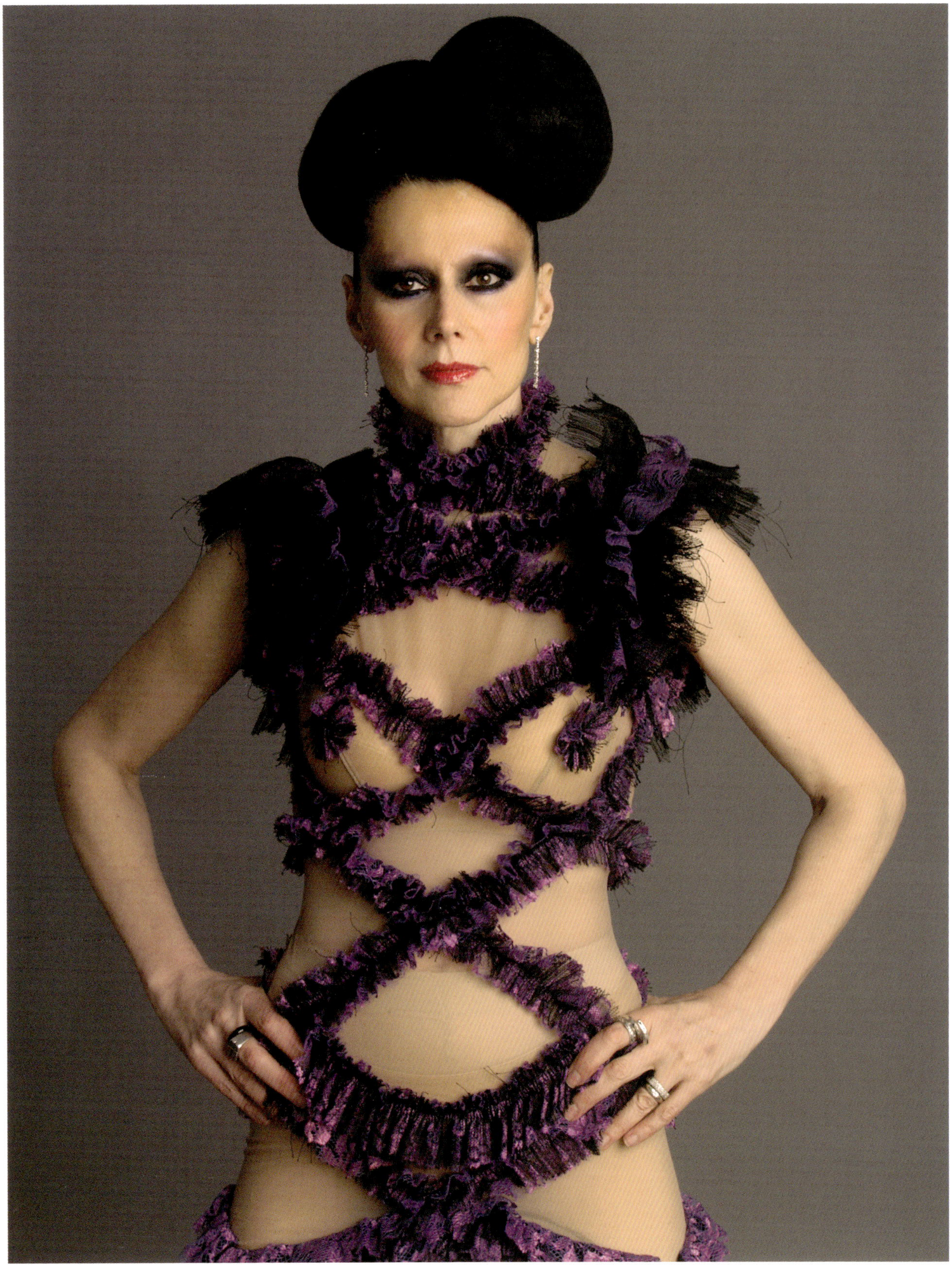

SUSANNE BARTSCH Nightlife Doyenne

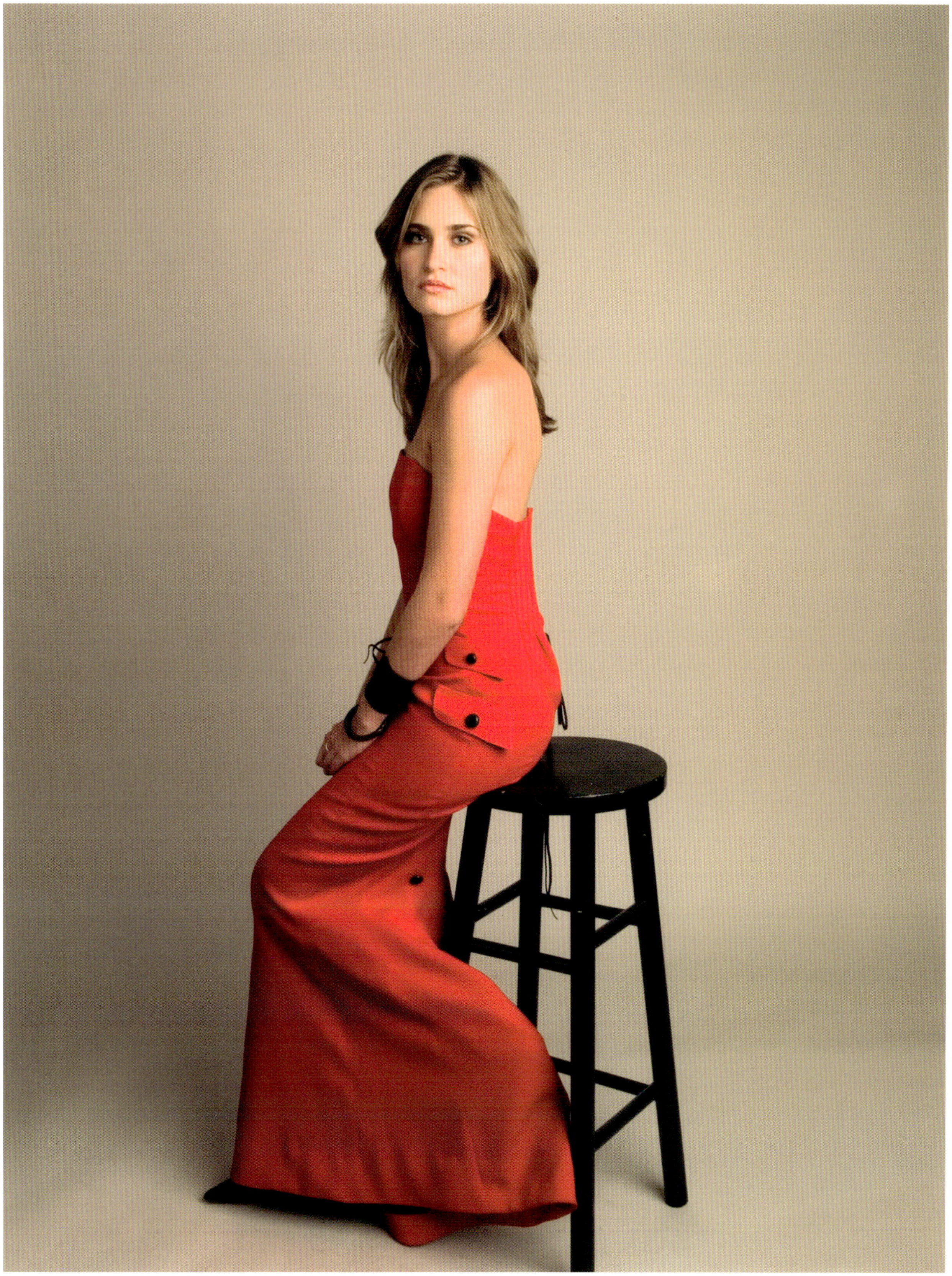

LAUREN BUSH Model

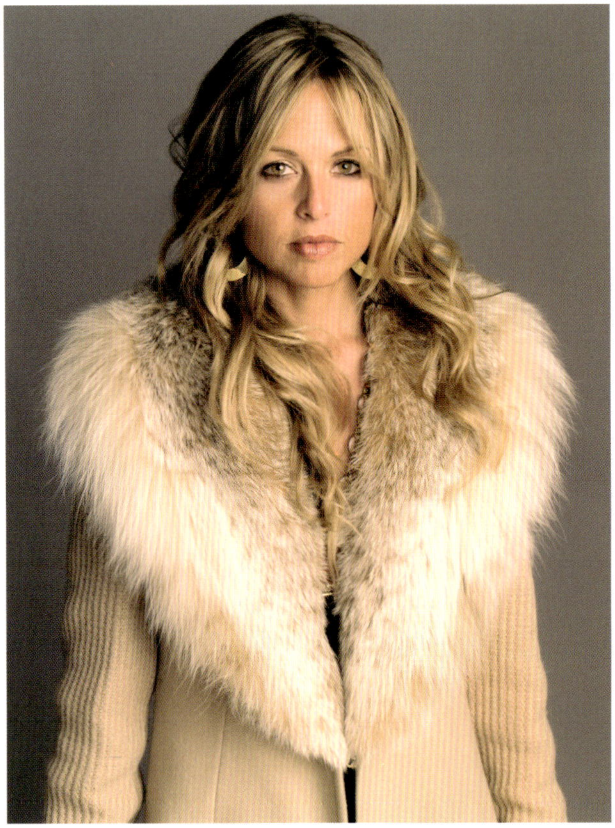

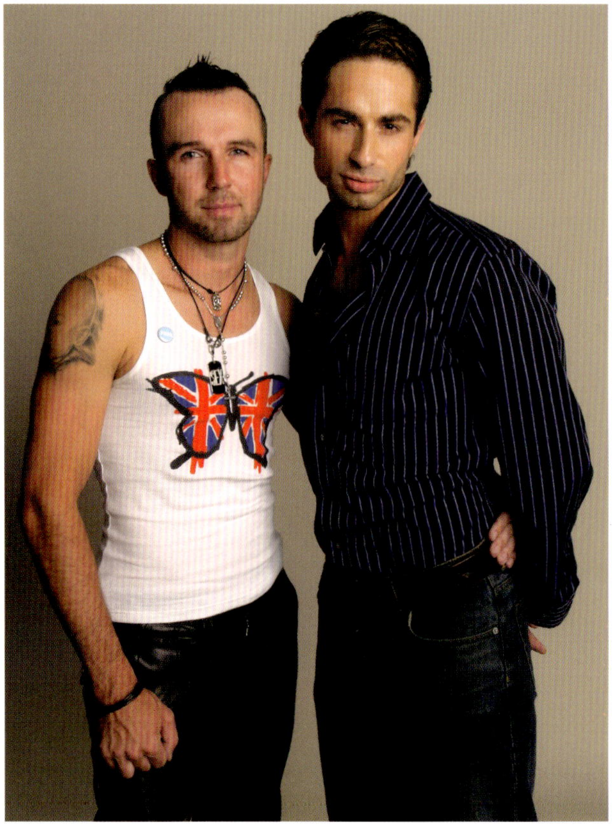

RACHEL ZOE Stylist

CHAD HUNT & MICHAEL LUCAS Adult Film Stars

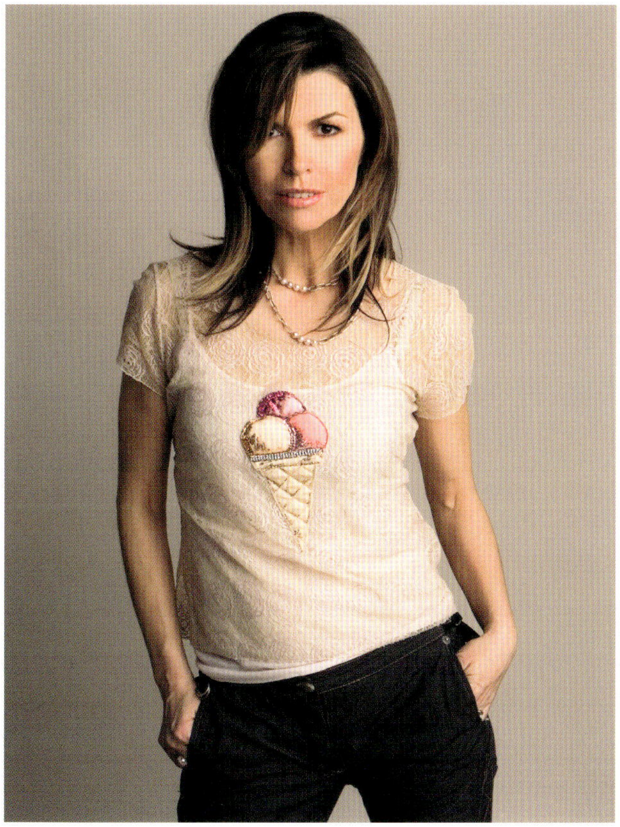

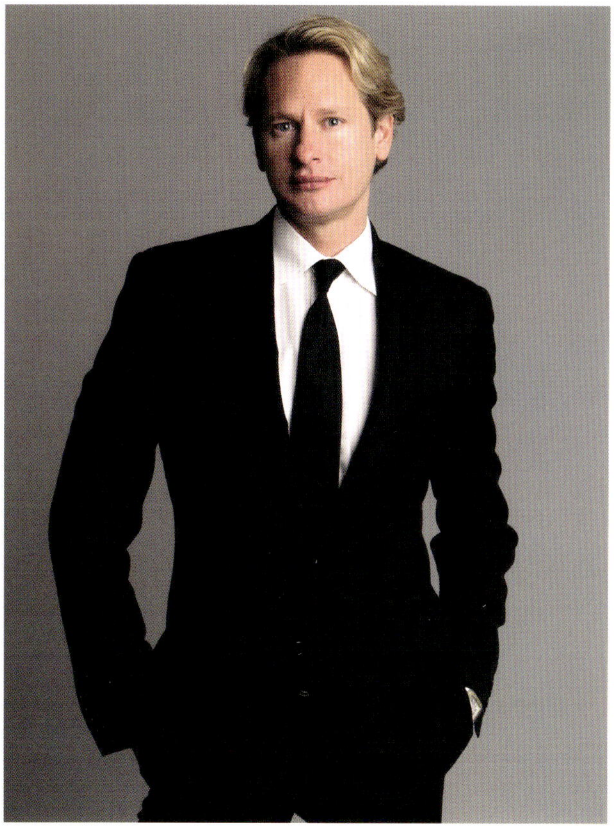

FINOLA HUGHES Style Star

CARSON KRESSLEY Style Master, Fab Five

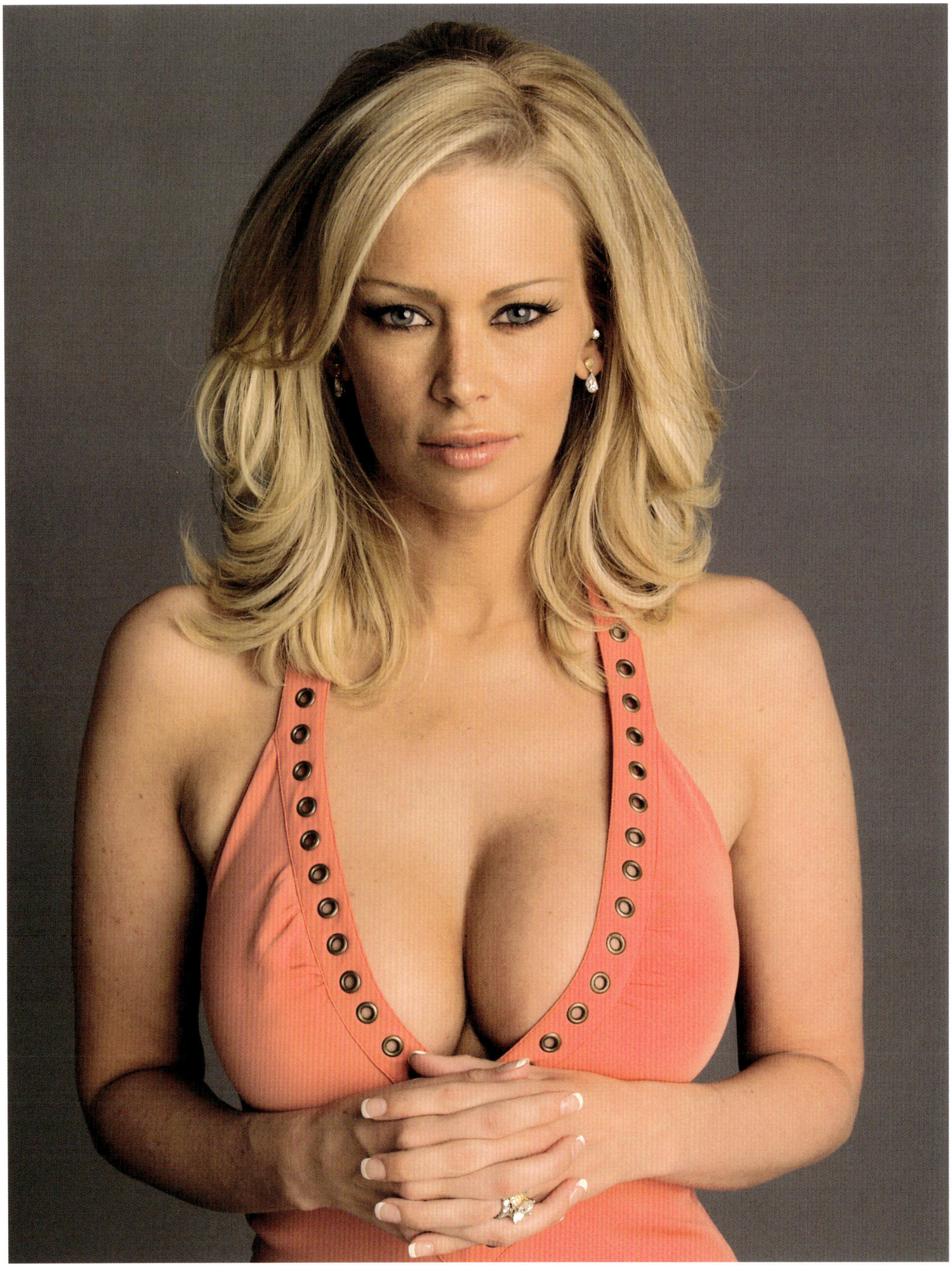

JENNA JAMESON Porn's Leading Lady

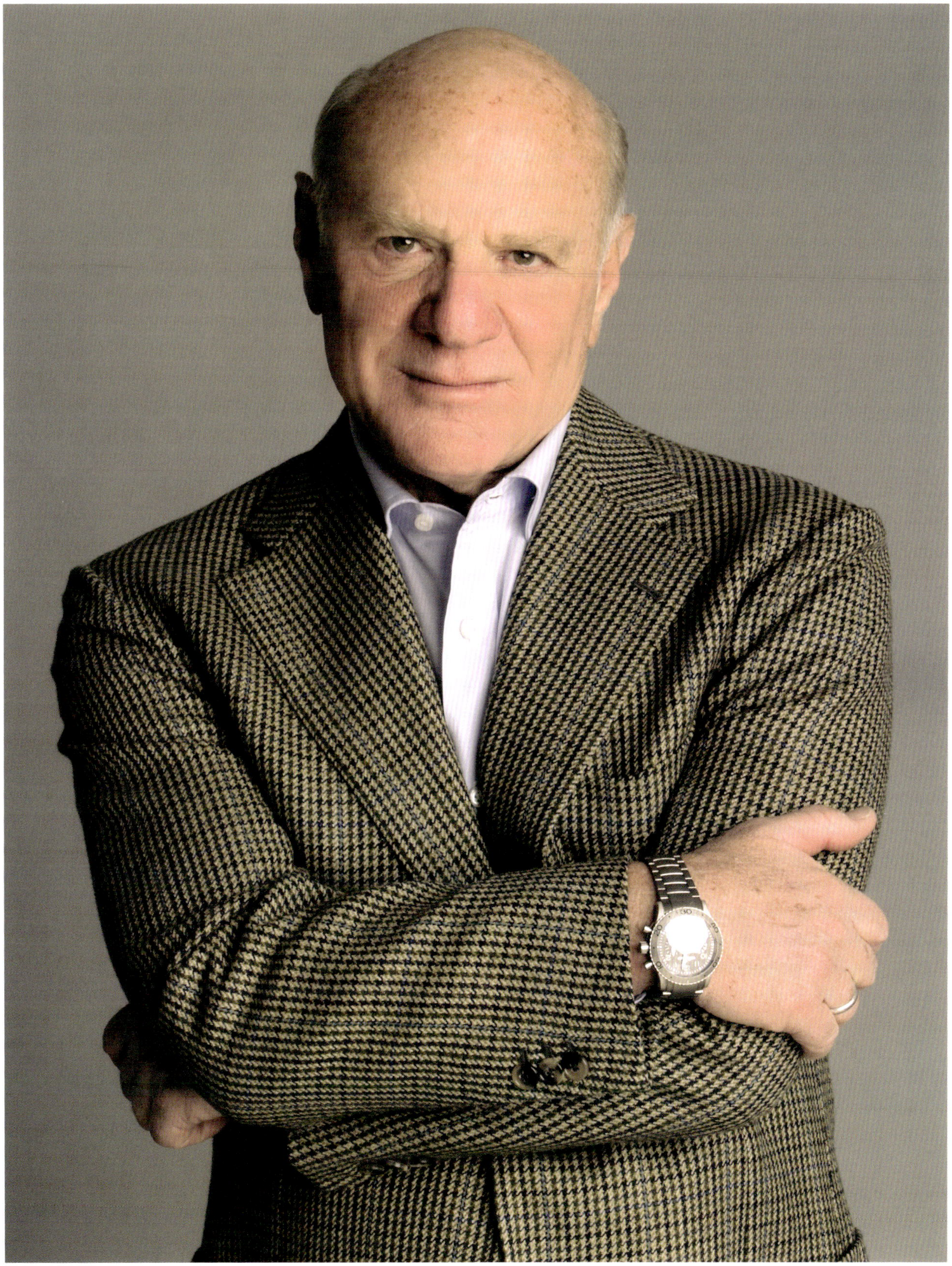

BARRY DILLER Media Giant

I love fashion and the way I can use it to represent different personalities and moods. I also love to try new styles and new designers. I'm always thrilled to be asked to wear some of the most beautiful designs of each season.

Social women have something to offer a designer, both as muses and as models. Designers don't just sell clothes; they offer a lifestyle. A collection represents this lifestyle and plays it out on the runway. Social women are then able to essentially model the designs in real life, thereby translating this lifestyle into something tangible and approachable.

My mother, grandmothers, and family friends have helped me develop an innate sense of taste, which I hope complements the designs I wear. But the best part of being considered a social in New York is the opportunity to forge relationships with so many talented people in the fashion industry. New and established designers have become my friends. I've known Peter Som, for example, since he first began, and look at him now!

I love to wear the clothing of designers I know; it gives me a connection to the whole process, which makes me acutely aware of the amount of work that went into what I'm wearing. It is nice to be able to help a new designer get noticed by wearing his or her clothes out and maybe getting photographed. And who knows? One might wear the dress of a new designer today who becomes the next Oscar or Carolina tomorrow. And to say I was able to wear his or her designs first reminds me that I am a very lucky girl.

I'm particularly fortunate to live in this fashion playground, New York City, where, for one week, two times a year, editors, buyers, photographers, fashionistas, and film and television stars gather to preview the seasonal creations of today's top fashion designers. I see this week—Olympus Fashion Week—as a chance for both industry icons and emerging talent to showcase their collections under one roof, or, in this case, one tent.

Though a show usually lasts just fifteen to twenty minutes, all eyes and attention are focused intently on each individual designer and his/her collection. I have been very lucky to be seated front row at a number of these shows, which has allowed me to see and literally feel the anticipation and excitement of the runway experience on a very intimate level.

And while being out front is amazing, being backstage is an even more remarkable experience. For the last two seasons, I have had the extraordinary experience of walking the Heatherette show. It was so amazing to see Fashion Week from this perspective. I was stunned to realize firsthand the pressure on the designers for those few minutes of visibility. Zippers might break, shoes might be too large, or a model might miss her mark.... I became well aware of the awesome responsibility of the designers and their models to present the best show possible.

Nothing will match the rush and exhilaration of walking down a runway at Fashion Week!

TINSLEY MORTIMER

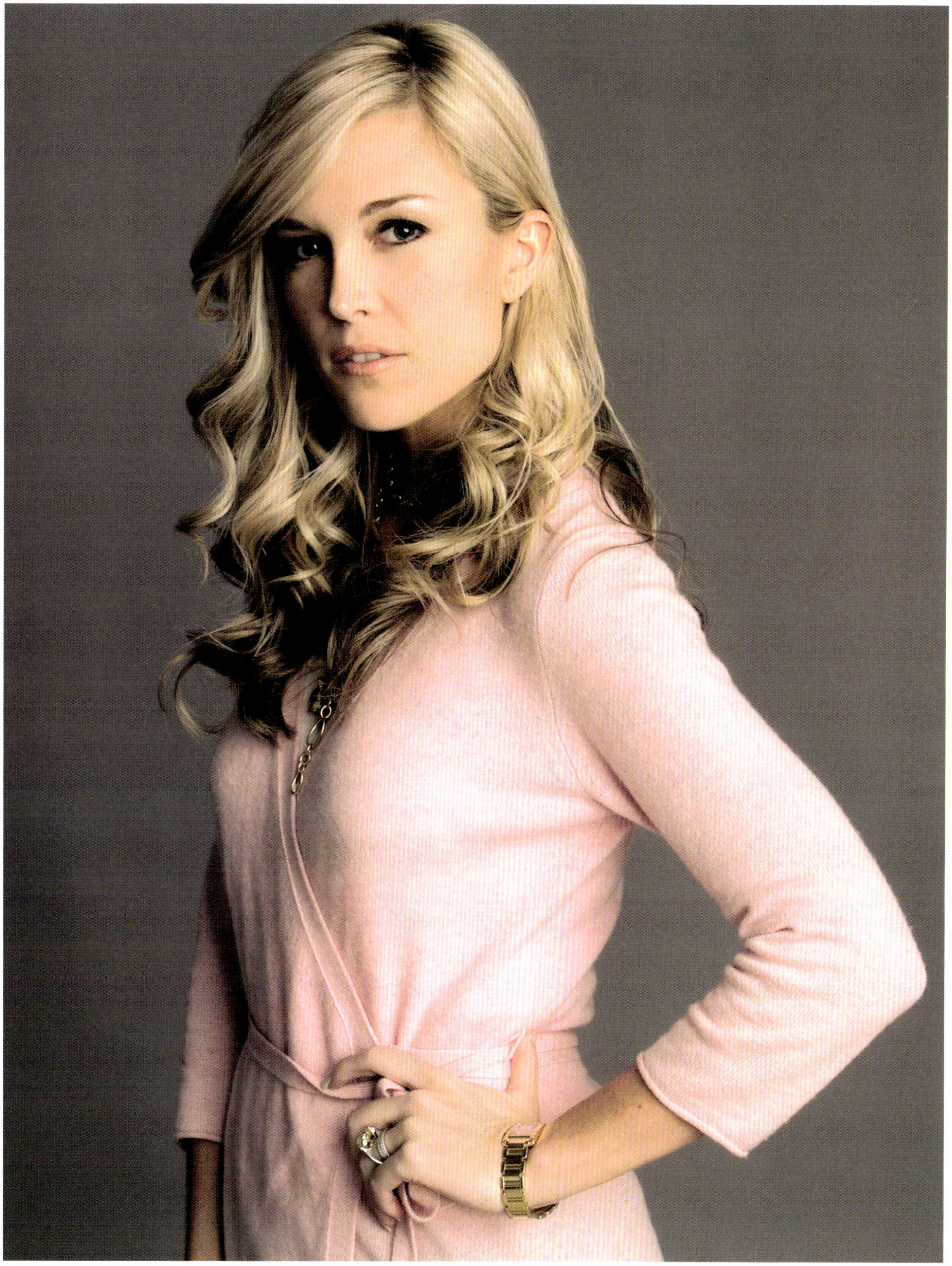

TINSLEY MORTIMER Socialite

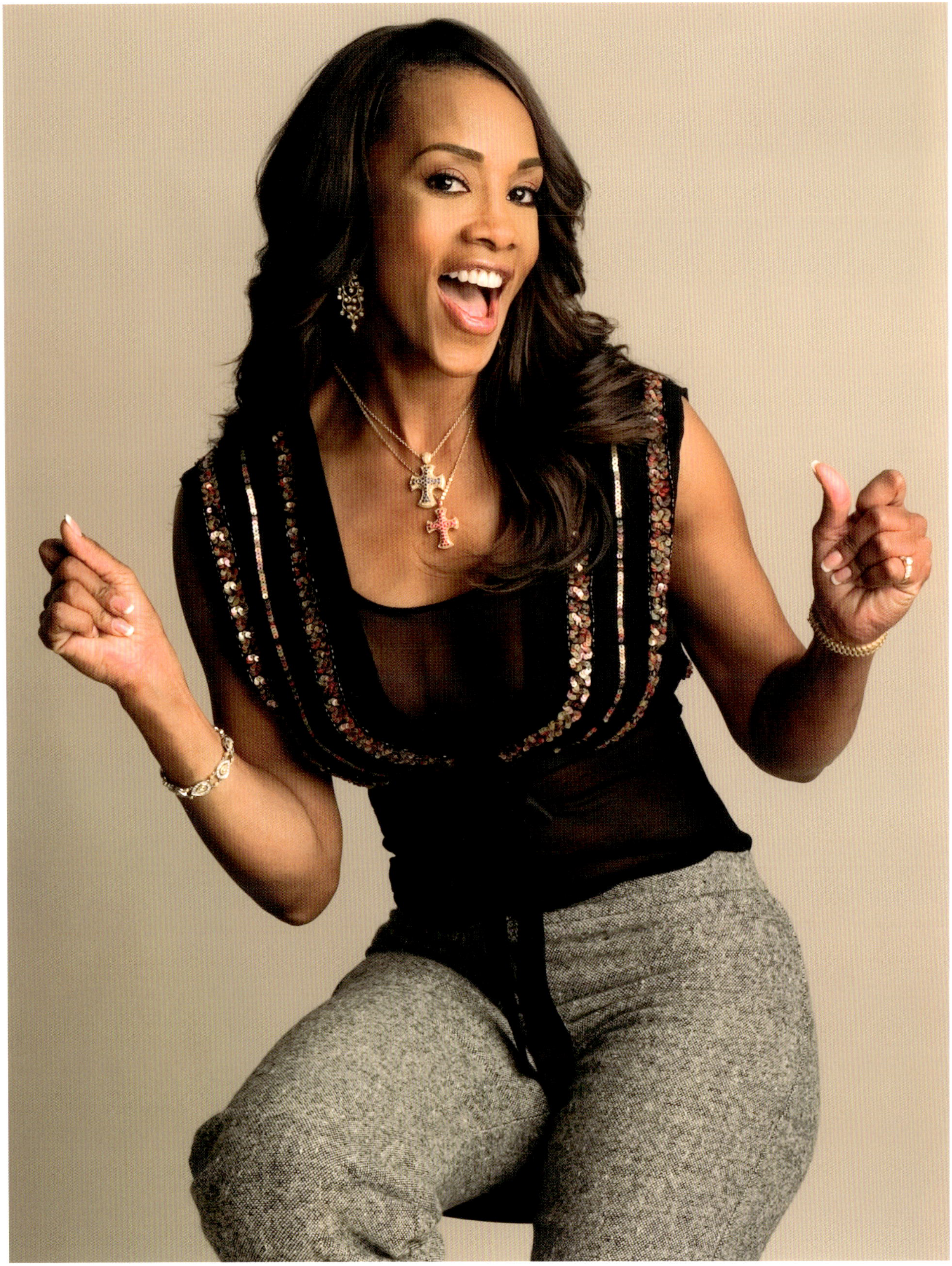

VIVICA A. FOX Actor

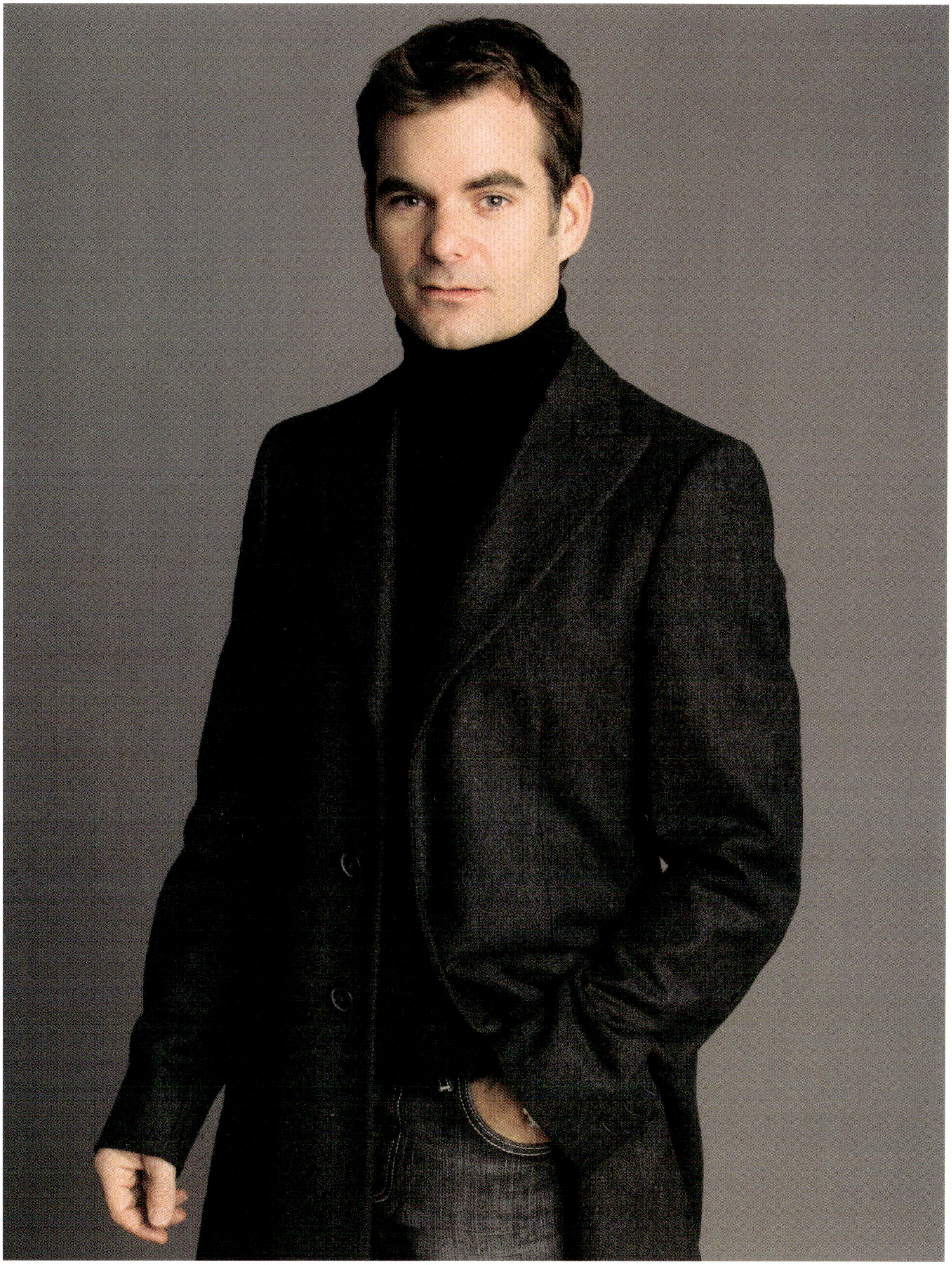

JEFF GORDON NASCAR Driver

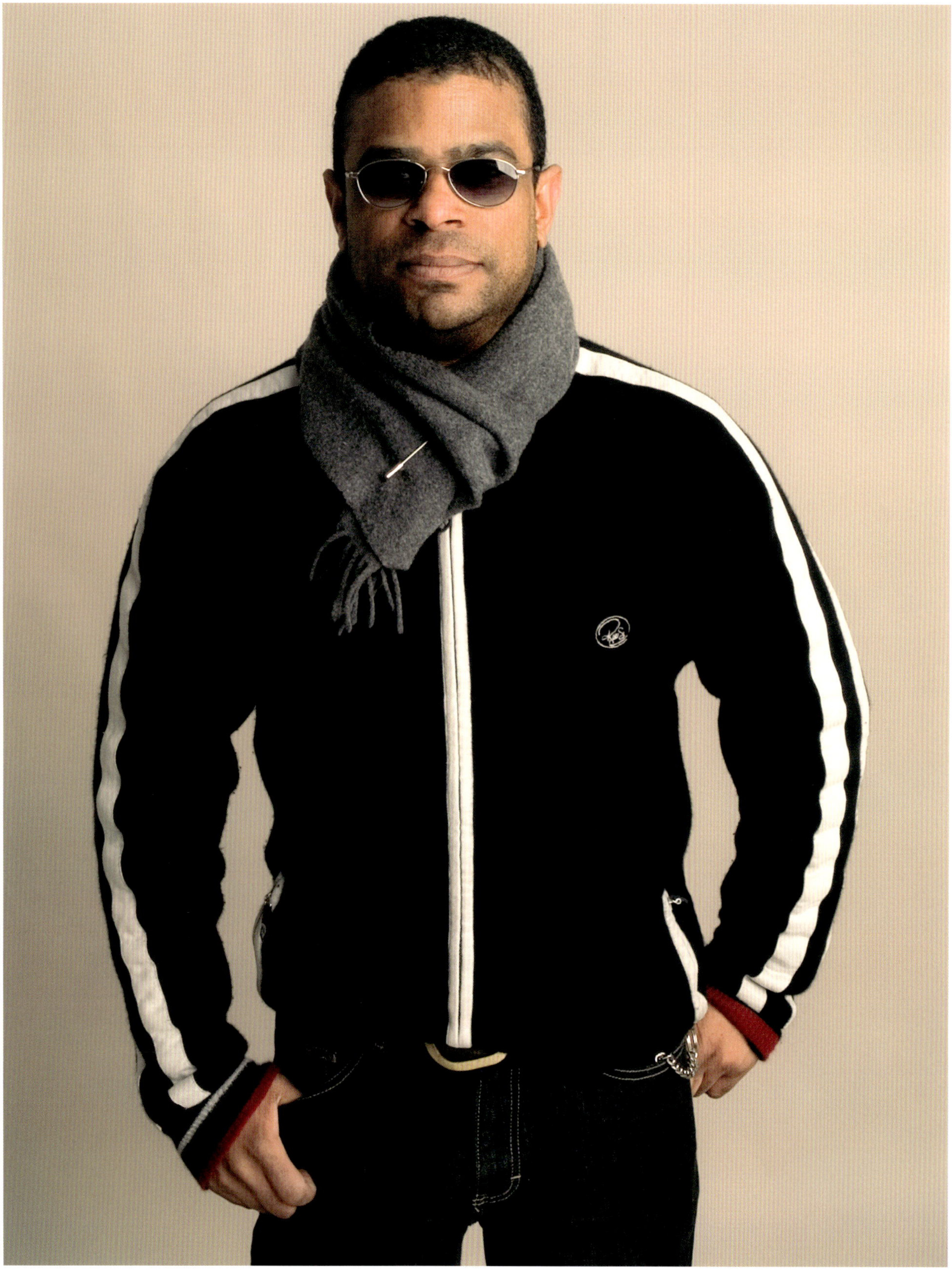

GEORGE WAYNE Contributing Editor, *Vanity Fair*

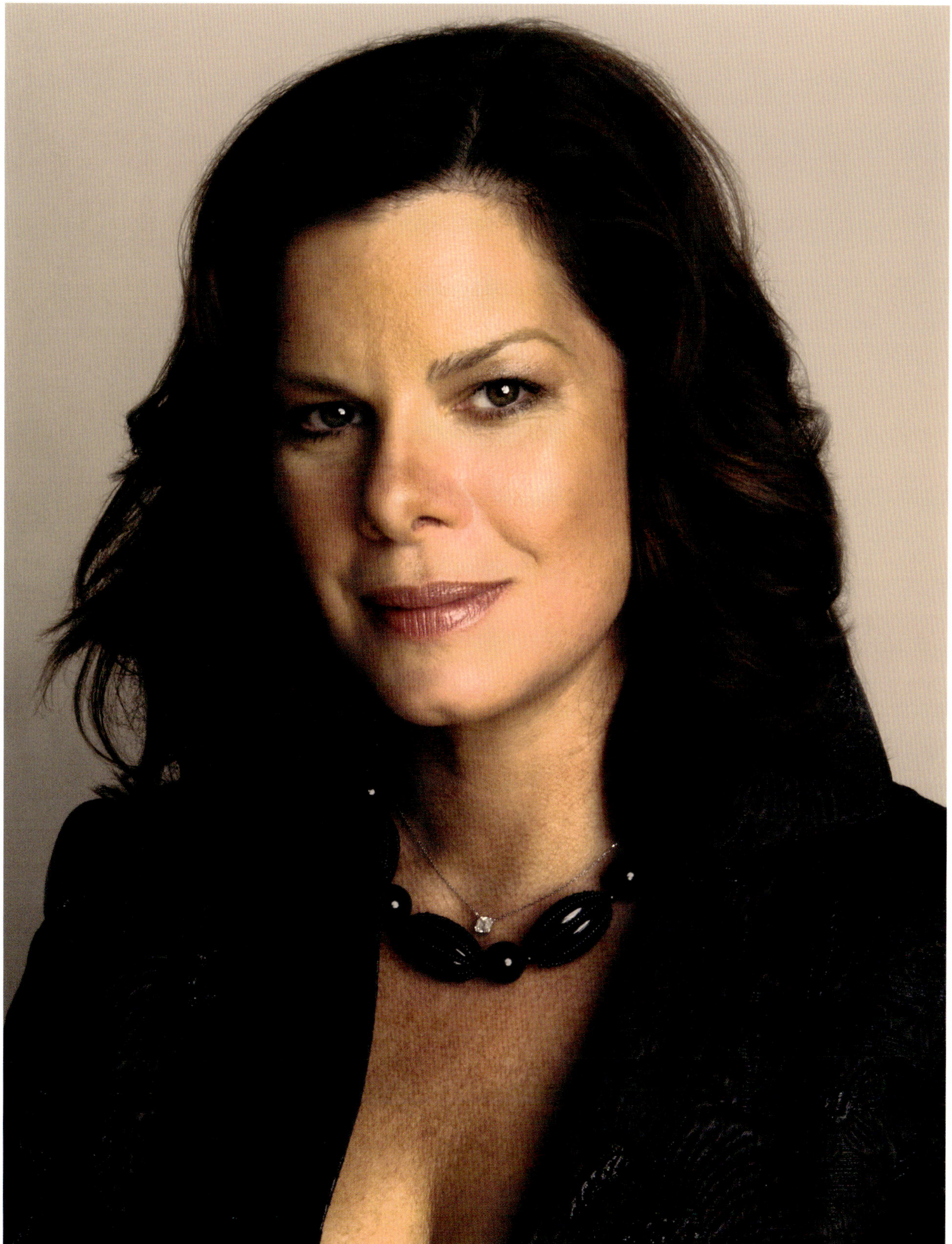

MARCIA GAY HARDEN Actor

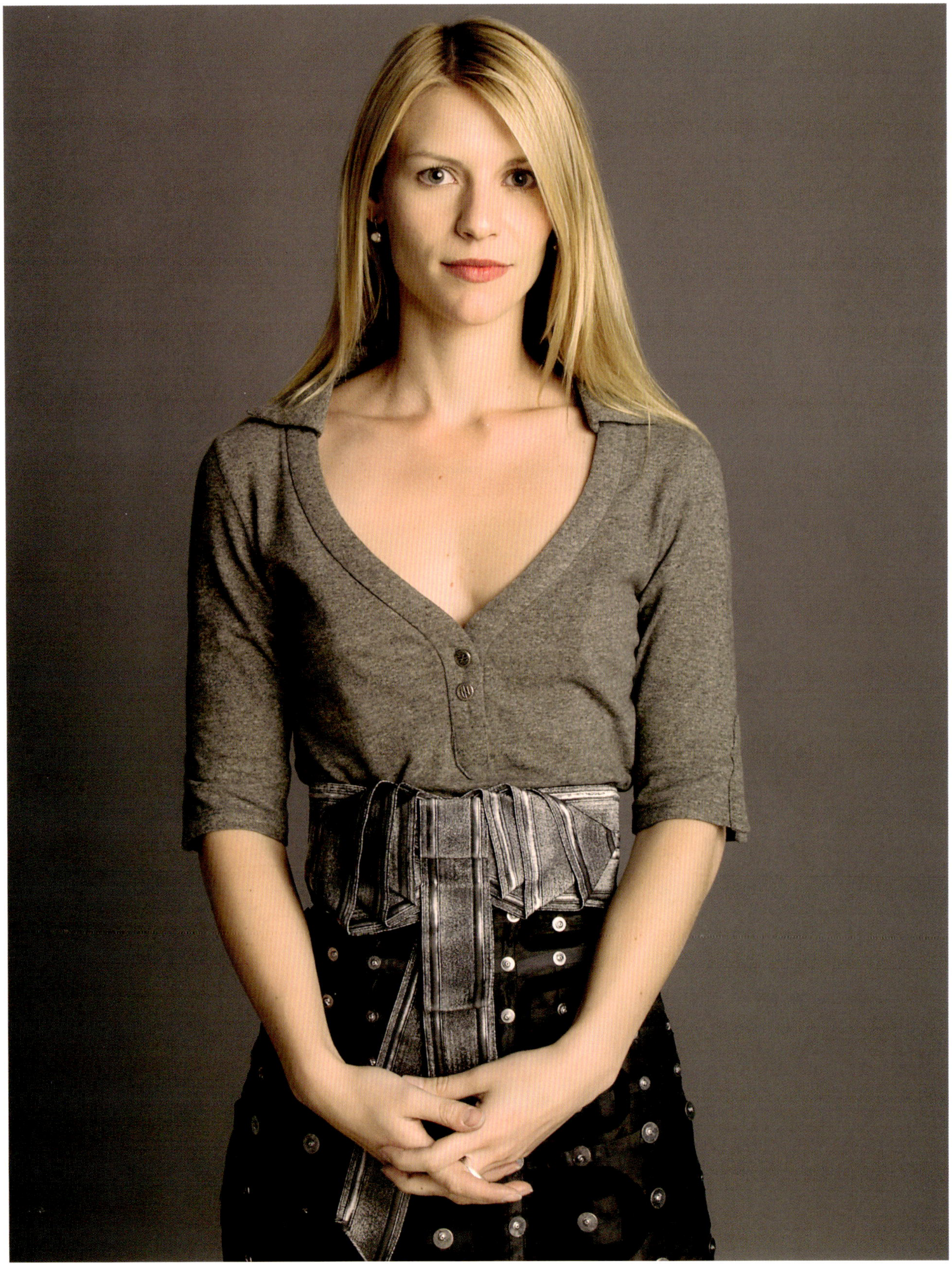

CLAIRE DANES Actor

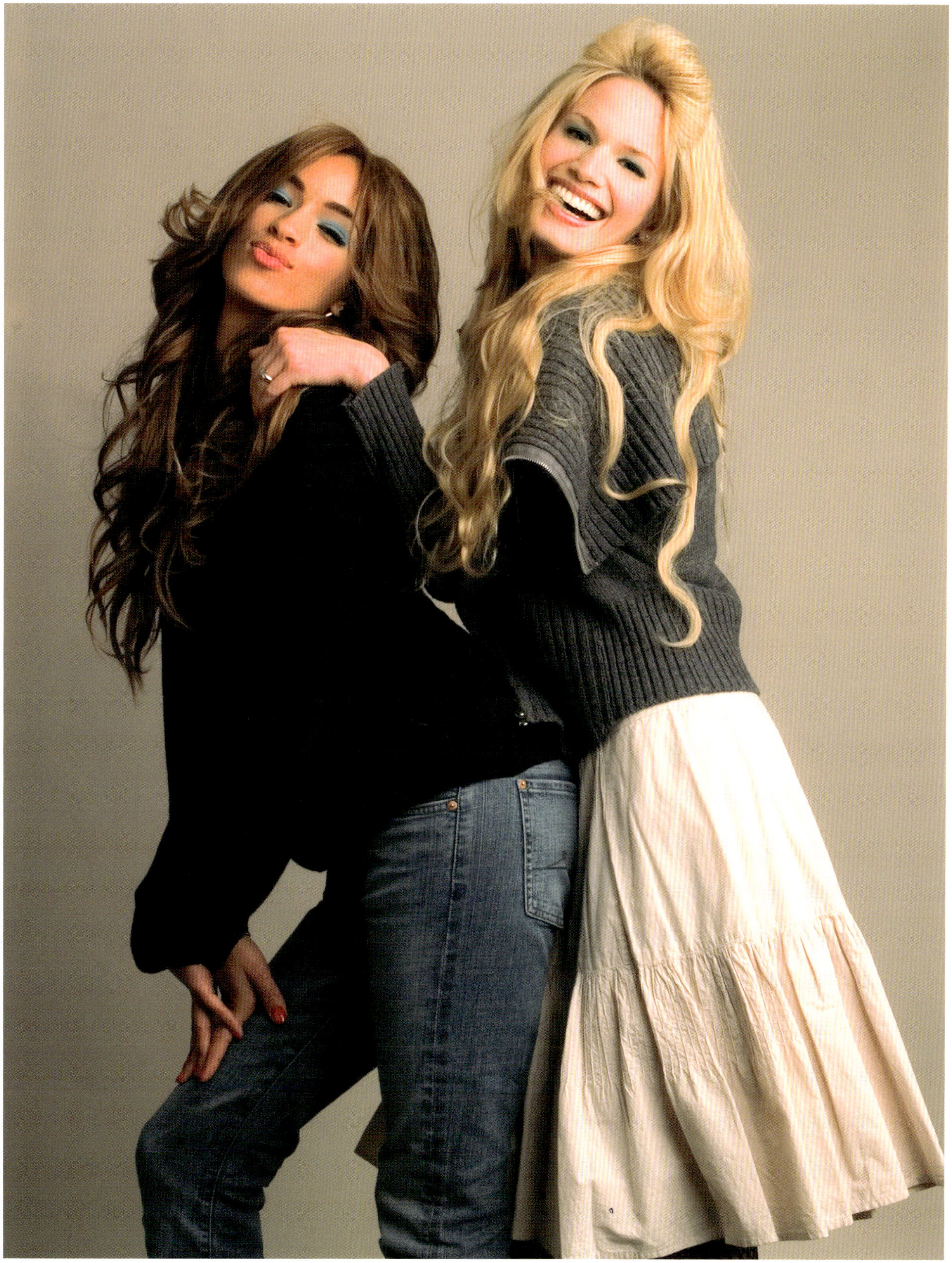

MICHELLE DE SWARTE & VICKY ANDREN Models

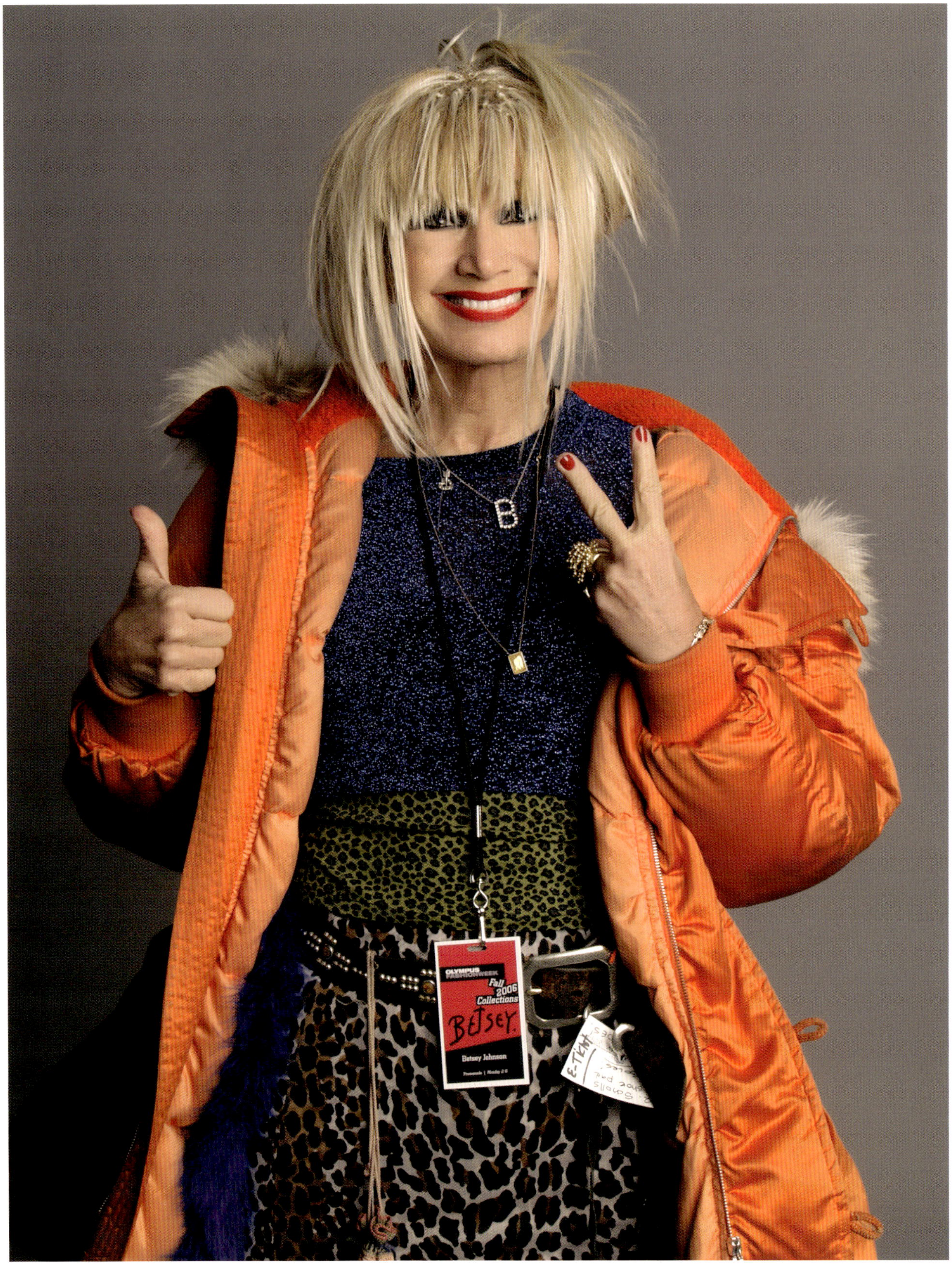

BETSEY JOHNSON Designer

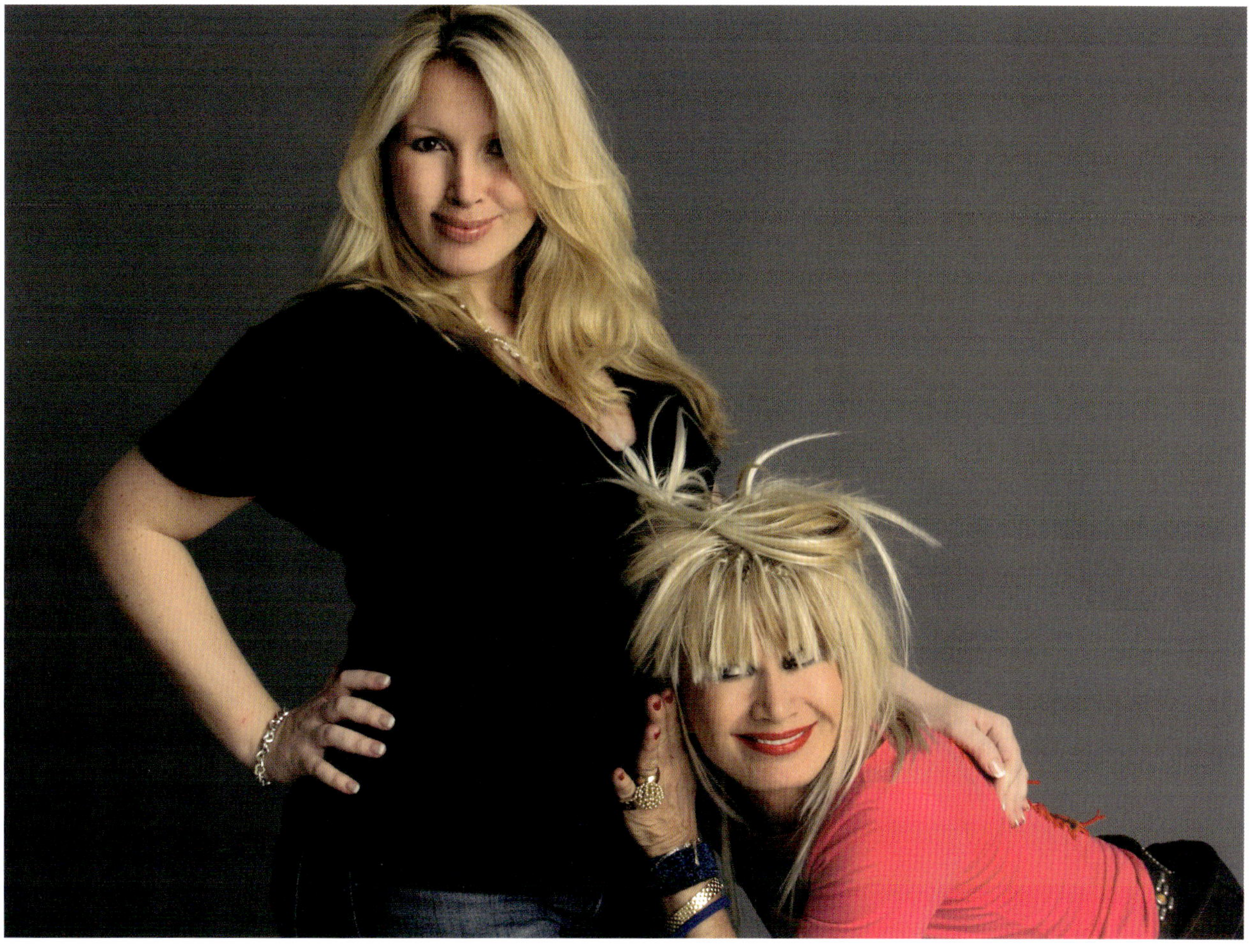

LULU JOHNSON, LAYLA MARGULIES & BETSEY JOHNSON Designer with Daughter & Granddaughter (in utero)

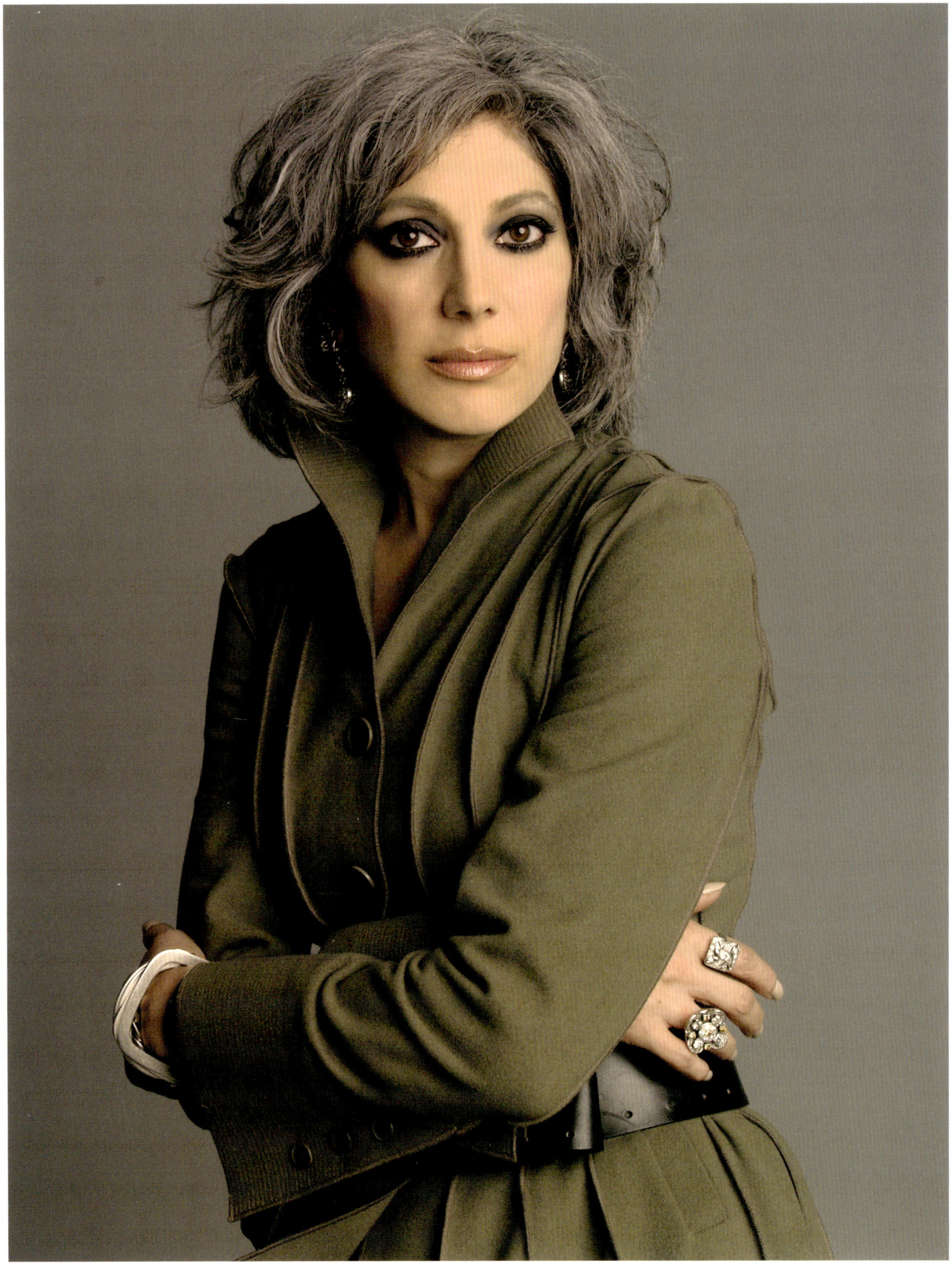

LAUREN EZERSKY Journalist

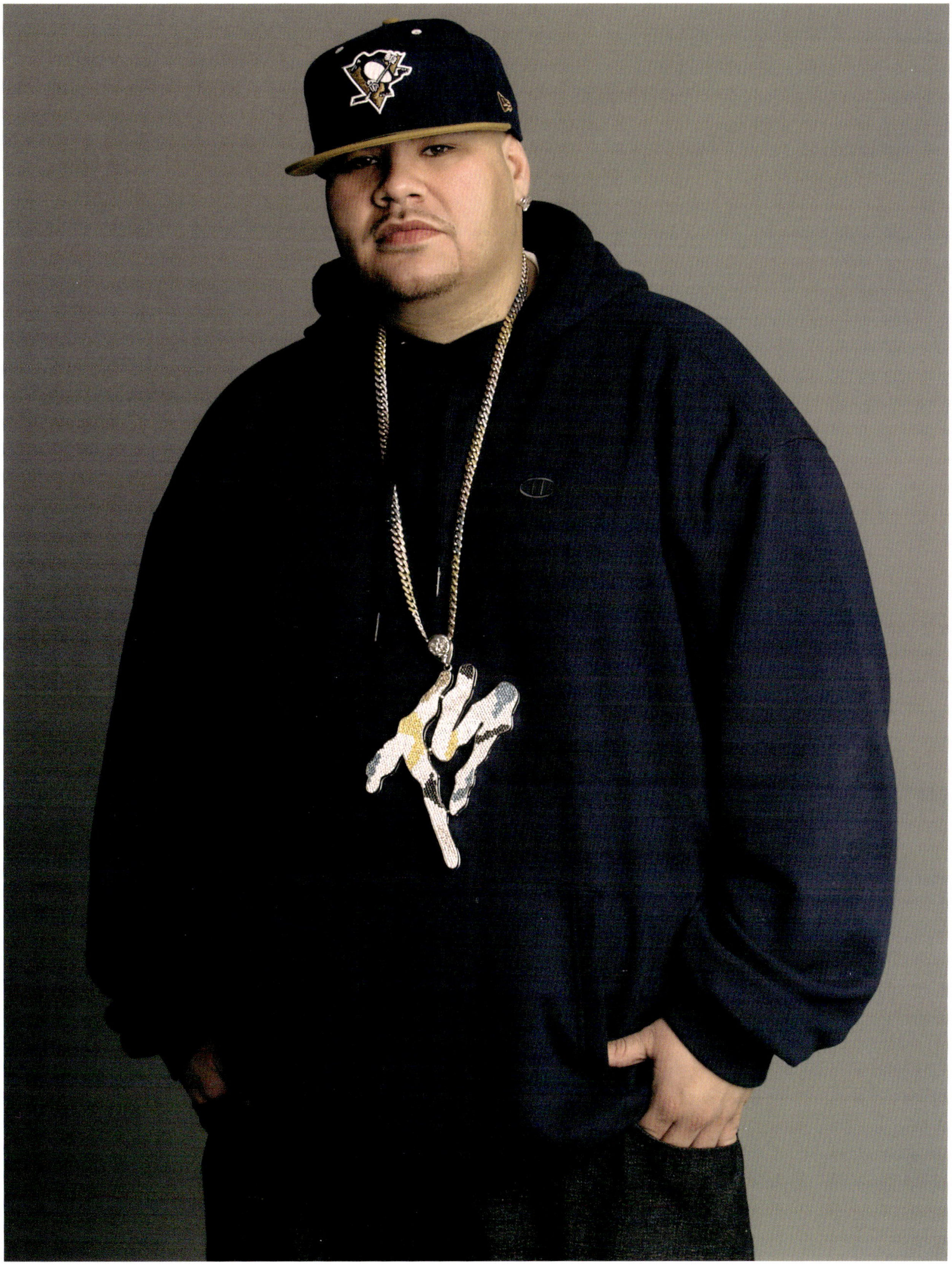

FAT JOE Rapper

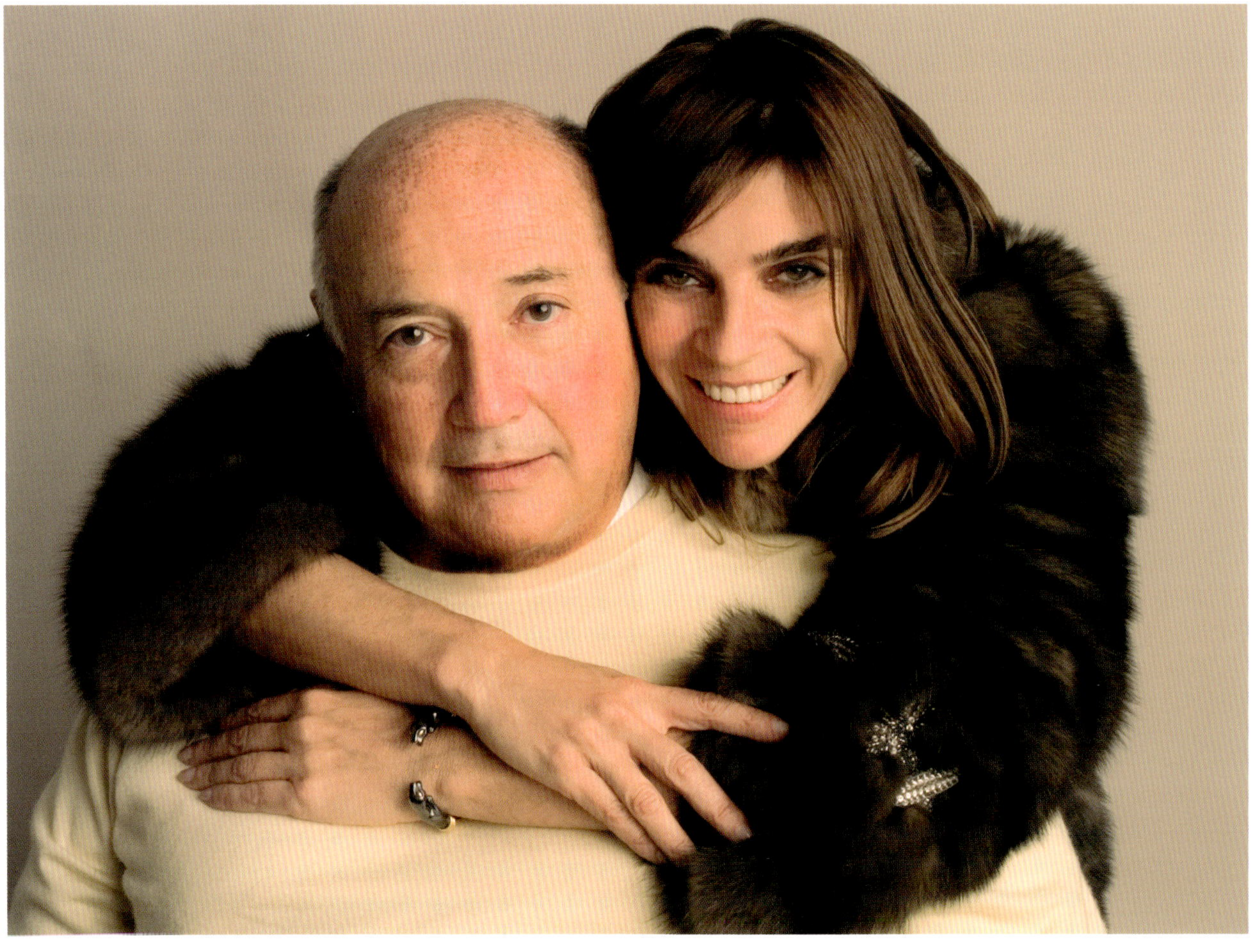

KAL RUTTENSTEIN (1936–2005) Senior Vice President of Fashion Direction, Bloomingdale's
CARINE ROITFELD Editor in Chief, French *Vogue*

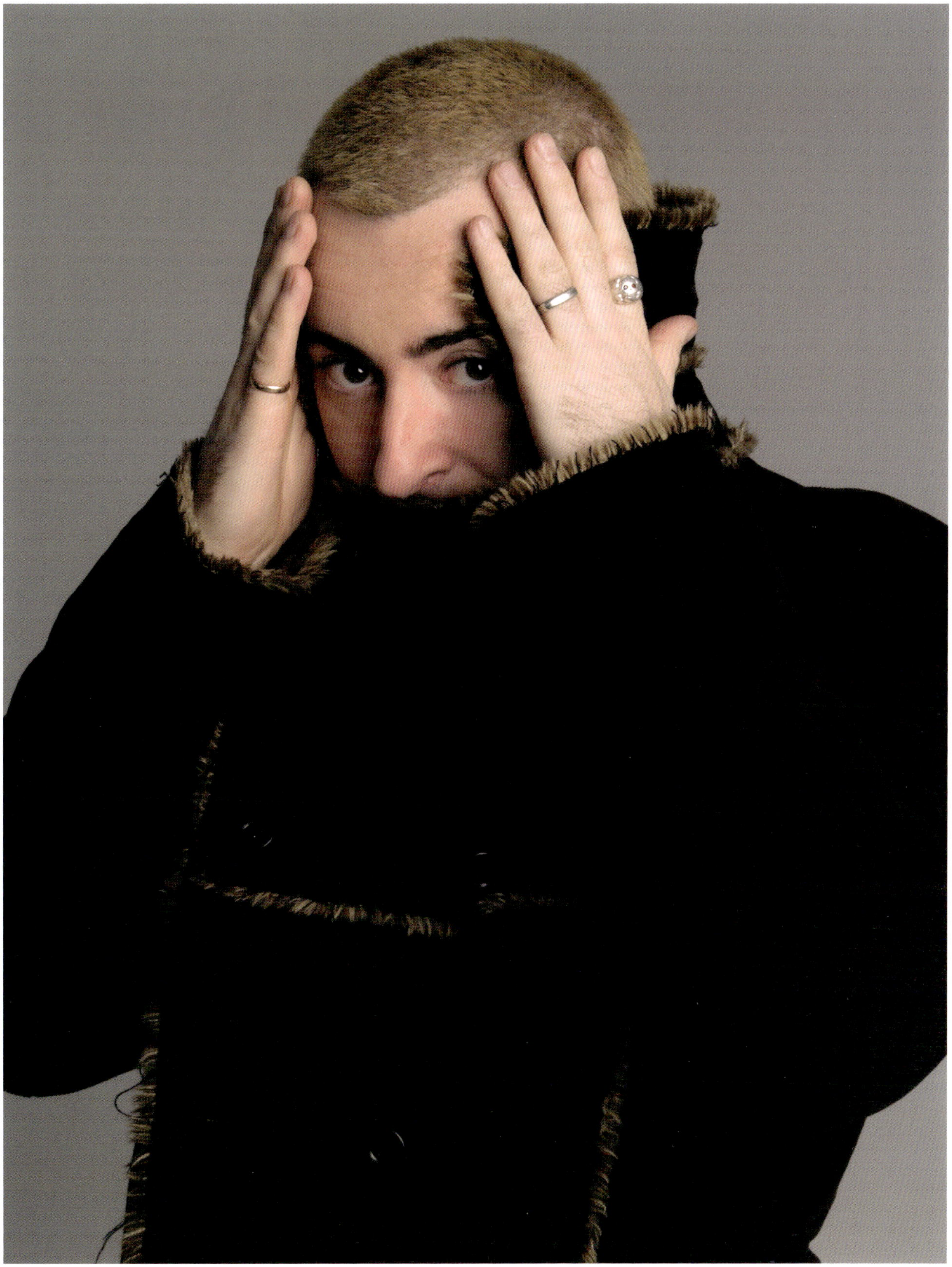

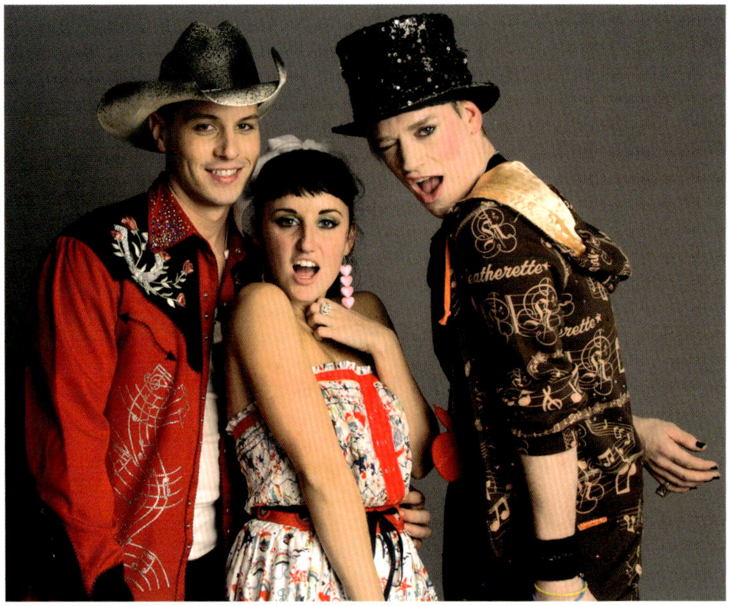

Traver and Richie with PR Maven Aimee Phillips

Showing at Bryant Park for the first time was a total dream come true. For as long as I [Richie Rich] can remember, I have been obsessed with fashion, so when I first moved to New York City I totally crashed the Todd Oldham show at Bryant Park. I remember standing in the back row freaking out that I was even there with all those amazing people. It was such an unforgettable experience.

When I walked into the tents the first time we showed there and saw everyone with Heatherette credentials, I couldn't believe we'd made it. Of course, even though I was in such awe that first time, it now feels like home!

One of our most memorable backstage moments was from our Spring/Summer 2005 show. It was the first time we were in the tents, and our big surprise at the end of the show was supposed to be Naomi Campbell walking for us as the grand finale. Naomi had to present onstage at Fashion Rocks the same night and no one was confident that she could make it in time. Paris Hilton had shown up right before showtime, which was an amazing surprise even for us! Paris wanted to walk, so we gave her two looks in the show. Toward the end of the show, Naomi still hadn't shown, so we figured she wasn't making it. Naomi's finale dress was made entirely out of mirrored plastic stars with a bikini underneath, so while our friend and muse Amanda Lepore walked the runway, we put Paris in Naomi's dress for the finale.

While the models were prepping for the finale, Naomi burst into the backstage area and frantically started looking for her dress. We stalled by sending poor Amanda back out on the runway while we grabbed the dress and bikini off Paris and stuck it on Naomi, threw Paris' second look back on her, and sent her out to stall some more while we got Naomi into the complicated dress. She didn't have time to get the bikini top under the dress, so she threw it up in the air and slid out onto the catwalk to a standing ovation and cheers like we've never heard at a fashion show. It was a total surprise to everyone that she made it and it was totally a magic Bryant Park moment.

There's truly only one Bryant Park, and even though we've shown in some really wonderful locations—a gigantic mall in Moscow, on the beach in Miami, in a real circus ring in L.A.—there's just such an amazing air about the tents. You can't replicate it anywhere else in the world.

HEATHERETTE

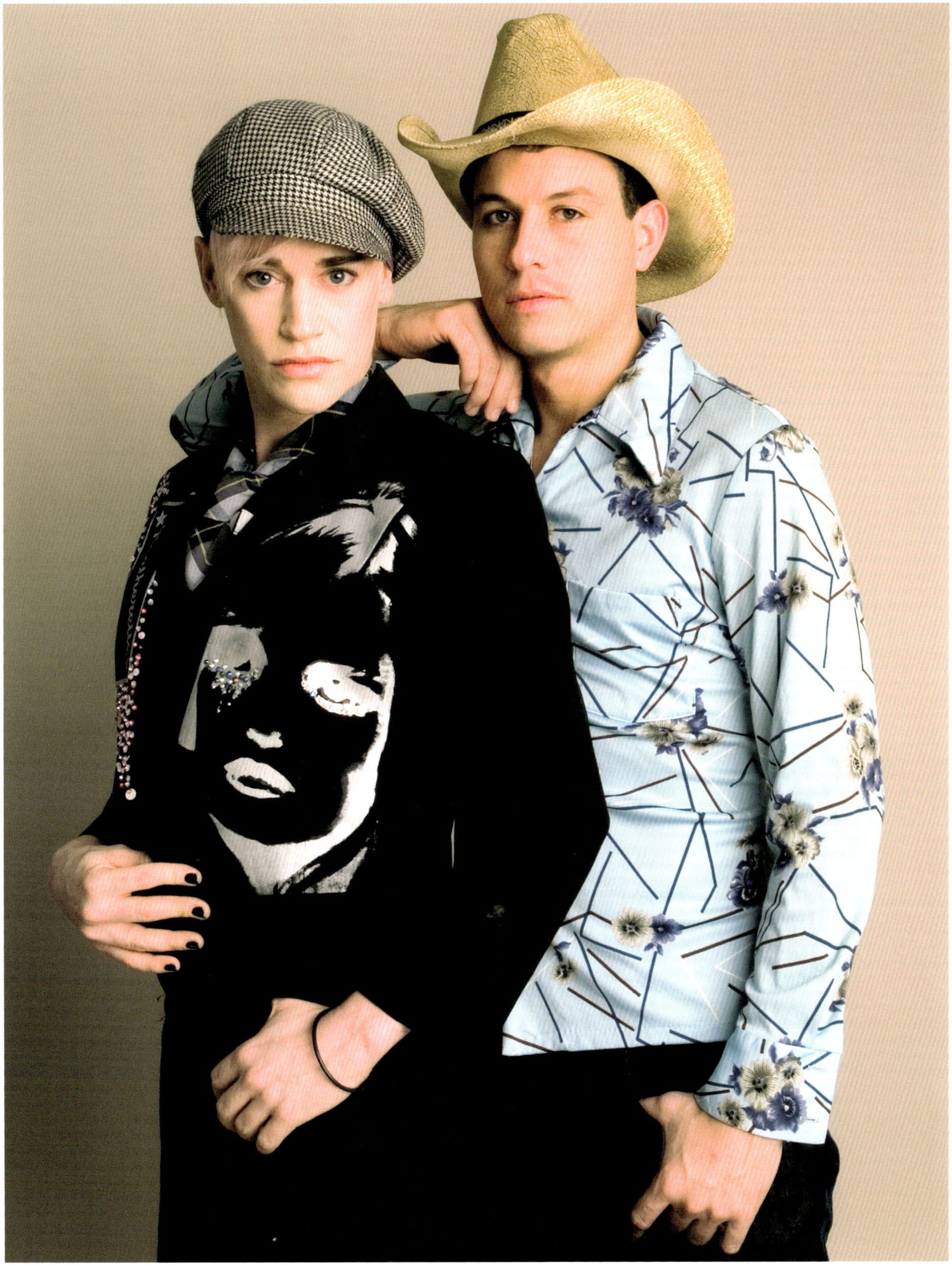

RICHIE RICH & TRAVER RAINS Designers, Heatherette

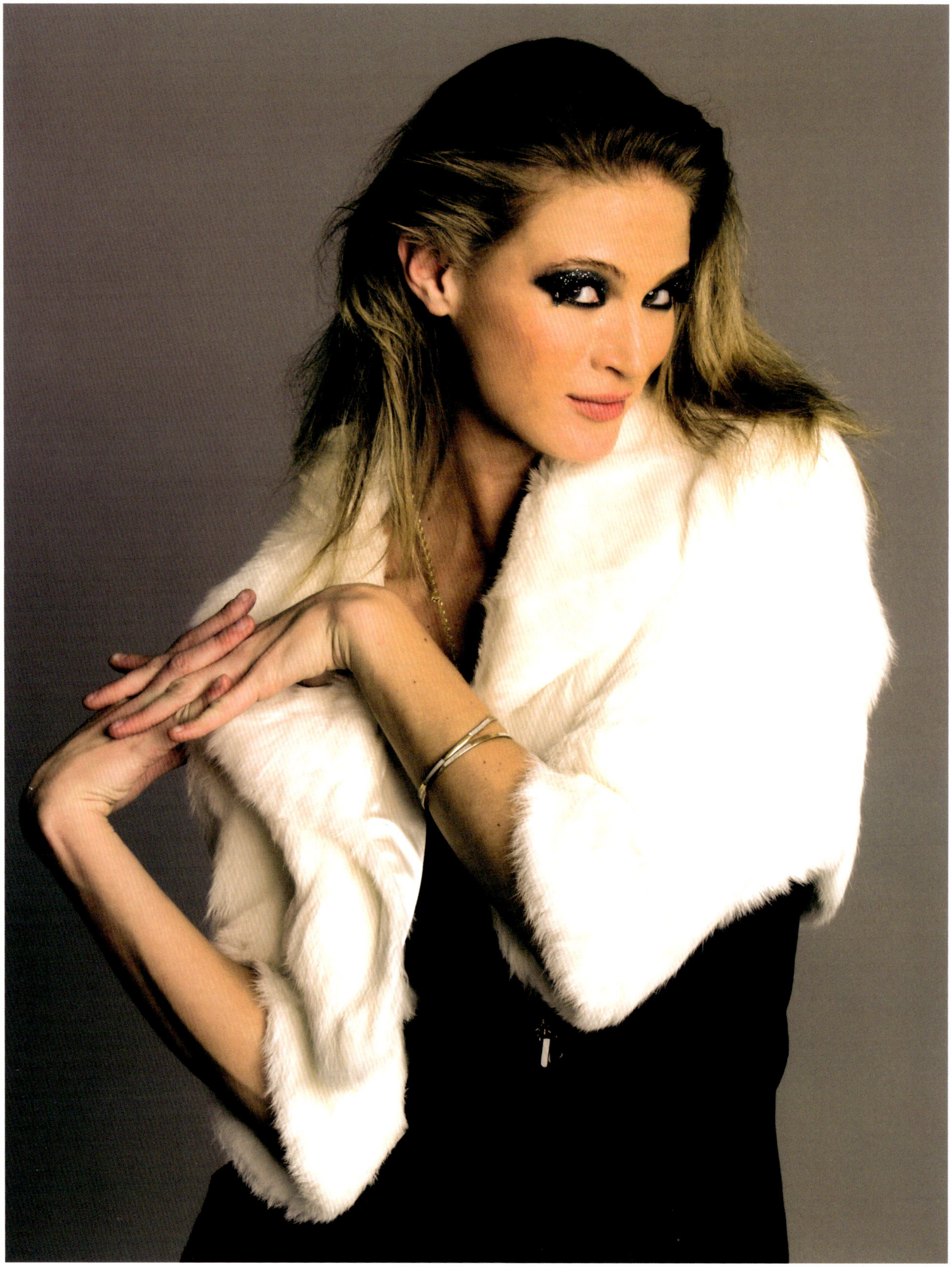

MICHELLE BUSWELL Model

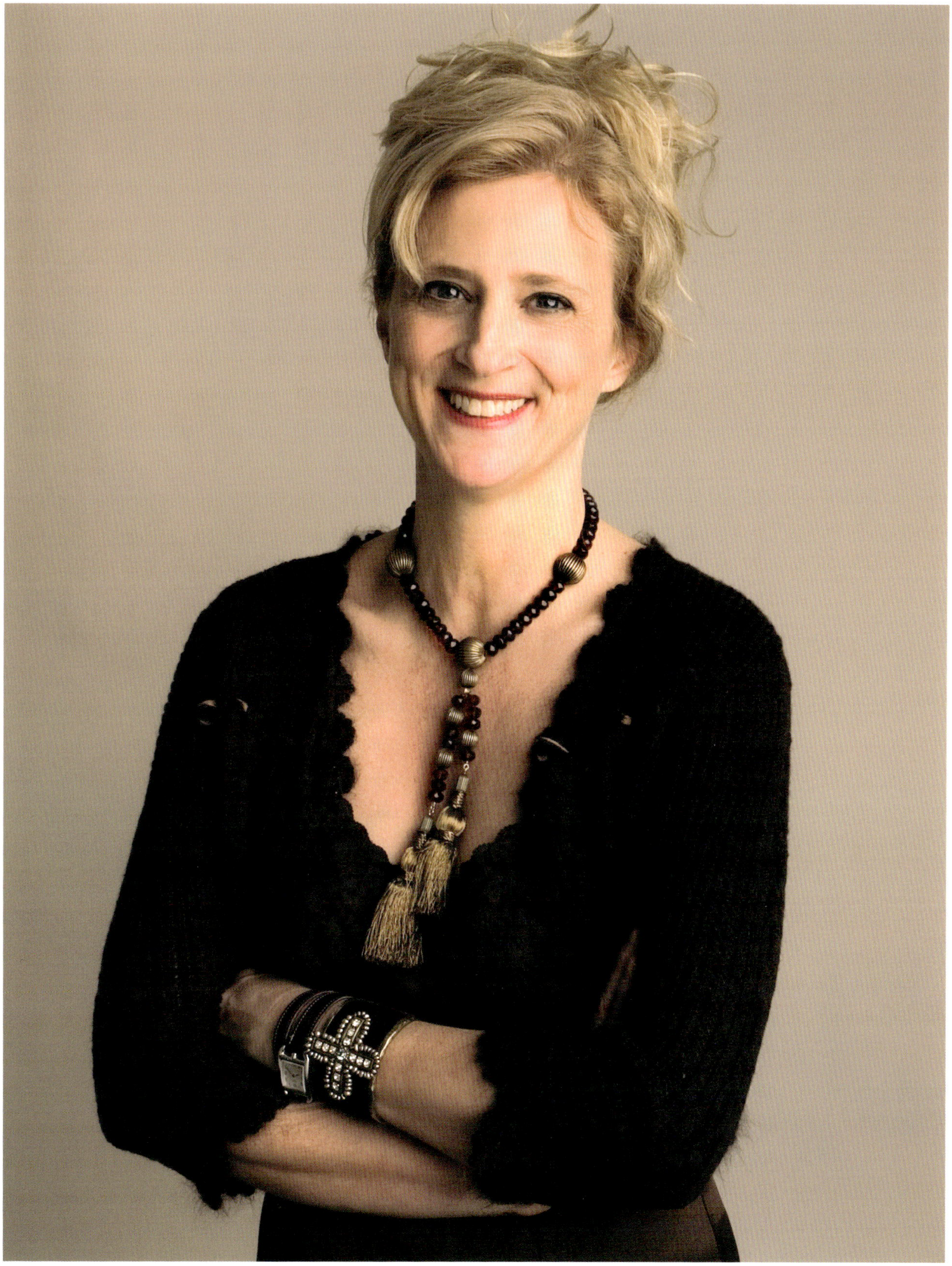

NANETTE LEPORE Designer

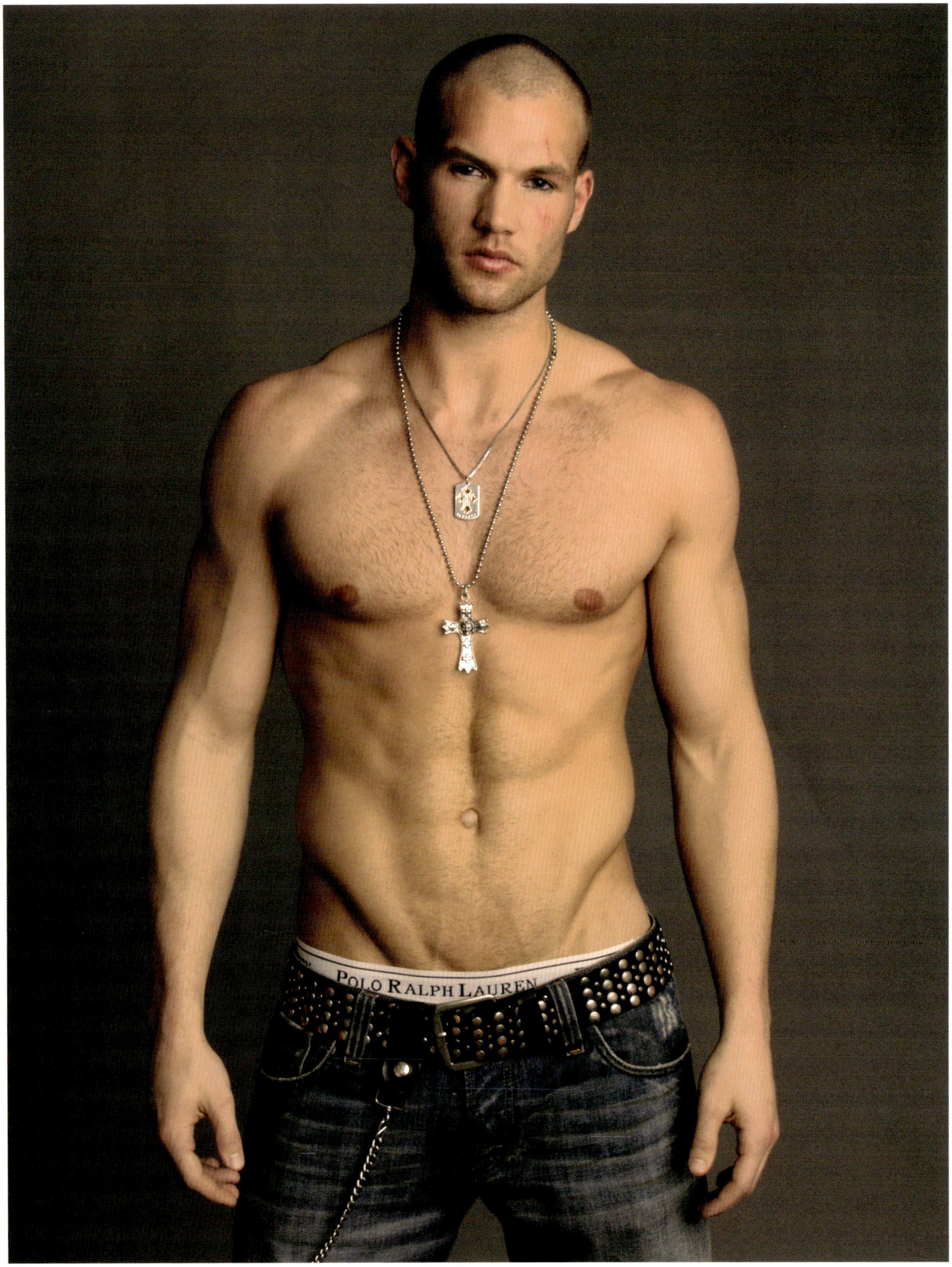

LUCAS KERR Model

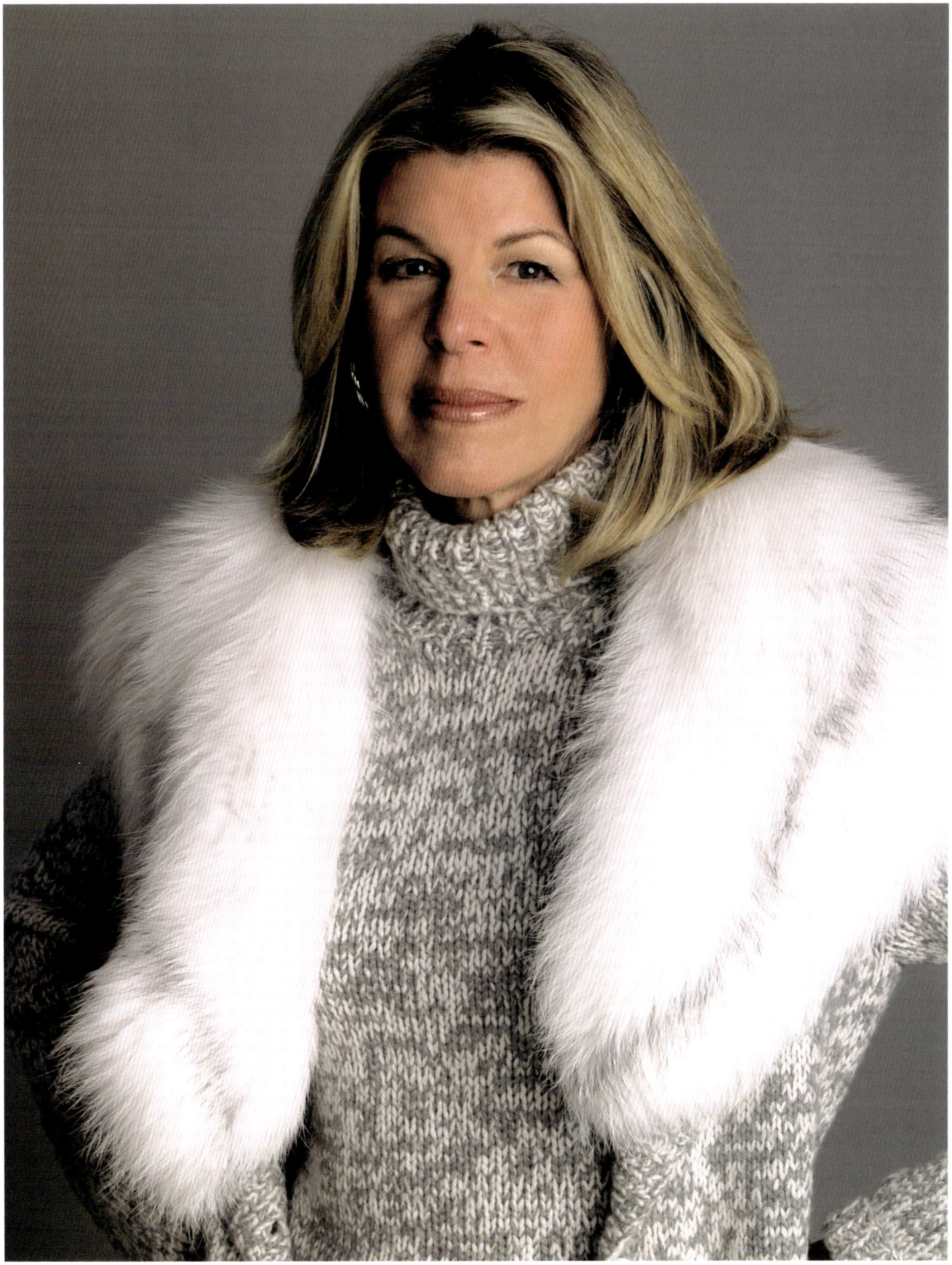

JAMEE GREGORY Socialite

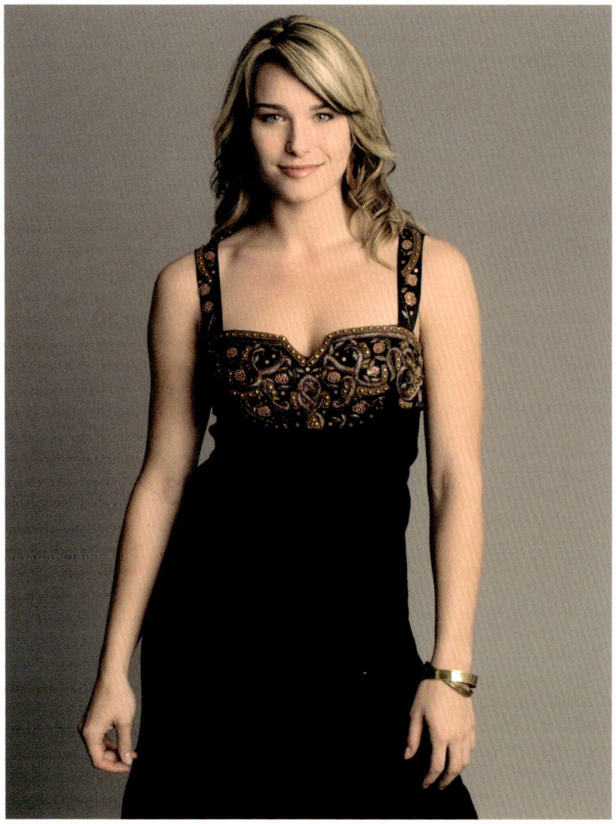

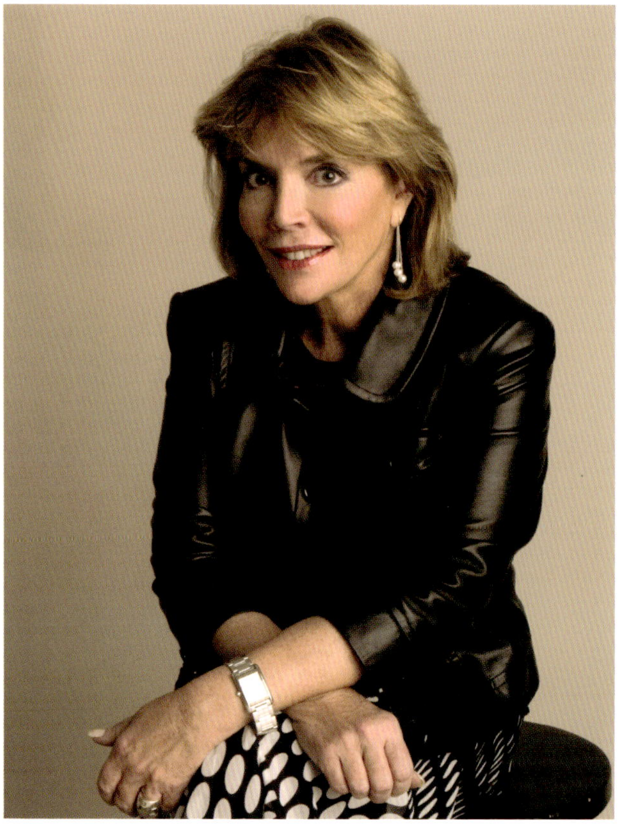

CALLIE STYDAHAR Correspondent, *Full Frontal Fashion* JUDY LICHT Host, *Full Frontal Fashion*

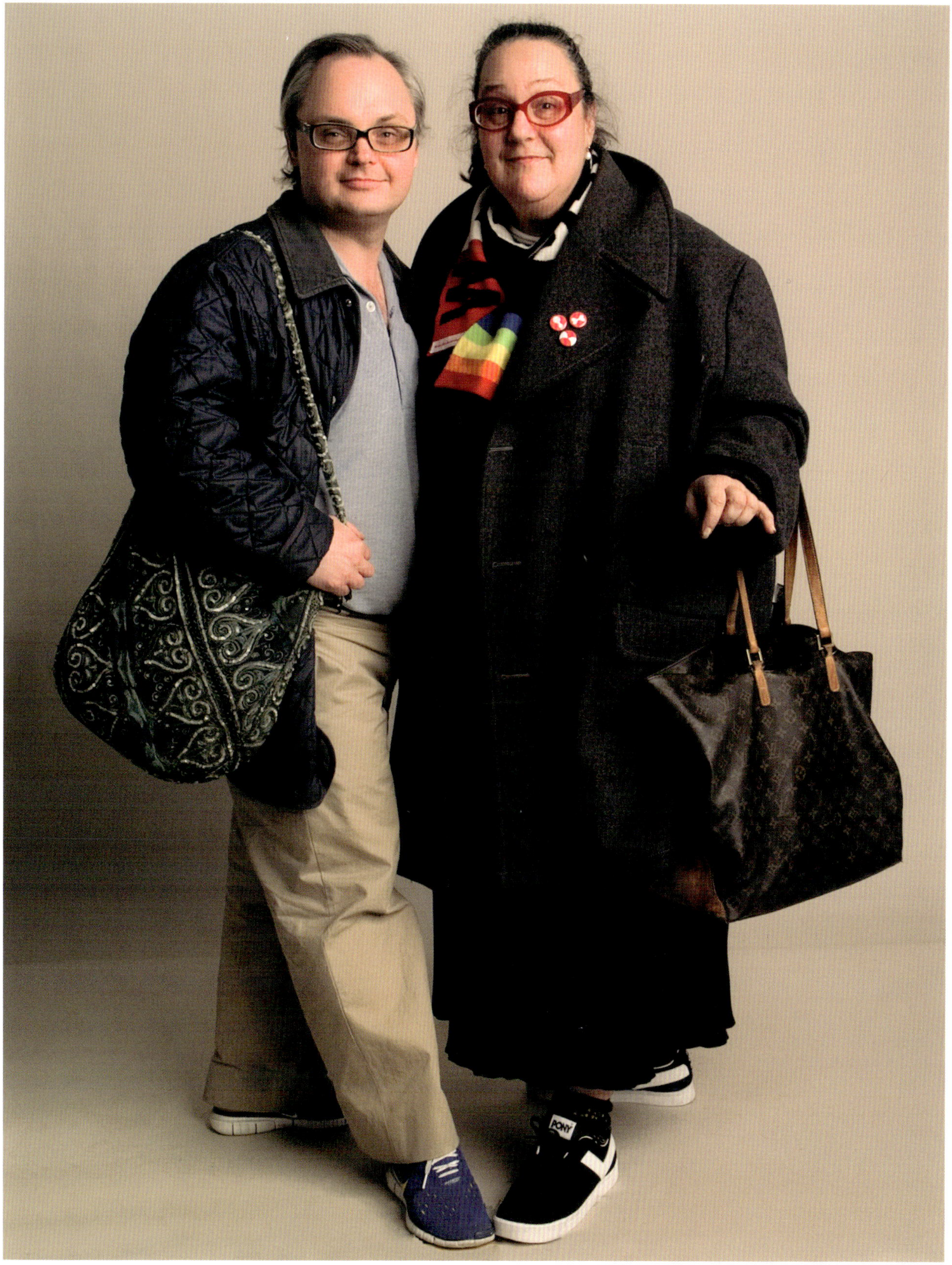

MICKEY BOARDMAN & KIM HASTREITER *Paper* People

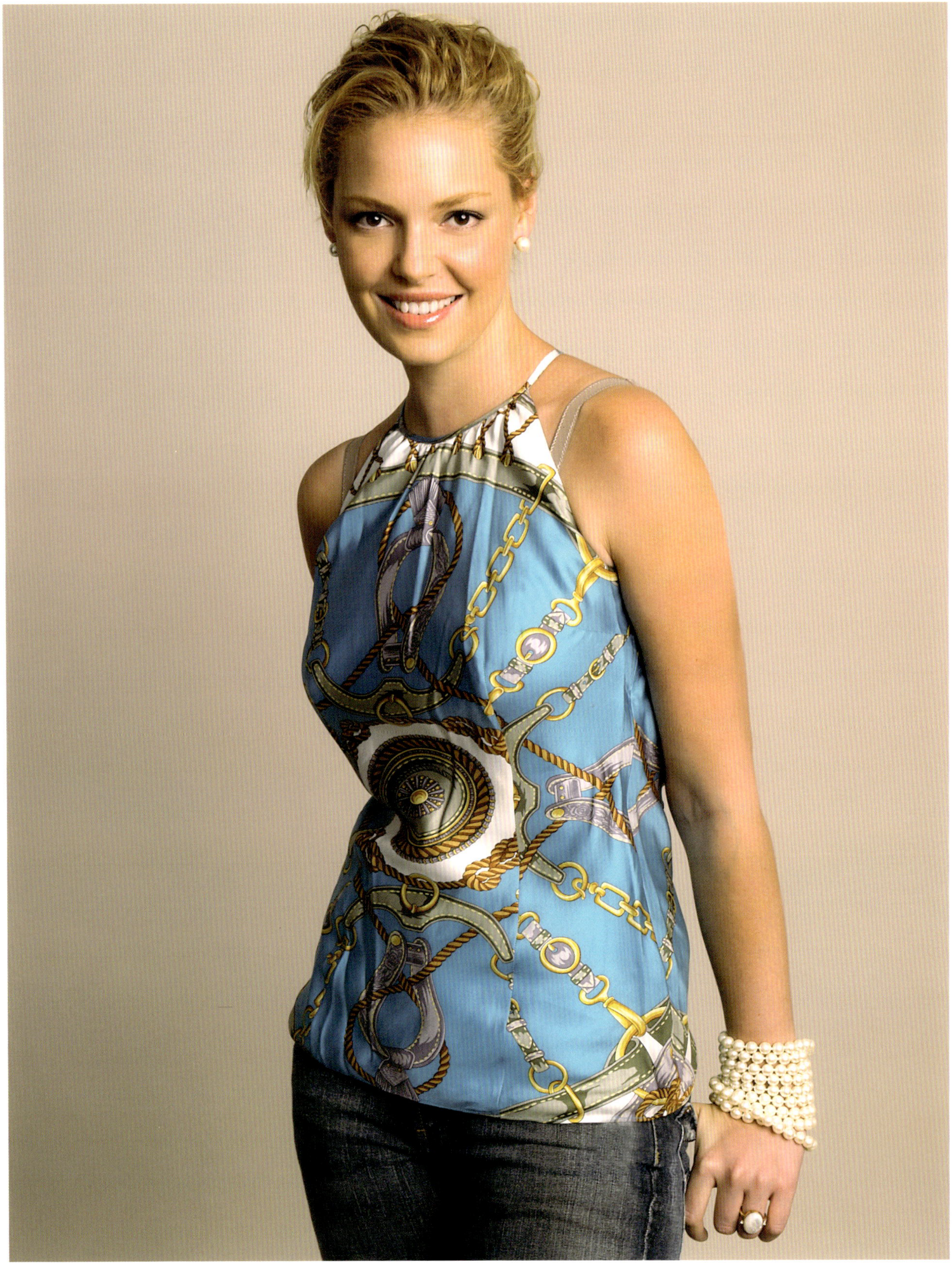

KATHERINE HEIGL Actor

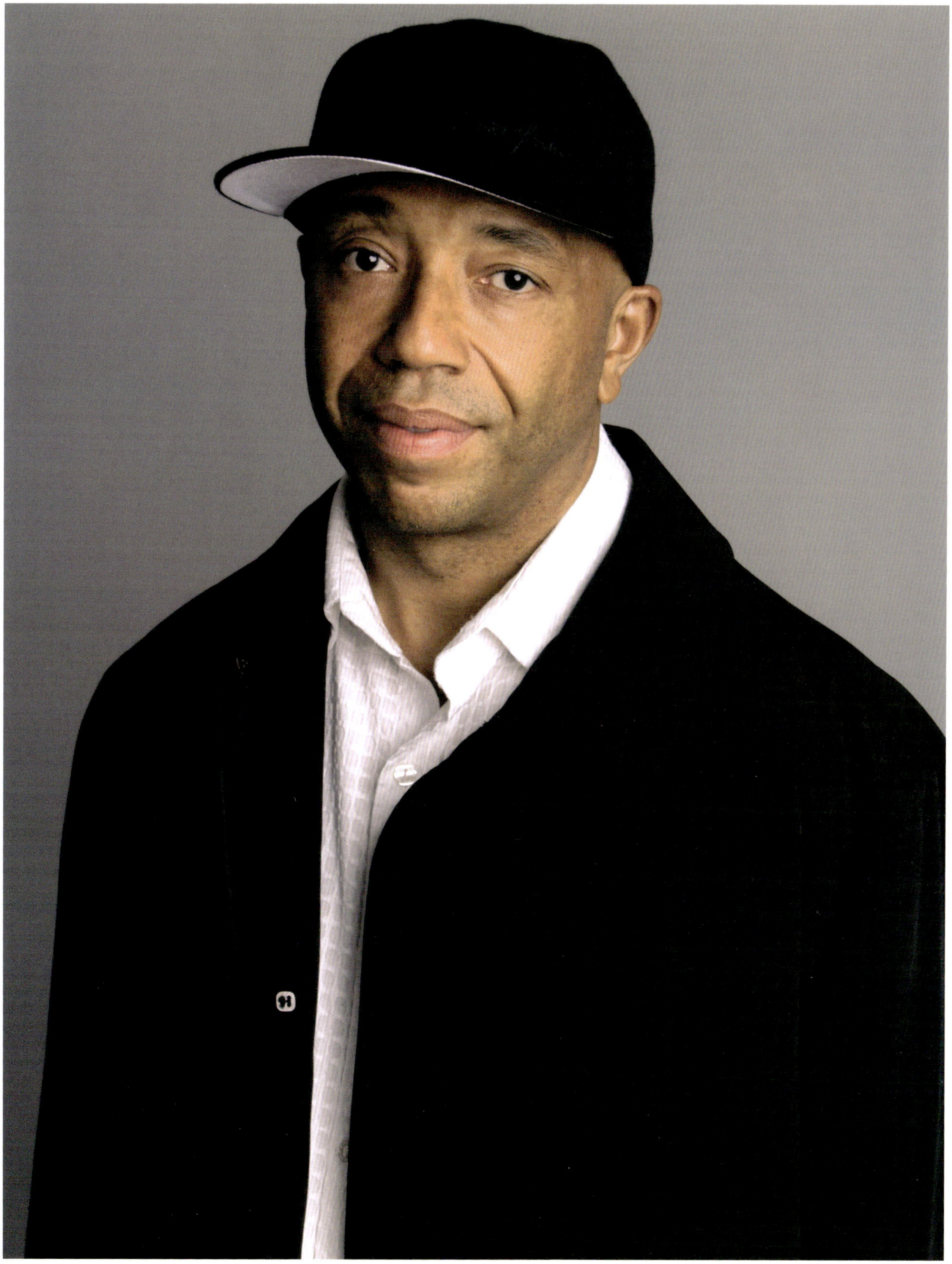

RUSSELL SIMMONS Entrepreneur

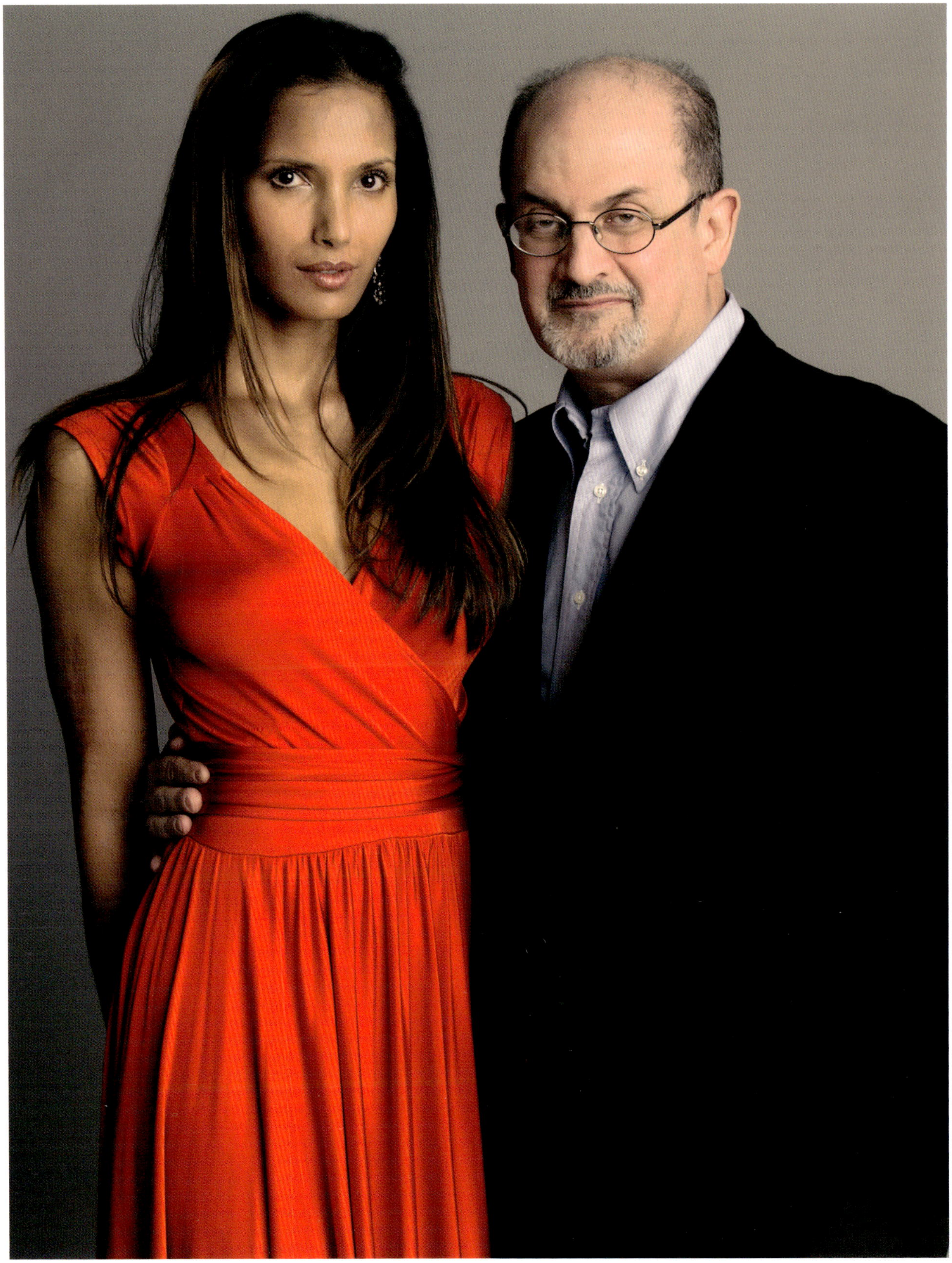

PADMA LAKSHMI Model/Actor
SALMAN RUSDHIE Author

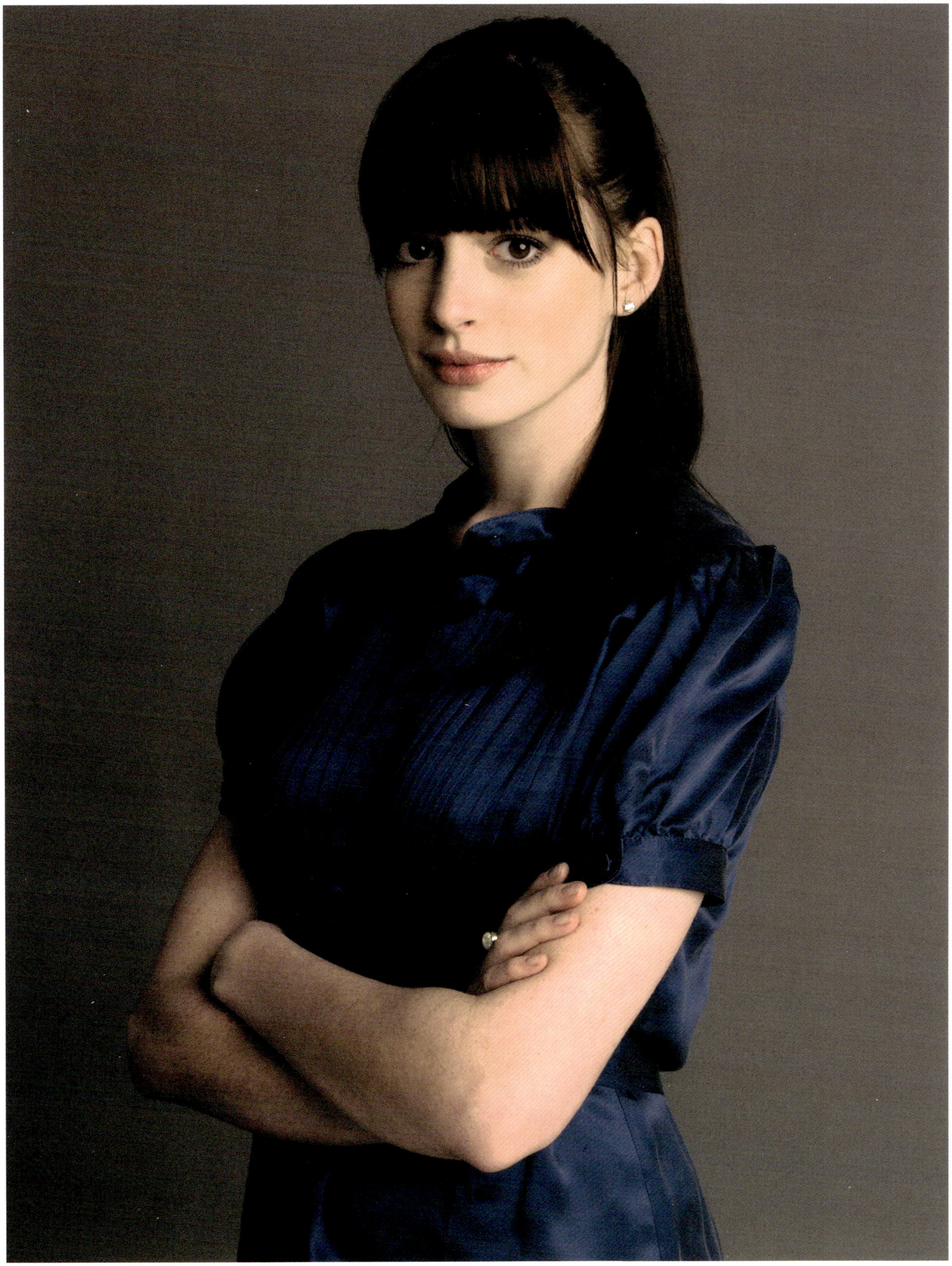

ANNE HATHAWAY Actor

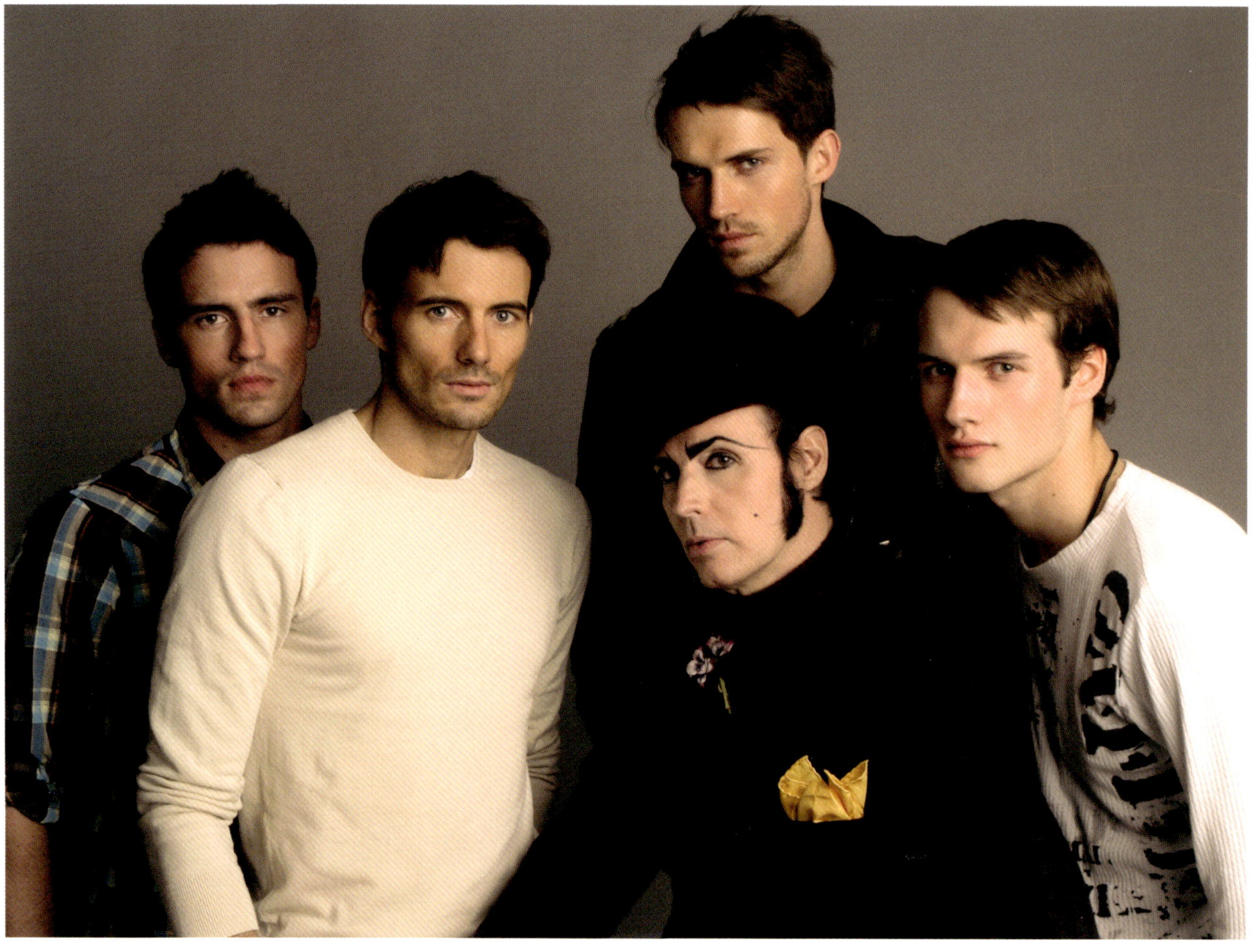

Patrick with models Michael Brager, Alex Lundqvist, Andrew Cooper, and Fabian Elsner

Dandy is what dandy does. Being the dandy of New York City, Fashion Week is a special time for me because, as a true dandy, my fashion sense and style is key. In addition to people watching on the streets of Manhattan, viewing the latest collections from a diverse group of designers at the tents is very inspirational to me.

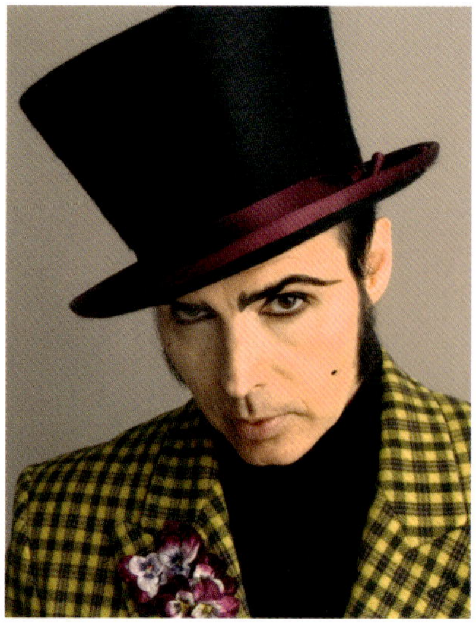

Watching from the front row gives me a bird's-eye view of details in fabrics, tailoring, and styling. Being a dandy, I like to take chances and set myself apart—and being myself hopefully helps others dare to be unique. That's what great style and fashion sense is truly about.

Fashion Week is my time to revel in my passion and work my own runway. I plan my outfits well in advance of the week. It's a long process because it's head-to-toe and all in the mix. The right hat with the right suit, tie, shoe, and boutonniere adds to my dandified self-expression. I know I get looks, but it's my performance art and I love it.

And the greatest form of flattery? Being photographed.

PATRICK MCDONALD

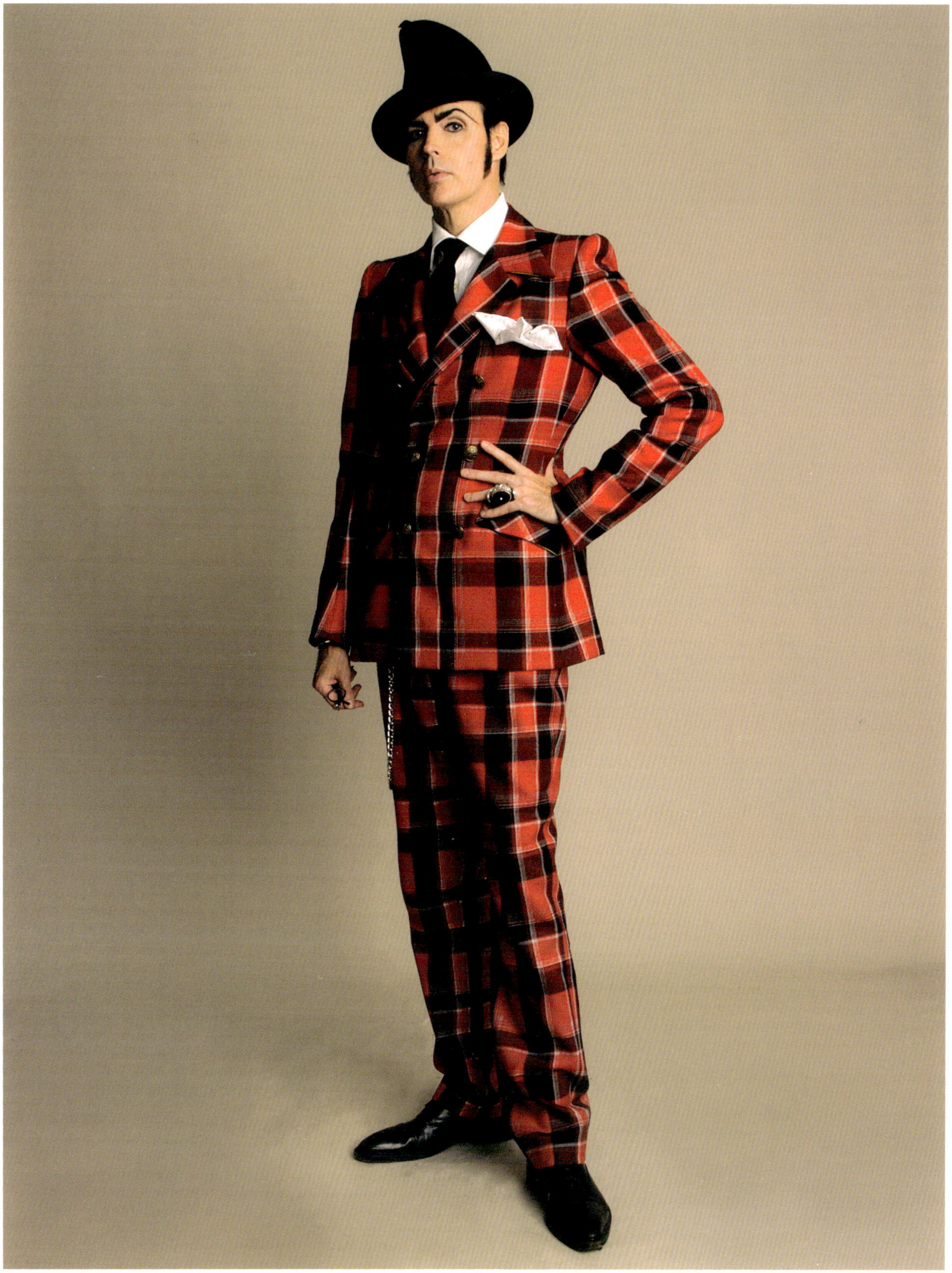

PATRICK MCDONALD Dandy

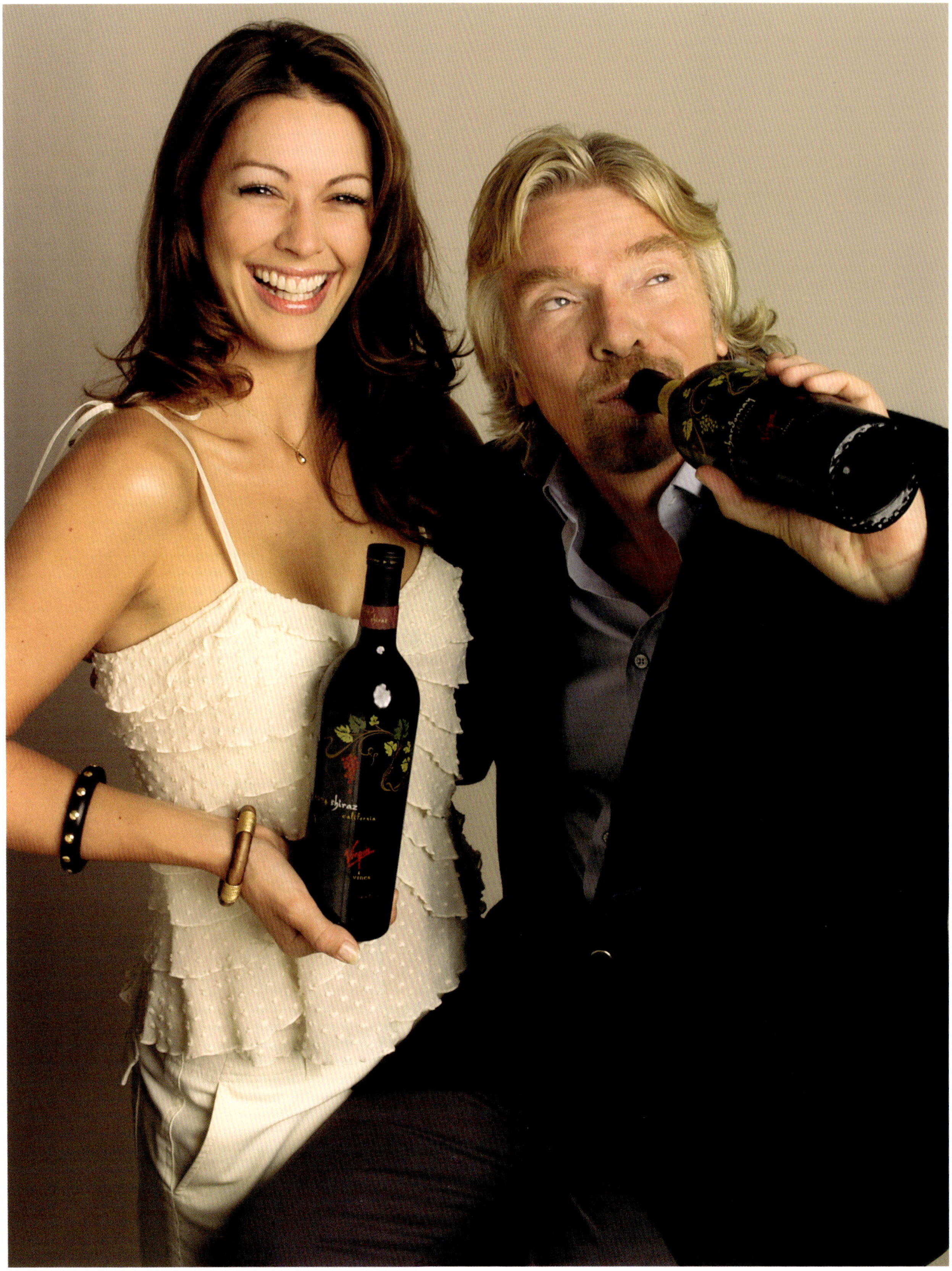

LOUISE GRIFFITHS Telly Beauty
RICHARD BRANSON #1 Virgin

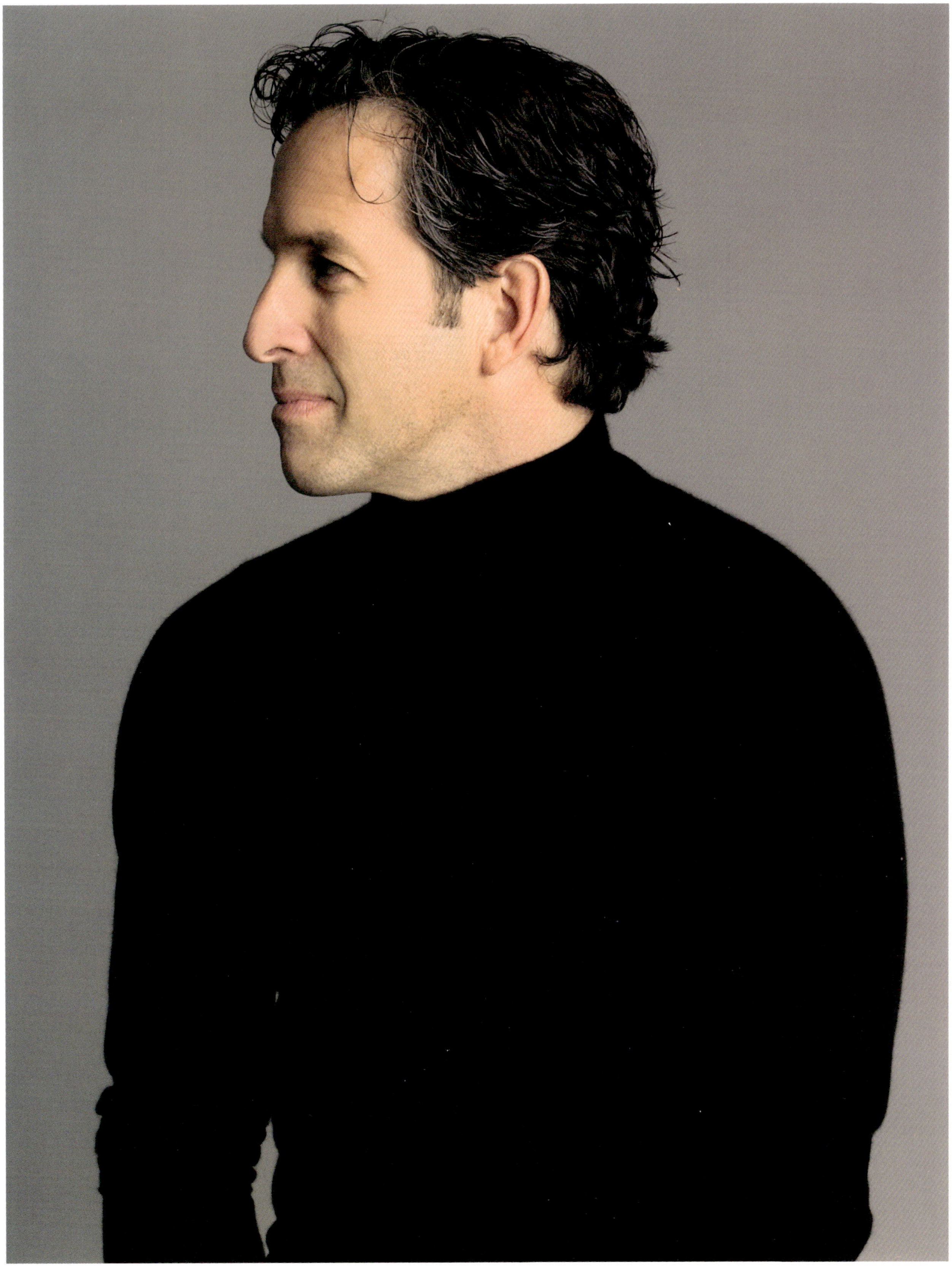

KENNETH COLE Designer

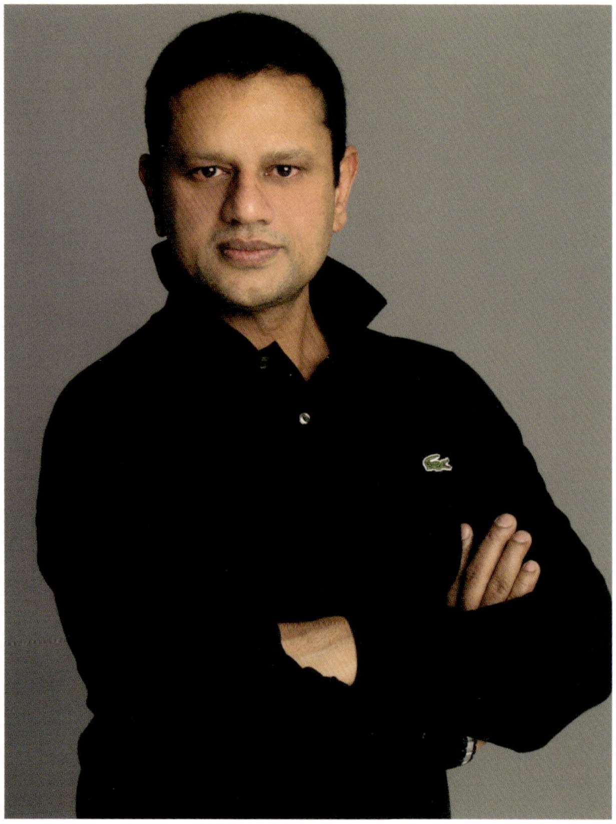

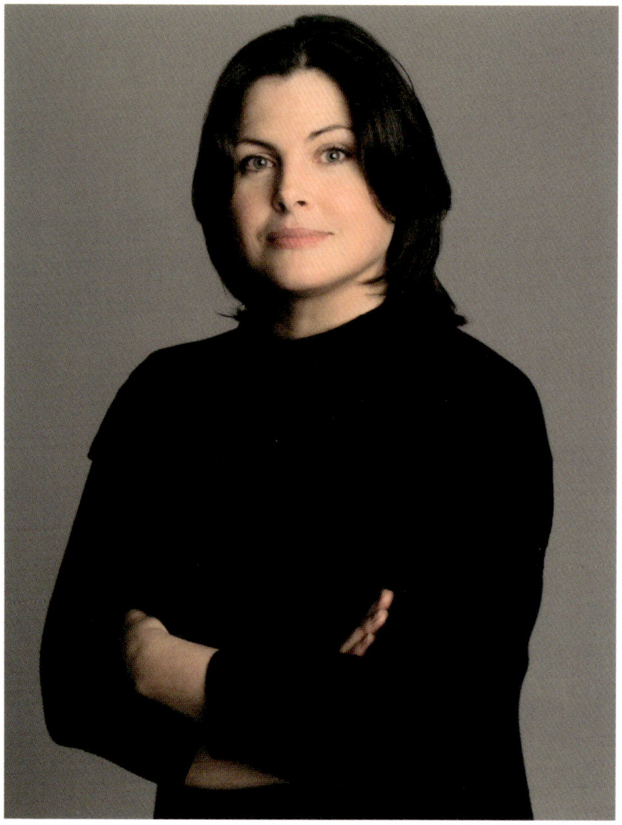

NAEEM KHAN Designer

CYNTHIA STEFFE Designer

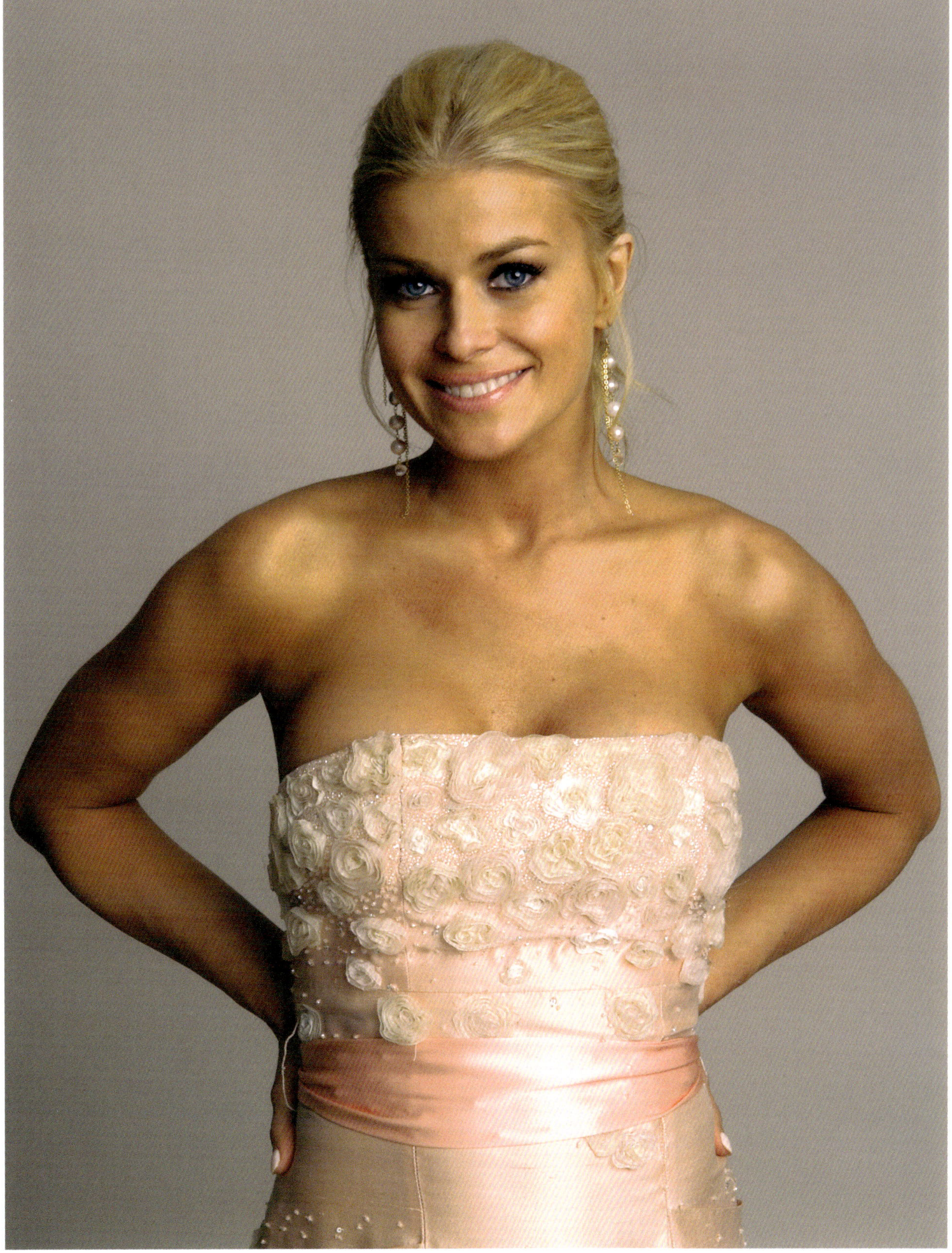

CARMEN ELECTRA Actor

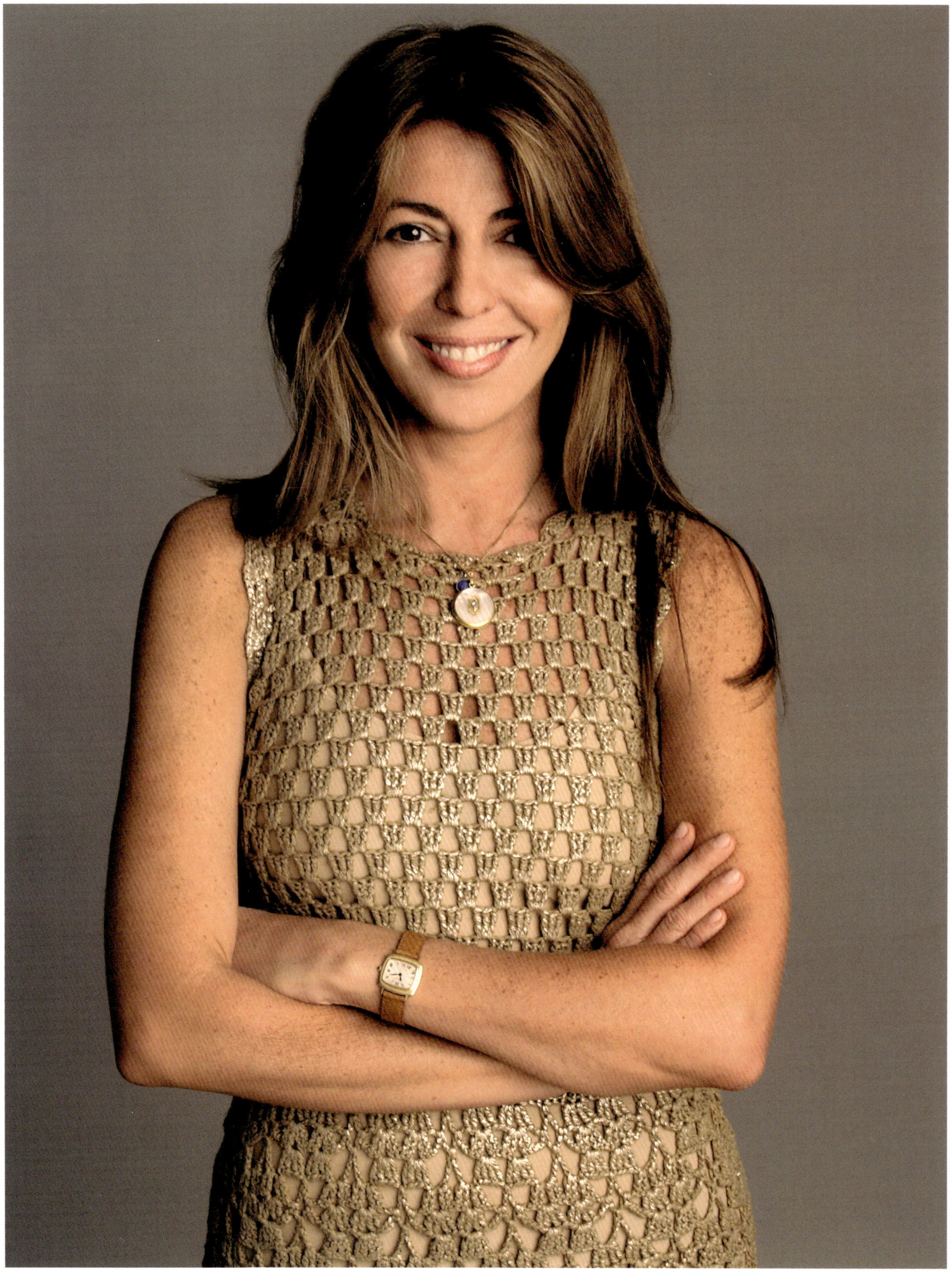

NINA GARCIA Fashion Director, *Elle*

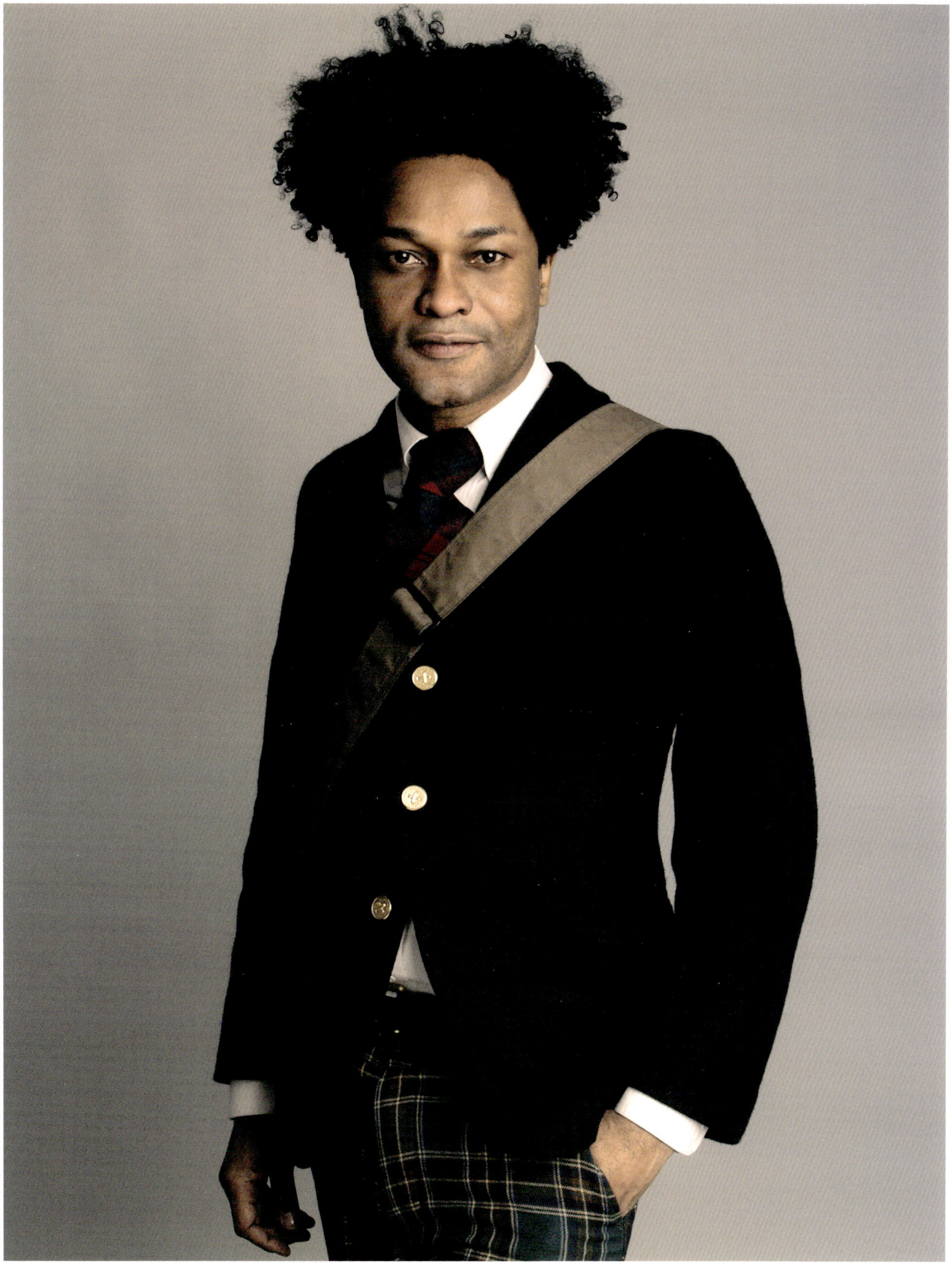

IKÉ UDÉ Artist/Editor, *aRUDE*

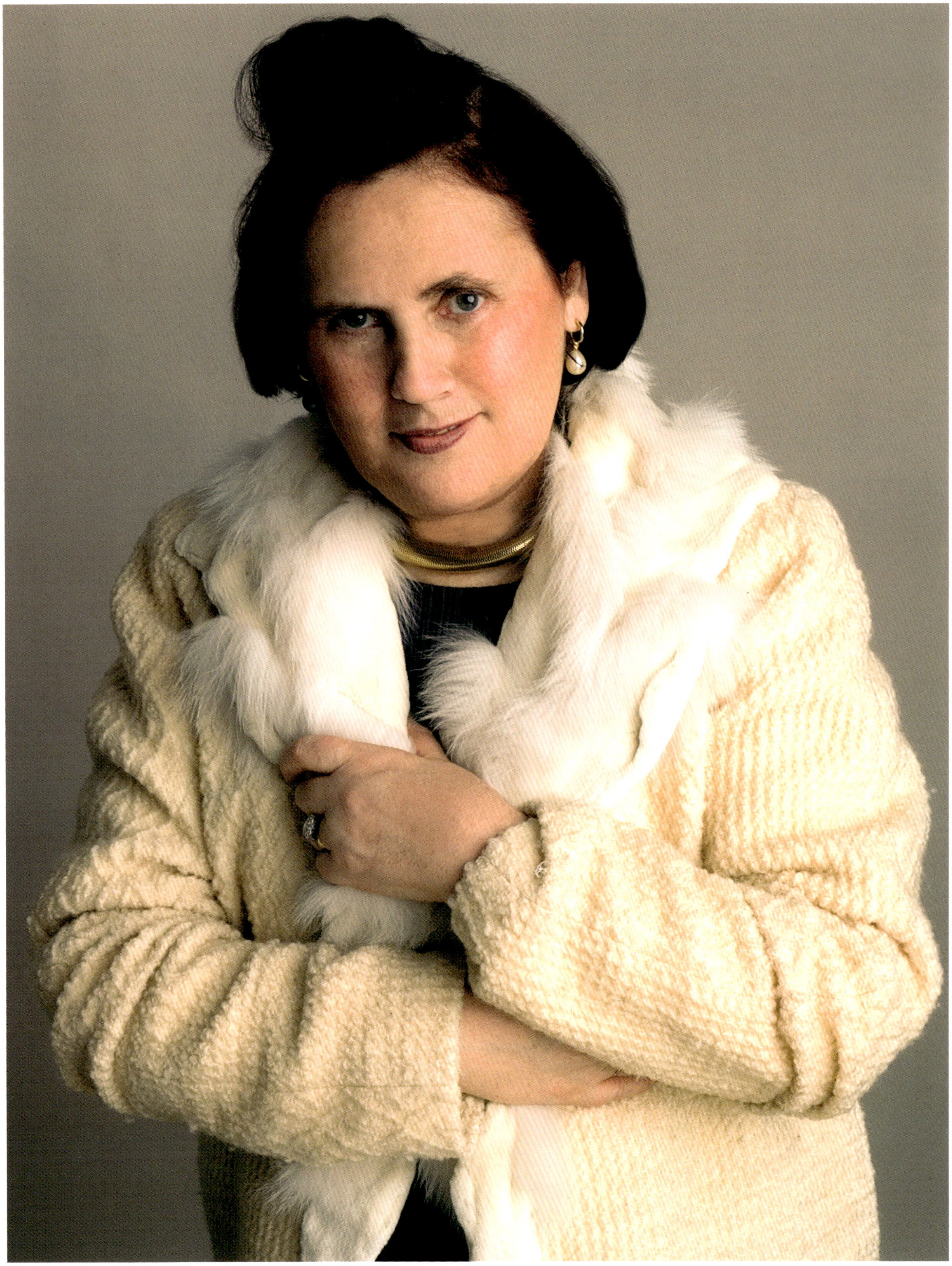

SUZY MENKES Fashion Editor, *International Herald Tribune*

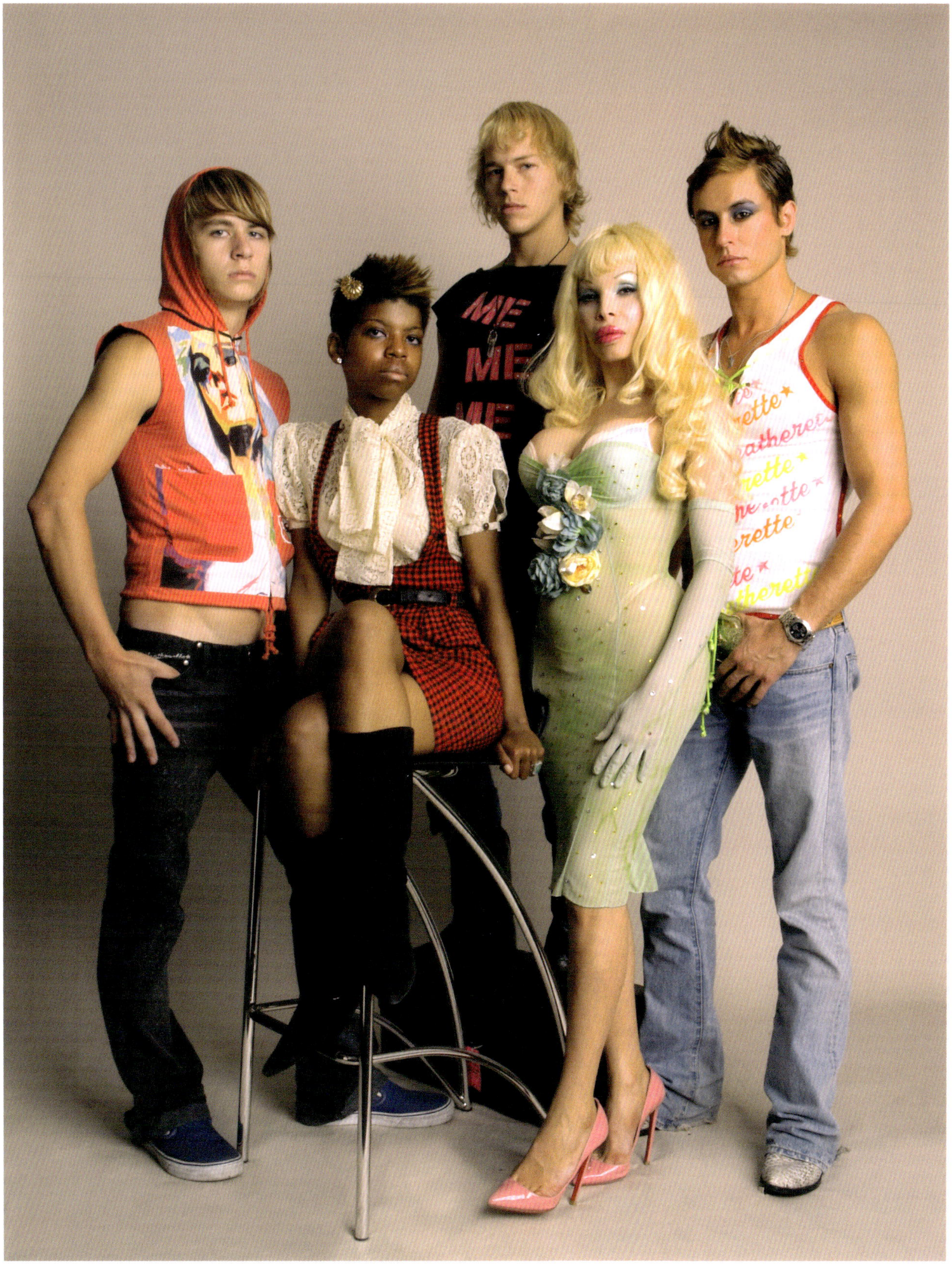

AMANDA LEPORE Muse
ZACKERY, NICOLE, JOE & GALEN Club Kids

INDEX

THE FRONT ROW

THE PHOTOGRAPHER

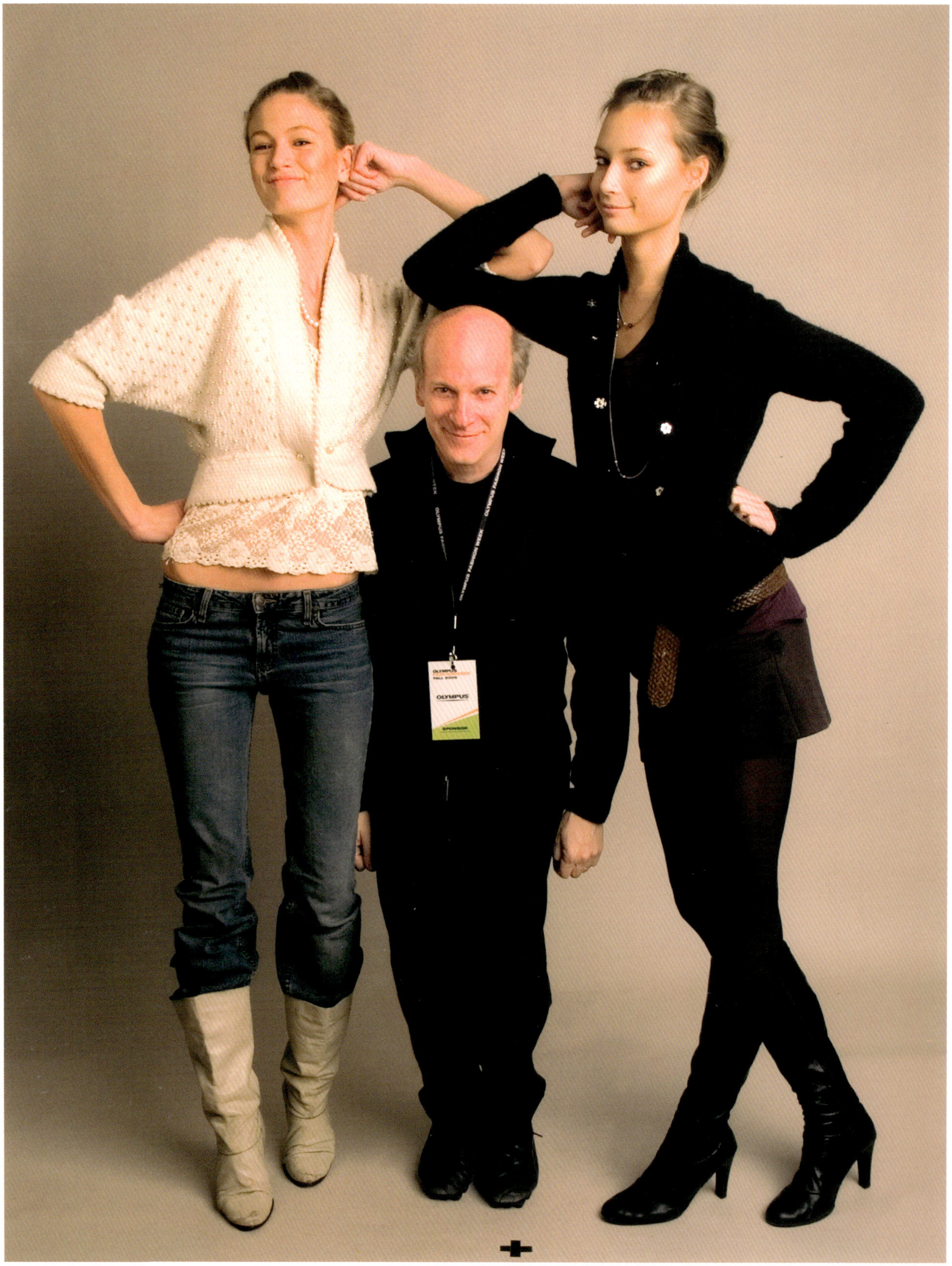

TIMOTHY GREENFIELD-SANDERS Crouching Photographer
MICHELLE BUSWELL & TIIU KUIK Towering Models

For three fashion seasons in a row, I photographed more than 200 individual subjects using a simple light source, a neutral-colored paper seamless, and a sturdy Olympus E-Series digital SLR camera. My cozy studio, courtesy of my friends at Olympus, was a safe harbor in the frenetic storm that takes place every six months in New York City's Bryant Park.

So many people made this project and this book possible. Some of them deserve special mention.

THE SUBJECTS: Thank you all for finding the time to sit for me and for giving me your utmost attention while there was such excitement all around us. A portrait depends so much on the subject trusting the photographer, and I am deeply indebted to each of you for that trust.

THE CREW: Mark Mahaney is an extraordinarily gifted photographer (he was recently honored in *American Photo* as one of the top ten upcoming talents) and his efforts over the years as my assistant have been immeasurable. Chad Batka has also been enormously supportive and an indispensable part of my team. Color master Dan Colish graciously shared his expertise with us for the production of *Look*. Susan Dwyer deserves many thanks as well.

OLYMPUS: This project would not have been possible without the ongoing support of Olympus. I would especially like to thank Mark Gumz, president and COO of Olympus America Inc., for his belief in me and my work. Thanks also to Mark Huggins, Chris Sluka, Deborah Klein, Jennifer Lyons, John Knaur, and Rich Pelkowski.

THE MVPS: First and foremost, Chad Thompson from MVPGroup was vital to this project. Chad and his team worked alongside me 24/7 from day one. The friendship, support, and encouragement from Chad and his highly organized majordomo, Alexander Cole, are very much appreciated. Thanks also to Kim Arbuckle for her support.

THE ANCHORWOMAN: The work done by Katie Couric and everyone associated with the Entertainment Industry Foundation's National Colorectal Cancer Research Alliance is extraordinary. I am delighted to have become a part of their efforts through our collaborations at Olympus Fashion Week, and I am most grateful to Katie for writing for this book.

THE FASHION QUEEN: Fern Mallis has been on my side from the first day we met. None of this could have happened without her. She keeps the show running and does it with a keen intelligence and an eye on the big picture. I am grateful to her entire IMG Fashion team, especially Leigh Bokser, Zach Eichman, Marli McCleary, Lynn Longendyke, Christina Neault, Guia Golden, and the OBO crew. And special thanks to Fern's colleagues at IMG Models, Ivan Bart and Peter Knell.

THE MAGAZINE EDITOR: When I started this project, one of my first calls was to Martha Nelson, the editor of Time Inc.'s PEOPLE Group. Martha immediately, sight unseen, agreed to publish a selection of my portraits in the magazine. Her faith in me and my work and the exposure that *People* brought to these images is immeasurable. Martha, thank you and your team: Susan Kaufman, Chris Dougherty, Diane Clehane, Duane Pyous, and Nicky Ferguson.

THE ACTOR: Alec Baldwin, a brilliant actor and a comic master, is also a great friend. His wonderful and ironic view of the fashion industry was indispensable to this book. Thank you, Alec, for always being there for me and my projects.

THE WRITER/EDITOR: Simon Dumenco is a dear and trusted friend who always finds time for me and for my many demands. Thank you, Simon, for your insightful writing and editing for this book and for your generosity of spirit. Thanks also to your expert team—Matthew Weingarden and Timothy Hodler—who lent their publishing expertise to *Look*.

THE DESIGNERS: Many designers contributed to the success of *Look*, but I am especially grateful to Zac Posen and Heatherette's Richie Rich and Traver Raines for their wonderful essays. They each, of course, face almost unimaginable pressure every Fashion Week—so their gracious and lucid perspectives on what goes into showing at Bryant Park are all the more remarkable.

THE SOCIALITE: Tinsley Mortimer's front-row seat at Fashion Week is well deserved. Her devotion to the fashion world (particularly emerging designers) and her support of numerous charities are very much appreciated. I am delighted to have her in this book.

THE DANDY: Throughout this project no one brought more color and style to my studio than Patrick McDonald. I am always amazed by his never-ending parade of designer ensembles. Thank you, Patrick, for sharing your dandy's view from the front row.

THE BEAUTIFUL PEOPLE: Hair and makeup artists Robbie Contreras, Federico Calce, and Piera Canu stood by in my backstage studio to make the beautiful people even more beautiful. I am grateful for their patience, skill, and camaraderie.

THE PROTECTORS: For the past three seasons, a crackerjack team of security experts has kept my studio at Bryant Park safe and sound. Thanks to Ty, Alexi, Joe, and the many others for standing by to make all run smoothly for us.

THE POWERHOUSE TEAM: *Look* would not have been possible without the skill and expertise of Craig Cohen and his colleagues at powerHouse Books. A special thanks to art director Kiki Bauer, whose long hours and gifted eye have made this book so beautiful.

THE FAMILY: Very special thanks are due to Karin, Isca, Liliana, and Sebastian.

ACKNOWLEDGMENTS